This book offers an extensive critique of individualism in psychology, a view that has been the subject of debate between philosophers such as Jerry Fodor and Tyler Burge for many years. Rob Wilson approaches individualism as an issue in the philosophy of science, and by discussing issues such as computationalism and the mind's modularity, he opens the subject up for non-philosophers in psychology and computer science.

Professor Wilson carefully examines the most influential arguments for individualism and identifies the main metaphysical assumptions underlying them. Because the topic is so central to the philosophy of mind, an area generating enormous research and debate at present, the book has implications for a very broad range of philosophical issues, including the naturalization of intentionality, psychophysical supervenience, the nature of mental causation, and the viability of folk psychology.

*Cartesian Psychology and Physical Minds* will prove a useful guide for philosophers and cognitive scientists seeking a sustained discussion of individualism.

D1565195

CAMBRIDGE STUDIES IN PHILOSOPHY

# Cartesian Psychology and Physical Minds

# CAMBRIDGE STUDIES IN PHILOSOPHY

General editor ERNEST SOSA

*Advisory editors*
Jonathan Dancy    University of Keele
Gilbert Harman    Princeton University
Frank Jackson    University of Melbourne
William G. Lycan    University of Carolina, Chapel Hill
Sydney Shoemaker    Cornell University
Judith J. Thomson    Massachusetts Institute of Technology

RECENT TITLES

# Cartesian Psychology and Physical Minds

## Individualism and the Sciences of the Mind

Robert A. Wilson
Queen's University

CAMBRIDGE
UNIVERSITY PRESS

Published by the Press Syndicate of the University of Cambridge
The Pitt Building, Trumpington Street, Cambridge CB2 1 RP
40 West 20th Street, New York, NY 10011–4211, USA
10 Stamford Road, Oakleigh, Melbourne 3166, Australia

First Published 1995
First paperback edition 1997
Printed in the United States of America

*Library of Congress Cataloging-in-Publication Data*

Wilson, Robert A. (Robert Andrew)

Cartesian psychology and physical minds : individualism and the
sciences of the mind / Robert A. Wilson.

p.   cm. – (Cambridge studies in philosophy)

Includes bibliographical references and index.

ISBN 0-521-47402-7

1. Philosophy of mind.   2. Individualism.   3. Human behavior.
I. Title.   II. Series.
BD418.3.W54   1995
128′.2 – dc20                                          94–36307
                                                            CIP

A catalog record for this book is available from the British Library.

ISBN 0–521–47402–7 Hardback
ISBN 0–521–59734–X Paperback

*For Selina*

*Say "some"*

# Contents

viii

# *Preface*

This is a book about individualism in psychology, a view that has generated much debate in the philosophy of mind over the last twenty years and that is pivotal for other issues in contemporary philosophical psychology: the naturalization of intentionality, the autonomy of psychology, the supervenience of the mental on the physical, the nature of mental causation, the viability of commonsense or 'folk' psychology, and the forms the cognitive sciences can and should take.

I have adopted a perspective on individualism that has not, in my view, received its due, one that approaches individualism in psychology from the viewpoint of the philosophy of science and attempts to identify and discuss the chief metaphysical intuitions that individualism rests on. I have also tried to make the book more accessible to those working in the cognitive sciences without compromising its philosophical audience so as to put some substance into the often glib hope expressed on jacket covers of books in the philosophy of mind: 'This book will be of interest to psychologists and cognitive scientists'. Although the reader will find a healthy dose of quotations to illustrate views that I discuss and the occasional comparison of my particular views to those of others, I have made only brief textual citations to relevant literature in the field and have kept notes to a minimum. This way, I should manage to annoy everyone.

I have benefitted from detailed comments in the early stages of this project from Sydney Shoemaker and Robert Stalnaker, to both of whom I am grateful. The book bears more than remnants of their critical analysis and is much the better for their gaze; I owe more to Sydney and Bob than specific points and objections (though these too). Ed Stein and J. D. Trout gave me encouraging comments on earlier forms of many of the chapters, and I feel fortunate in having such good colleagues at a distance as my friends.

Earlier versions of particular chapters were read over the last three years at Cornell University, Monash University, the University of Auckland, and Queen's University, as well as at meetings of the Pacific Division of the American Philosophical Association, the Canadian Philosophical Association, the Society for Philosophy and Psychology, and the Southern Society for Philosophy and Psychology. For helpful discussions of bits and pieces, many thanks also to Richard Boyd, Andrew Cling, Mark Crimmins, Frances Egan, David Field, Carl Ginet, Wayne Henry, Terence Horgan, Terence Irwin, Frank Keil, Bernie Kobes, Jim Lipton, Joe Moore, Dave Robb, Dion Scott-Kakures, Sergio Sismondo, and Brian Smith.

Finally on the intellectual debt side of the balance sheet, I would like to thank John Heil and three anonymous referees for detailed comments on the penultimate version of the manuscript. There is good reason to think that none of them will be completely satisfied with the final result.

Versions of the following chapters have appeared previously, and I thank the relevant publishers and editors for permission to reprint the material here:

Chapter 2: 'Individualism, Causal Powers, and Explanation', *Philosophical Studies* 68 (November 1992), pp. 103–39. Copyright 1992 Kluwer Academic Publishers. Reprinted by permission of Kluwer Academic Publishers.

Chapter 3: 'Wide Computationalism', *Mind* 103:351–72. Reprinted by permission of the editor of *Mind* and Oxford University Press.

Chapter 5: 'Against *A Priori* Arguments for Individualism', *Pacific Philosophical Quarterly* 74, 1 (March 1993), pp. 60–79. Reprinted by permission of the journal.

Chapter 8: 'Causal Depth, Theoretical Appropriateness, and Individualism in Psychology', *Philosophy of Science* 61, 1 (March 1994), pp. 55–75. Reprinted by permission of the Philosophy of Science Association.

An earlier, shorter version of Chapter 7 was prepared for and accepted by *Synthese,* but was later withdrawn due to an unusually long delay between acceptance and the likely date of publication.

Figures 1 and 2 on pgs. 81 and 82 are reproduced from *Preception*, 2nd. ed., by R. Sekules and R. Blake by permission of the publisher. (McGraw-Hill, 1990.)

# 1

# Introduction: What is individualism in psychology?

Individualism in psychology is a view about what mental states are, a view about how mental states are to be individuated, classified, taxonomized, or typed. It is a substantive, plausible, and controversial view that, over the last twenty years, has been the focus of much debate in the philosophy of mind. This introductory chapter has four aims: to clarify what individualism is; to explore why it is an extremely plausible view; to explain why, nonetheless, individualism is a controversial thesis about individuation in the sciences of the mind; and to set out the scope and limits of this book.

## 1. NEGATIVE AND POSITIVE CHARACTERIZATIONS OF INDIVIDUALISM

In a frequently quoted passage, Tyler Burge characterizes individualism as the view that 'the mental natures of all a person's or animal's mental states (and events) are such that there is no deep individuative relation between the individual's being in states of those kinds and the nature of the individual's physical or social environments,' (1986a:3–4). According to Burge's formulation, individualism makes a *negative* claim: that the way mental states are individuated is not significantly affected by factors external to the individual who instantiates those states. Individualism is a view about the nature of mental states, a view about what's *not* strictly relevant to their individuation.

What Jerry Fodor calls *methodological solipsism* provides the same sort of negative characterization of individualism. Methodological solipsism is the doctrine that psychology ought to concern itself only with *narrow* psychological states, which do not presuppose 'the existence of any individual other than the subject to whom that state

1

is ascribed' (Fodor 1980a:244).[1] The sense in which psychological states don't presuppose the existence of other individuals is that what those states are, how they are individuated and taxonomized for the purposes of psychological explanation, doesn't presuppose anything in particular about the external world of the individual who has those states. As Fodor reminds us, discussing the Cartesian possibility of prevalent deception, 'there is an important sense in which how the world is makes no difference to one's mental states' (1980a:228). It is how a person *conceives of* the world that determines what that person does. Any taxonomy of psychological states developed within the cognitive sciences should reflect this fact, and individualism expresses a constraint on taxonomy that ensures that this will be so.

These negative characterizations of individualism draw a contrast between the mental or psychological states *of individuals* and the physical and social environments in which such individuals are embedded. Psychological states are, as it is sometimes put, *in the head,* and in taxonomizing psychological states, formulating psychological kinds, the distinction between what is inside the head and what is outside of it is significant. (Hence individualism is sometimes called *internalism* and its denial *externalism* about the mind.) Put epistemologically, the distinction between the knowing subject and the world known is important for taxonomy and explanation in psychology. As I shall explain more fully in §6, for this reason individualism is motivated in part by a *Cartesian epistemology,* according to which the thinking subject is at best contingently embedded in a physical and social world; the proper investigation of such a knower or cognizer should abstract away from this contingent fact (cf. Burge 1979, 1986b, 1988; Lepore and Loewer 1986:595; Recanati 1993:ch. 12).

Stephen Stich's *principle of autonomy* provides a contrasting *positive* characterization of individualism. Stich says:

The basic idea of the principle is that the states and processes that ought to be of concern to the psychologist are those that supervene on the current, internal, physical state of the organism. . . . [A]ny differences between organisms which do not manifest themselves as differences in their current, internal, physical states ought to be ignored by a psychological theory. . . . [H]is-

---

1 Fodor's characterization of narrow psychological states is taken from Putnam (1975:220), who in introducing the term 'methodological solipsism' initiated recent discussions of individualism in psychology. Note that the term 'methodological solipsism' was used in the early work of the positivists, most notably in Carnap (1928); see §64 of that work for further references.

torical and environmental facts will be psychologically relevant only when they influence an organism's current, internal, physical state. (1983:164–5)

Individualism, as expressed in the principle of autonomy, is the view that mental states must supervene on the intrinsic physical states of the individual in whom they are instantiated. The principle of autonomy states a necessary condition for classifying two mental state tokens as states of different psychological kinds, and so offers a sufficient condition for the classification of two mental state tokens as states of the *same* psychological kind. Two mental states should be classified as belonging to different psychological kinds only if they are 'manifested in' or, in some intuitive sense, correspond to internal physical differences in the creatures in which those states are instantiated; conversely, if two mental states do not correspond to different intrinsic, physical bases, then they are states of the same psychological kind.

Individualists sometimes state their view in terms of how *doppelgängers* must be treated by a scientific psychology: Doppelgängers, individuals sharing all of their intrinsic physical properties, *must* be taxonomized under the same psychological kinds. For mental states to be of different psychological kinds, they must supervene on different intrinsic physical properties; intrinsic physical identity entails psychological identity. This understanding of the principle of autonomy suggests that individualism is also motivated in part by a *physicalist ontology* (see Horgan 1987; Kim 1982).

Just beneath the surface of these negative and positive formulations of individualism is the view of individualism as a *constraint* on individuation and explanation in psychology (cf. Putnam 1975:220). I will now say something more explicit about why such a view of individualism is plausible.

## 2. INDIVIDUALISM AS A CONSTRAINT ON PSYCHOLOGICAL EXPLANATION

A constraint delineates an initial space of options. It can be thought of as a rule dividing what we might call *admissible* possibilities from *mere* possibilities: It both rules out certain options, the mere possibilities, and in so doing tells us which options constitute admissible possibilities. An intuitive example may help to clarify this Janus-faced feature of constraints before we move on to consider constraints on taxonomy and explanation in particular.

Suppose that you want to go somewhere in particular – Oognadatta, as it may be. There are an infinite number of ways in which you can satisfy your desire, each of which specifies a number of parameters, such as mode of transportation, route to be taken, speed at which you might travel, dates and cost of travel, and duration of the journey. Even if there is a sense in which there is an infinity of options here, if you are like most of us, travel anywhere (let alone to Oognadatta) is constrained by those parameters that create the initial space of options. If you want to get there within a few days, that rules out the glorious trip by camel you had dreamt of, as well as many other possible ways of getting to Oognadatta; if you have little money for the trip, then hiring a private jet will be ruled out. The same parameters whose values constrain your travel options also determine which means of travel are admissible possibilities.

The common talk of constraints in the sciences, including psychology, can also be understood in terms of this Janus-faced feature of constraints. For example, evolutionary biologists are faced with a number of constraints on the space of options they can entertain in formulating hypotheses about particular evolutionary phylogenies. There are constraints from population genetics concerning, for example, the speed of genotypic change in a population; from geology, such as the past location and movement of land masses; and from genetics, such as the stability of particular genomes over time. Such constraints create a *manageable* space of alternative hypotheses about the evolutionary past by counting some options as mere possibilities.

Likewise, developmental psychologists often talk of constraints on various aspects of development. These are rules that govern the developmental path of particular capacities and conceptual structures; they both describe something about a developmental process and prescribe something about theories of that process. For example, the child's development of *biological* knowledge appears to be constrained by domain-specific principles that change over time as the child's conception of the biological develops (Carey 1985; Keil 1989). The constraints circumscribe the set of possible conceptions of biology that the child has at a given developmental age. Possible theories of the developmental process themselves are directed by the existence of such constraints, which partition the space of theoretical options into those that are admissible and those that are merely possible. Note that the Janus-faced nature of these constraints in both evolutionary biology and developmental psychology not only rules out certain theoretical options in the science but also, in doing so, makes theory development possible.

These sorts of constraints on scientific explanations are, broadly speaking, *empirical* constraints: they derive from empirical data and constrain particular empirically testable hypotheses and theories. Other constraints on scientific explanation are not so clearly empirical. The sort of case I have in mind here is typified by *behaviorism* as a putative constraint on psychological explanation, in both its 'methodological' and 'philosophical' varieties. Methodological behaviorism is the view that any psychological state posited in a psychological explanation is to be explicated in terms of observable stimuli and responses; philosophical behaviorism is the view that mental state terms are to be defined as stimulus–response pairs (or, more plausibly, sets of such pairs). Such constraints demarcate a space of options about the nature of psychological or mental states into those that are admissible and those that are not (hence one can talk of violating the constraint imposed by behaviorism). But their status is not clearly empirical in the way in which the constraints on evolutionary biology and developmental psychology are. (We will return to the status of behaviorism as a constraint on psychological explanation in Chapter 10.)

What *sort* of constraint is individualism? In many ways, I think it should be viewed as imposing the same sort of constraint that behaviorism imposes, though this view, appropriately clarified, will emerge as a conclusion of this book rather than serve as one of its premises. The status of individualism as either an empirical or an a priori constraint on psychological taxonomy will be a theme very much in the background in Part I, and the relationships between behaviorism and individualism will be a theme in the concluding chapter. For now, let me say something fairly uncontroversial about individualism as a putative constraint on psychological taxonomy and explanation.

The view of individualism as a constraint on how we can categorize mental states and processes for psychological explanation, one that rules out certain ways of taxonomizing mental states and psychological explanations, is implicit in both the negative and positive characterizations of individualism given in §1; individualism specifies a minimal necessary condition that explanations in psychology must meet. Like other constraints, however, it should not be viewed only in terms of what it rules out; in delimiting the space of admissible taxonomies and explanations in psychology, it makes genuine psychological explanation possible. As a constraint on psychological explanation, individualism is both substantive and plausible. In the next section, I discuss the plausibility of accepting individualism as a constraint on taxonomy and explanation in psychology by identifying some of the deep intuitions often invoked in support of it. These intuitions draw on both the negative and positive characterizations of individualism and lead us to a more complete understanding of the individualist's view of the nature of both the mind and psychology.

## 3. THE MIND OF THE INDIVIDUALIST

Kent Bach articulates some of the central intuitions underlying individualism as follows:

What is outside a person's mind is irrelevant to psychology. Regardless of how the world is in comparison to how it is represented as being and regardless of how it may change while the person's psychological states remain the same, everything is the same as far as psychology is concerned. According to MS [methodological solipsism], the psychologically appropriate way to individuate types of beliefs, desires, and other intentional states is by their contents, not by relations the subject has to things in the world, which could have been different without affecting content. . . . What matters is how the subject represents the world, not how the world actually is. (1982:123)

The familiar fact that one can continue to think about something when that thing is absent (or even when it does not exist) is, I think, part of what Bach is referring to here. Our mental representations of the world need not correspond to how the world is, and the former rather than the latter determine our cognitive behavior. As cognizers we carry around symbols for things in the world that enable us to engage in relatively *experience-independent* thought. Kim Sterelny makes this point about cognition succinctly: 'Cognition is information processing, but cognitive operations must be tuned to the physical, intrinsic features of the states that *code* that information, for they have no direct access to the distal causes of those intrinsic features' (1989:75).

In a paper sympathetic to individualism that focuses on Fodor's methodological solipsism, Colin McGinn, echoing Fodor's own remarks about the *inaccessibility* of the semantic properties of mental states, says:

The following question arises [for Fodor]: in virtue of what do beliefs play a role in the agent's psychology? And, it seems, Fodor contends, that there can be only one answer to this question: beliefs play a role in the agent's psychology just in virtue of intrinsic properties of the implicated internal representations – the semantic *relations* between representations and things in the world must be irrelevant to the psychological role of beliefs. More precisely, the causal role of a belief must depend upon, and only upon, those properties of representations that can be characterized without adverting to matters lying outside the agent's head. (1982:208)

As McGinn goes on to say, according to this view, '[i]t is not *what* is encoded that matters to causal role, but what it is coded *into*' (1982:210). Michael Devitt spells out the individualist's view of *psychology* more explicitly:

In psychology, we are concerned to explain why, given stimuli at her sense organs, a person evinced certain behavior. Only something that is entirely supervenient on what is inside her skin – on her intrinsic internal physical states, particularly her brain – could play the required explanatory role between peripheral input and output. Environmental causes of her stimuli and effects of her behavior are beside the psychological point. The person and all her physical, even functional, duplicates must be psychologically the same, whatever their environments. Mental states must be individuated according to their role within the individual, without regard to their relations to an environment. (1990:377)

These varying expressions of individualism – that mental states are intrinsic; that it is the representation of the world, not the world itself, that is relevant to psychology; that psychologically relevant states must supervene on the current internal physical states of the organism – share a common core. Psychology involves abstracting over the mental states of *individuals*: It is concerned with identifying the cognitive contribution of the individual to her own behavior. As such, it is the *causal powers* of an individual's mental states that are relevant to psychological taxonomy and explanation. How an individual's states interact with one another, and how they, in turn, cause that individual's behavior are, after all, facts about that individual. Individuals form their particular mental states in various ways, but it is their being in those states rather than how they came to have them that is relevant to their subsequent behavior. Since psychology is concerned in large part with predicting and explaining cognitive behavior, it ought to ignore any difference between individuals that does not itself make a difference to the role that some mental state plays in the causation of behavior.

7

Even if individuals live in significantly different worlds, they can be partially (or, in principle, wholly) psychologically identical, where this implies that they are to be regarded as instantiating some (or, in principle, all) of the same psychological kinds. If two mental states have the same causal powers, then, according to the individualist, psychology ought to classify or taxonomize those particular mental states as being of the same kind. Facts about the history or environment of an individual are relevant to mental causation and mental taxonomies, as Stich says, only insofar as such facts are manifested in the internal physical states of the individual. We can distinguish between states that respect the constraint of individualism, these being, in Stich's terms, *autonomous,* and states that do not. Individualism says that psychology ought to be concerned only with autonomous psychological states.

Stich (1983:165) highlights the intuitive distinction between autonomous and non-autonomous states by considering an individual and the *replacement* of that individual, a physical replica of that individual. An individual and her replacement will differ in many properties, particularly their historical properties, and, when they are located in different environments, may even behave differently. But since they are physically identical in constitution, replacements have the same *dispositions* to behave; an individual and her replica have the same behavioral *potential*. If an individual does $A$ in $E_1$, then her replacement must also do $A$ in $E_1$, even if the replacement is not, in fact, in $E_1$. Placed in identical environments, physically identical individuals must behave in the same way. There is an intuitive difference between the sorts of properties and states that replacements share, such as their disposition to behave, and the sorts of properties that they differ in, such as when they were born or whether they are located three miles from a burning barn. Since psychology is interested in explaining the dispositional behavior of individuals *across* environments, it ought to concern itself only with the types of properties and states that replacements share. The constraint of individualism attempts to demarcate just such autonomous properties and states.

With these claims about individuals and explanation in mind, individualism might be thought of as a particular instance of a general taxonomic principle governing scientific explanation, something like the following: Only entities that share the same causal powers ought to be grouped together in a scientific explanation. In fact, Fodor himself has made this claim, a claim that is the focus of the next

8

chapter: '[I]ndividualism is a completely general methodological principle in science; one which follows simply from the scientist's goal of causal explanation and which, therefore, all scientific taxonomies must obey' (1987:42–3). An individual and her replacement, since they are physically identical, share the same composition, mass, height, and biological functions. For the purposes of taxonomy in physics, chemistry, biochemistry, biophysics, or biology, an individual would be treated the same way as her duplicate, for two individuals sharing these types of properties have the same causal powers so far as each of these disciplines is concerned. Each of these properties is an intrinsic property of the individual whose behavior is being explained. Psychological categories, *whatever* they are, must be subject to the same general constraint. For the purpose of formulating projectible generalizations, one taxonomizes objects and properties by their causal powers. And causal powers supervene on the intrinsic, physical states of the individual instantiating those powers.

One point seldom explicitly registered is that since taxonomies in an individualistic psychology individuate mental states in accord with their causal *powers,* individualistic taxonomies treat the causes and effects of any mental state in different ways. Taxonomy will be forward-looking in that it *must* reflect what mental states themselves can cause, that is, other mental states and behaviors. Yet it will be backward-looking only insofar as the causes of mental states make a difference to what those mental states themselves can cause. Thus historical and other relational properties are relevant to an individualistic taxonomy of psychological states, as Stich says, 'only when they influence an organism's current, internal, physical state' (1983:165).

This suggests one way in which individualism is a stronger, that is, more restrictive, view than functionalism in the philosophy of mind, even 'narrow' or 'short-armed conceptual role' functionalism (Block 1986:636). Functionalism, the view that mental states are individuated by their total causal or functional roles, does not distinguish between the causes and effects of mental states in determining whether two mental states are of the same kind. A functionalist would distinguish two mental states, $S_1$ and $S_2$, if $S_1$ could only be caused by $C_1$ and $C_2$, whereas $S_2$ could only be caused by $C_3$, even if the total effects of $S_1$ and $S_2$ were identical across all possible circumstances. Since the functional role of a state includes both its tendency to be caused and its power to cause, states such as $S_1$ and $S_2$ that differ in the former will be taxonomized differently, even if they agree in the latter. An individualist, by contrast, could not offer a taxonomic scheme distinguishing states such as $S_1$ and $S_2$, since such states have identical causal powers. Since individualism is, in this respect, a stronger view than functionalism, individualism imposes a constraint on individuation that is not derivable from functionalism alone.

In this section, I have concentrated on both the intuitions that motivate and support individualism and the conception of the mind and psychology that individualism expresses. If I have done my job well, individualism should appear intuitively plausible. *Of course* individualism is a constraint on psychological explanation; how could it not be? We need a Cartesian psychology for the investigation of physical minds. There might seem, then, little reason to think that individualism is a *substantive* constraint on psychological taxonomy and explanation. But by examining what individualists deny or are committed to rejecting, one can see just why the individualistic constraint on taxonomy is not only substantive but quite contentious.

## 4. CONSEQUENCES OF INDIVIDUALISM

One reason for contention is that the constraint individualism imposes on individuation in psychology is violated by our commonsense belief-desire explanations of behavior (Stich 1978a); what is often called our *folk psychology* invokes a notion of wide content. Before explaining why folk psychology violates individualism, a note on the term 'folk psychology' itself.

Both philosophers (e.g., Churchland 1979; Lewis 1972), and psychologists (e.g., Gopnik 1993; Wellman 1990) have viewed our commonsense or folk psychology as a *theory* about the inner mental life and behavior of agents. What is meant in saying this is often not clear, but a minimal consequence is that folk psychological explanations at least appear to be both systematic and predictive in the way that *scientific* explanations are: Folk psychology is structured by positing basic theoretical entities, such as beliefs and desires, whose interactions with one another are regular and make it possible to predict what people will feel, think, or do in certain circumstances. Such minimalism about conceiving of folk psychology as a theory – a minimalism I shall presuppose in talking of folk psychology – is compatible with thinking that folk psychological explanations are interpretational or narrative in their form (Davidson 1980, 1984), depend on empathy or simulation (Gordon 1986) or involve an irreducible phenomenological aspect (Goldman 1993); it is also compatible with thinking that folk psychology is a badly mistaken theory about individuals.

Stich has argued that the propositional attitudes, particularly belief, have historical, contextual, and 'ideological' features built into their very conception, and this fact about them results in a conflict with the principle of autonomy. Since Stich takes the principle of autonomy to be a constraint on psychological explanation he concludes that 'folk psychology has taxonomized states too narrowly, drawing distinctions which are unnecessary and cumbersome when we are seeking a systematic causal explanation of behavior. To believe that p is to be in an autonomous functional state *and* to have a certain history, context, and ideological relation to the ascriber' (1983:170). Only the property specified in the first of these conjuncts, being in an autonomous functional state, respects the autonomy principle, and only this type of property should constitute the subject matter of psychology proper. Explanation in psychology should be individualistic or *narrow,* not non-individualistic or *wide.*

Stich's primary concern in the 1978 paper referred to at the beginning of this section was to identify a conflict between folk psychological ascriptions and the principle of autonomy. One weakness of that paper is that it relies on the premise that '[i]f a belief token of one subject differs in truth value from a belief token of another subject, then the tokens are not of the same type' (Stich 1978a:357). The centrality of this view about belief individuation to folk psychology can reasonably be questioned. For example, indexical and demonstrative beliefs would seem to be counter-examples to the claim that Stich's premise makes (as Stich himself acknowledges in an appendix to his paper, which attempts to defend the premise). In fact, since the assumed premise is false in the intra-personal case – the truth value of a belief can change over time because of a change in the world – it seems an unreasonably stringent necessary condition on individuation in the interpersonal case. Tyler Burge (1979, 1982a, 1982b, 1986a) has, however, provided a convincing defence of the view that folk psychological notions *are* sensitive to physical, linguistic, and social factors that does not rely on this premise. Like Stich, Burge thinks that folk psychological notions themselves are not individualistic. That is, folk psychological mental states are individuated, in part, by factors that are not fixed by the internal, physical states of the individuals who instantiate them.

11

To bring out why, consider the following variation on the original Putnam (1975) and Burge (1979) thought experiments introduced, in part, to show that folk psychology is not individualistic. Suppose there is an individual, Rex, much like us, who comes into regular contact with *water*, calls it 'water', and knows that others in his community call it 'water'. Rex will have various *beliefs about water*, including beliefs such as the following: that water runs through the taps, that there is water in the local swimming pool, that he uses water to wash his car (occasionally), that water tastes better when it is diluted with scotch. It is plausible to think that Rex has beliefs about water in particular, not, say, some stuff that is phenomenally similar to water, because it is *water* that surrounds Rex. (By parity of reasoning, had Rex been surrounded by that other stuff, he would have had beliefs about that stuff, not about water.) Folk psychology is *intentional:* We individuate folk psychological states, such as belief and desire, in part by their *contents,* and the contents of at least many such states are specified by reference to things that are outside the heads of the individuals in whom those states are instantiated.

Thus we can see why folk psychology violates the methodological solipsism formulation of individualism. To see why it also violates the principle of autonomy formulation, we need to consider the case of doppelgängers. A graphic way to do so is to consider the fancy of Twin Earth. Suppose that there is a place very much like Earth, *Twin Earth,* with stuff on it very much like water, twin water (or *twater*), at least in the sorts of properties that people like Rex can detect, but is not water. Then, a Twin Earth individual who is physically identical to Rex, Twin Rex (or *T-Rex*) has beliefs about twater. But now, comparing Rex on Earth with T–Rex on Twin Earth, we have a case in which there is, *ex hypothesi,* an identity in intrinsic physical properties but a difference in folk psychological states; thus we have a case showing that folk psychological taxonomy violates the principle of autonomy. Burge (1979, 1986a) has argued, convincingly in my view, that these conclusions are general in two ways: (a) they apply to beliefs about a range of things (e.g., arthritis, contracts, sofas), not just those about natural kinds, and (b) the fancy of Twin Earth is not crucial, since one can formulate the thought experiments in terms of an individual in her actual environment and that individual in a counterfactual environment.

One problem with folk psychological individuation being non-individualistic is that it implies that being a member of one linguistic community rather than another, or living in a world with one type of stuff on it (water) instead of another (twater), are properties that determine what one's folk psychological mental states are, that is, what kinds they are instances of. What I shall call the *standard intuition* about molecularly identical duplicates who are causally connected to different kinds of stuff is that they have folk psychological states with *different* contents. Yet properties such as living in a world with one type of stuff on it (water) rather than another (twater) appear to play no real causal role in the life of the individual, and taxonomizing mental states partially in terms of them does seem, as Stich says, to individuate mental states too finely. If one is an individualist and accepts that folk psychological individuation is non-individualistic, as for example both Stich and Fodor do, then one must either reject or advocate the revision of folk psychological explanation. For the most part, individualists have conceded that folk psychology is at least in part wide; the locus of debate has been the significance of this feature of folk psychology.

Though the view that folk psychology is wide is shared by many individualists and non-individualists, it is not a universal view. For example, John Searle (1983:ch. 8) and Brian Loar (1988a) are individualists who reject this view; Peter Unger (1983, 1984) also questions whether folk psychological ascriptions are non-individualistic. These philosophers all reject the standard intuition about the Putnam–Burge Twin Earth thought experiments, an intuition that both presupposes and supports the causal theory of reference. Searle defends a descriptivist theory of reference over a causal theory; Loar argues that the thought experiments show only that psychological ascriptions have a non-individualistic, *social* content in addition to an individualistic, *psychological* content; Unger argues against the causal theory on the grounds that it fails to account for important 'secondary intuitions' (1983) and argues for a broad conception of philosophical inquiry that allows for what he calls *semantic relativity* (1984), a conception of philosophical semantics that undermines the significance of the causal theory of reference. Also, some have argued directly against the externalist conclusions that have been drawn from the thought experiments (Crane 1991; Elugardo 1993), others have argued against the *relevance* of the thought experiments to conclusions about psychological kinds (Cummins 1991). Except in passing, I shall not discuss these challenges to the standard intuition about the twin cases.

One reason for restricting the discussion in this way is that even though there may be a sense in which doppelgängers *are* in the same psychological state, more puzzling is that there seems also to be a clear sense in which they are in different psychological states. There is at least an aspect to our ordinary folk psychological explanations for human behavior that is not individualistic. How are we to make sense of this if individualism is a general constraint on psychological taxonomy and explanation? If we accept individualism as such a constraint, then even aspects of folk psychological taxonomy and explanation that are wide are problematic, something not to be explained but explained away. These positions must recognize at least a prima facie conflict between individualism and (aspects of) our folk psychology.

A second reason is that the conflict between individualism and the types of ascriptions made in folk psychological explanations of action is quite general. The conflict is neither solely nor essentially one between *folk* psychology and individualism. This is not to say that much, if not most, of the debate over individualism hasn't centered on folk psychological notions; on the contrary, it has. The point, rather, is that the conflict itself is more general than has often been supposed by individualists and non-individualists alike; it is not only the propositional attitudes that violate the constraint of individualism. Differences in the semantic or representational properties, particularly the truth, reference, and content, of mental states do not in themselves constitute or imply differences in the internal physical states of individuals. This is true of *any* mental state that can be described as having representational content, whether or not it is a propositional attitude, such as a belief or desire.

We can see this by generalizing the recipe for Twin Earth cases. Consider our two individuals, Rex and T-Rex, who are physically identical but exist in environments that differ in some way that they cannot detect. Rex will have mental representations, folk or otherwise, that are about something on Earth, something that is not, *ex hypothesi,* on Twin Earth at all, whereas T-Rex's mental representations will be about something on Twin Earth. Hence the contents of their representations are different. Since, *ex hypothesi,* Rex and T-Rex are physically identical, this difference is not manifest in their internal physical states. The mental states of Rex and T-Rex, described in terms of content, are not supervenient on the internal physical states of those agents. So, accepting individualism in psychology, explanatory ascriptions of content, including those made by folk psychology, are not taxonomically relevant for the discipline of psychology.

## 5. FRAMEWORK AND SCOPE

An individualist who thinks that this complete generalization of the Twin Earth argument is valid will be likely to explore the possibility of developing psychological explanations that are *content-free*. Such an individualist takes there to be a conflict between the individuation of mental states *by content* and the constraint of individualism. The radical option of a content-free, individualistic psychology is one that Stich thinks defensible; his *syntactic* theory of mind provides the foundations for one way in which an individualistic psychology could be developed.

Few individualists do accept a complete generalization of the argument, however. Perhaps the most prevalent individualist response to the standard Twin Earth intuition has been to argue that individualism is compatible with *some* notion of content, even if not with ordinary, folk psychological, wide content.[2] Rather than accepting Stich's syntactic theory, based as it is on a radical abandonment of content, such philosophers pursue a more conservative, revisionary path, advocating a notion of *narrow content*. Narrow content is a notion that is compatible both with individualism and with the view that content ascriptions play a genuine explanatory role in psychology. This notion of content is distinct from, inter alia, the truth conditions that mental states have, for the truth conditions of, say, a belief clearly flout the constraint of individualism. As the thought experiments about individuals like Rex and T-Rex indicate, the truth conditions for beliefs of physically identical agents can vary. Yet if individualism is true, psychology ought to be concerned solely with the sorts of properties that physically identical agents, were they to exist, would share. The revisionary version of individualism claims that there is some notion of content that *does* abide by the constraint of individualism.

As the existence of both content-free (syntactic) and intentional (narrow content) versions of individualism indicates, we can distinguish two questions about explanation in psychology. First, does

---

2 Those making such a response include Block (1986), Devitt (1990), Field (1978), Fodor (1982, 1987:ch. 2, 1991a), Loar (1981:chh. 4, 7, 1988a), McGinn (1982), Segal (1989a, 1991), and White (1982, 1991:ch. 2).

individualism actually impose a constraint on psychological explanation? We have spent the bulk of this chapter examining the motivations behind an affirmative answer to this question. Second, ought psychology to refer to an individual's mental contents at all in explaining cognitive behavior? This is a question about the relevance of *intentional* or *representational* properties to psychological explanation. If one does think that such properties are relevant to explanation in psychology, one is faced with the *problem of intentionality:* What are intentional properties, and what place do they have in a naturalistic worldview? Since the questions about individualism and content are distinct, note that both individualists and non-individualists who think that reference to mental contents is a necessary part of psychological explanation must face the problem of intentionality.

The principal issue with which I shall be concerned is the significance of individualism *for psychological explanation.* Thus I shall not be primarily concerned to evaluate claims of the form 'content of type *X* is narrow/wide', as some other philosophers have. For example, McGinn (1989:ch. 1) argues that perceptual or phenomenological content must be shared by doppelgängers. By 'perceptual content' McGinn means the experiential content of mental states, what philosophers of a previous generation might have called the *sense data* of experience. Supposing that McGinn is right about perceptual content so understood, this is relevant to my interest in individualism here only if there is reason to think that such content plays some role in psychological explanation. More generally, the existence of narrow content does not support the view that individualism is a constraint on psychological explanation unless such content is crucial to psychological explanation.

Likewise, the existence of psychological states that have wide content does not imply that individualism is *not* a constraint on psychological explanation. Gareth Evans, for example, has defended a form of what he calls *Russell's Principle,* the view that 'a subject cannot make a judgement about something unless he knows which object his judgement is about' (Evans 1982:89). This principle is most plausible in cases of demonstrative, perceptual identification, though we need not concern ourselves here with the precise domain for which the principle holds. Evans argues that together with other plausible principles, Russell's Principle entails that there is some class of thoughts that gain their content from the subject's relation to *particular* objects in the world. To take Evans's own example (1982:90), consider a case in which a subject sees one of two identical steel balls. Supposing that he has no knowledge that could distinguish having seen one of the balls rather than the other, what sense does it make to say that his thoughts are about one rather than the other? If one takes such discriminating knowledge to be the result of informational links between the subject and object in question, as Evans himself does, then ascribing thoughts to the subject about *that* ball presupposes the subject's appropriate location in the world: Ascriptions of this type of content to an individual *do* presuppose the existence of some object external to that individual.[3] Even if Evans is right in thinking that the information-based version of Russell's Principle he defends holds for some types of mental states, this does not show that individualism fails to be a constraint on psychological explanation. To show *that,* one needs to argue that the ascription of these non-individualistic mental states plays some general role in psychological explanation.

Having offered both negative and positive characterizations of individualism, articulated part of the individualist's conception of the mind and psychology, and said why individualism is a plausible yet controversial constraint on psychological explanation, I offer some further reflections on the individualist's conception of the mind. It is a conception that draws on both Cartesian and physicalist intuitions.

## 6. INDIVIDUALS: CARTESIAN AND PHYSICALIST INTUITIONS

We have seen two distinct formulations of individualism. The principle of autonomy says that mental states must supervene on the intrinsic physical states of the individual in whom they are instantiated; the doctrine of methodological solipsism says that the taxonomies of mental states we form for the purpose of psychological explanation do not presuppose the existence of anything beyond the individual instantiating those states. Even though these two formulations of individualism are distinct, I shall not be concerned with articulating the *precise* nature of the distinction between them. Rather, I want to make two points about what they share as formulations of individual-

---

3 John McDowell also develops a version of this view, what Blackburn has called *strong singular thought theory.* See McDowell (1977, 1984, 1986) and the critiques of Blackburn (1984:ch. 9) and Segal (1989b); cf. also Noonan (1986) and Peacocke (1981).

ism, points that will elucidate both the presuppositions of the debate over individualism and the 'physicalist' and 'Cartesian' motivations for individualism to which I have already alluded.

As mentioned in §1, it is sometimes said that an individualistic taxonomy of mental states formulated in either of these ways locates mental states 'in the head'. Although there are respects in which this metaphor is misleading (see Chapter 6), it does articulate the idea that since *individuals* are the ultimate bearers of mental states, one ought to develop explanatory categories for mental processing and behavior that characterize mental states as being instantiated in a self-contained individual. The first point, then, is that were mental states to be located elsewhere in the body than in the head (say, in the heart), this would not significantly affect the debate over individualism. Importantly, there would still be a boundary marked by the sensory stimulations and basic bodily actions of an individual that, individualists claim, circumscribes the subject matter of psychology. More radically, someone who thought that talk of the location of mental states was at best metaphorical and at worst something like a category mistake – say, because she held that minds were not physically instantiated – could still be an individualist. (Since traditional dualism has few adherents today, and since even fewer combine dualism with an individualistic view of psychological explanation, I shall set to one side such a doubly Cartesian view in what follows.)

This raises a second point about our characterizations of individualism: They presuppose a substantive view about what sort of thing an individual is. Both individualists and their opponents have a clear notion of what sort of entity they mean by 'individual': It is something like an *organism* or *agent*. More specifically, individuals are presumed to be both *physically integrated* and *psychologically independent* entities.[4] That is, the individuals on whose intrinsic, physical states mental states supervene, or outside of whom one cannot refer in taxonomizing their mental states, have both spatial and causal integrity, as well as a certain autonomy from other entities in the world. To understand what 'integrity' and 'independence' mean here, and

---

4 Cf. McGinn (1989:15–24), who suggests that the denial of individualism is prima facie implausible because it involves denying that the mind is a substance, where substances are, in McGinn's terms, *bounded* and *self-subsistent*. I think that the *issue* of individualism, not just its acceptance, presupposes that individuals are physically integrated (roughly, McGinn's 'bounded') and psychologically independent (roughly, McGinn's 'self-subsistent').

to see that the question of whether individualism is a constraint on psychological explanation presupposes that both are features of individuals, consider creatures that lack these properties.

Consider, first, an individual whose brain or sensory organs are physically remote from her body, connected, perhaps, by radio waves over thousands of miles. Such an individual lacks the spatial and causal locality that physically integrated individuals like us have. This is not to suggest that such an individual could not have a mental life very much like those we have or, in principle at least, a mental life exactly like those we have. Yet there are worldly contingencies that such an individual's mental life is subject to that ours is not, and this blurs our intuitions about just what such a mental life would consist of. In particular, whether an individual with remote sensory organs has mental states that satisfy either the principle of autonomy or the doctrine of methodological solipsism is an issue that cannot be clearly formulated. What counts as inside and outside for such an individual? What *are* her intrinsic, physical states?

Perhaps more needs to be said about the idea that we are psychologically independent, for this idea is complex and identifies a characteristic distinctive of *thinking* beings. Much of our occurrent mental life is *chosen,* and what we choose to think, imagine, and remember, for example, is not determined either by what others think or by how the physical world is constituted. In what sense would our thoughts be *ours* were we not to have this sort of control? Although there are deep puzzles about the sense in which we are free to determine our actions by our beliefs and desires (our dispositional mental life, if you like), we do normally think of our ordinary actions as free from outside interference, as being 'up to us'. Turning from the first- to the third-person case, the individuals whose behavior we observe are *units of action,* originators of what they do; they are psychologically independent.

It is clearly possible for a creature with a mental life to lack this independence: There are possible creatures whose mental lives are systematically tied to one another, perhaps through mutual causal dependence or through their being coinstantiated in the very same physical stuff. An obvious point is that *we* are not such creatures. A less obvious point is that for individuals who lack the psychological independence that we clearly have, the debate over individualism cannot be expressed in terms of whether or not one accepts the principle of autonomy or methodological solipsism as constraints on psychological taxonomy and explanation. As in the case of creatures lacking physical integrity, for creatures lacking psychological independence there are no clear answers to the questions that underlie these formulations of individualism. Does reference to states that are shared by mutually dependent individuals violate methodological solipsism? Are shared physical states intrinsic to each of a pair of psychologically dependent individuals?

The conception of an individual as a physically and causally integrated entity that is psychologically independent also reflects two different sorts of motivation for individualism that I identified in §1. On the one hand, a physicalist worldview motivates a philosophical psychology that allows one to understand psychological agents *as* physical beings, highlighting what agents have in common with the rest of the physical world. Stated as the view that psychological states must supervene on intrinsic physical states, individualism can be seen as the application to psychology of a general physicalist constraint on individuation and ontology. This sort of motivation for individualism corresponds to viewing an individual as physically and causally *integrated,* for it is this property that individual agents share with other material entities.

On the other hand, individualism is also motivated by the idea that it is how an agent herself *conceives* of the world rather than the nature of the physical world itself that explains her actions. The ability of agents to conceive of the world at all is a feature that *distinguishes* them from other physical things in the world. In the Cartesian epistemological tradition, foundations for knowledge are indubitable posits, grasped or known in some way by the individual, whether such posits are clear and distinct ideas, as for Descartes himself, or the incorrigible sense data of the empiricists; the *justificatory* primitives to which the first person has privileged access are mental facts about an individual. It is this *type* of fact that the individualist thinks of as *explanatorily* primitive in psychology: Psychology should be concerned with identifying the cognitive contribution that an agent *herself* makes to her own behavior, where this contribution is distinct from that which the individual's environment makes. This distinction between an individual's mental life and her physical and social worlds is also at the core of the conception of individuals as psychologically *independent;* it is agents so conceived who are units of action.

Philosophers use 'individuate' in a number of different ways, and it may further clarify just what sort of view I take individualism to be by being more precise about what I mean in characterizing individualism as a view about individuation in psychology.

Traditional philosophical discussions of criteria for individuation are about particulars, usually objects, and focus on the issue of what makes a given thing the thing that it is. In this sense, when one individuates an object, one specifies *identity conditions,* that is, conditions under which a particular thing can be said to exist or to continue to exist. In such discussions, the focus is on what makes one thing at a particular time the *very same thing* as some thing at some other time; there is a concern with the nature of the links between what are thought of as successive temporal stages of one and the same object, and with the role that continuity plays in our concept or concepts of identity. The identity of indiscernibles can be seen as an abstract principle that provides a sufficient condition for the identity and individuation of objects in this sense of 'individuation'. Perhaps the most familiar philosophical location of this use of 'individuation' is in discussions of *personal* identity, where the various criteria (e.g., memory, bodily continuity, psychological connectedness) are proposals for what makes a particular person *that* person.

Individualism in psychology is *not* first and foremost a view about the individuation of particulars in this sense. Rather, individualism makes a claim about the individuation of *kinds of* particulars or, more simply, about the individuation of kinds, types, or categories. That is, individualism is a view about the classification of particular entities into kinds or categories. This is apparent in both formulations of individualism we have discussed: Both methodological solipsism and the principle of autonomy state constraints on the *taxonomy* of mental states. When philosophers of science ask questions about how, say, biologists individuate organs or organisms, they are asking questions about how these entities are categorized or taxonomized in the relevant science. The concern in such an inquiry is not with the identity conditions for particular entities but, if you like, with the identity conditions for kinds (or, generally, groups) of entities.

The distinction here is between what I shall call the *instantial* and *taxonomic* conceptions of individuation; individualism is a view about the latter conception. Individualism does not say anything directly about the identity of mental particulars, whether these be objects, states, or processes, and insofar as it has implications for what mental states *are,* it does so via a claim about explanations of behavior that invoke them. As a putative constraint on psychological explanation, individualism is a view about *taxonomic* individuation, since it is only by making a claim about the individuation of kinds of entities that it can offer a constraint on what specifications of mental states are to feature in psychological explanations.[5]

Although classic discussions of identity and individuation focus on objects, note that the same sorts of questions raised in such discussions can also be raised about other ontological types, such as properties. This is important here, for to view individualism as a putative constraint on the taxonomic identity of mental particulars might be thought to beg an important question in favor of the individualist. As Robert Stalnaker has pointed out to me, an anti-individualist might well balk at the idea that she is taking a position about mental *particulars* at all; rather, the debate about individualism is one about what sorts of psychological properties we can properly ascribe *to individuals,* where such individuals are the only particulars of concern, individualism being the view that such properties must supervene on the intrinsic physical properties of the individual. On this view of the issue, individualism can be construed as a view about the taxonomic individuation of mental or psychological *properties,* rather than the instantial individuation of their instances (see Chapter 6).

Viewing individualism as a constraint on taxonomic individuation has implications for the sense in which individualism is a *metaphysical* thesis about the mind. As my discussion in the previous section suggests, I do take individualism to have certain metaphysical presuppositions and implications. Yet I do not see individualism itself as the sort of metaphysical thesis that others have sometimes taken it to be. For example, Colin McGinn (1989:ch.1) has discussed what he calls 'internalism' and 'externalism'. (As McGinn uses them, 'internalism'

---

5 It may be tempting to think of the distinction I am drawing as the familiar distinction between numerical and qualitative identity. But a common way of understanding qualitative identity implies that two qualitatively identical entities share all of their phenomenal properties. Clearly, two entities could be of different kinds even were they to share all of these properties, and so qualitative identity does not entail taxonomic identity. Hence qualitative and taxonomic identity are distinct.

and 'externalism' are restricted versions of individualism and non-individualism, respectively: They concern the relation between an individual and her *non-conceptual* environment; see McGinn 1989:2n.) Comparing externalism to a particular criterion of personal identity, McGinn says that '[b]oth are metaphysical theses about the essential nature of the entities in question' (p. 3); that internalism and externalism are theses 'about the existence and identity conditions of mental states' (p. 3); and that 'the externalist holds that the mind is penetrated by the world, configured by it' (p. 10). My problem with these sorts of characterizations is not that McGinn conceives of individualism primarily as a view about instantial rather than taxonomic individuation; rather, he makes no distinction between the two, moving freely between what I am claiming are distinct senses of 'individuation'.[6]

Theses about instantial individuation concern the identity and individuation of particulars; theses about taxonomic individuation, such as individualism, concern the identity and individuation of kinds. Since it is particulars that are classified into kinds, these two senses of 'individuate' are not unrelated; the point here is that they are distinct. One way to show this is to make it plausible to see questions concerning instantial and taxonomic individuation as related in a certain way; two notions can bear *this* relation to one another only if they are non-identical. I think it is compelling to view questions about the individuation of a particular entity as *presupposing* a consideration of that entity as being of a particular kind (see Macnamara 1992; Wiggins 1980:chh. 1, 2). In this respect, questions concerning the taxonomic individuation of kinds are conceptually antecedent to those concerning the instantial individuation of particular things.

The main reason for thinking this to be true is that it is difficult to make sense of talk about individuative or identity conditions for entities *per se*. Rather, one can only talk of the identity conditions for particular things considered as things of a certain type. (If this is true,

---

6  There is a corresponding shift between two senses of 'constituent' throughout McGinn's book. For example, McGinn says that, according to the externalist, 'the world enters constitutively into the individuation of states of mind' (p. 9), the truth of which relies, I think, on a conception of constitution as a *taxonomic* relation of the sort that holds between properties (or kinds) and their instances. For the most part, however (e.g., pp. 5–6, 20–1, 41–3, 115n), McGinn conceives of constitution as an *ontological* relation of the sort that obtains between part and whole.

then even principles that govern identity that do not seem to refer to particular *kinds* of entities at all, such as the indiscernibility of identicals, are about the identity conditions of particular things qua things of certain kinds; I shall not attempt to develop or defend this intuition here.) Criteria for personal identity, for example, are criteria for the identity of particular *persons,*[7] and the centrality of that category for our personal lives and the moral issues they are immersed in has made the topic of personal identity a focus in discussions of identity.

To see the dependence of instantial individuation on taxonomic individuation, consider the traditional, first-person expression of the puzzle of personal identity: What is it that makes me *me?* Although this might appear to be a question about an entity *simpliciter,* this is only because the kind to which that entity belongs is implicit in the question posed. Suppose that, as an individual, I am considered as a concentrated, swarming mass of various biochemical properties rather than as a person. To the extent that the question of what makes me *me* has any sense at all on this supposition, it has a different significance than it normally does; it becomes a question that does not elicit the same interest as does the issue of *personal* identity.

We might think that we can pose a question about instantial individuation without presupposing that the object in question belongs to some category, that is, that it is a token of a type. Yet there seems no way in which one can *evaluate* a given criterion for instantial individuation without making an assumption about the type to which the given entity belongs. To take Hobbes's famous example, to determine whether a given ship at some time is the very same thing as the ship of Theseus, we must consider the object as a particular kind of thing, for example, *as a ship;* it is, *ex hypothesi,* the very same collection of planks. Bare particulars, spatio-temporal concentrations of matter that are not taxonomically individuated at all, don't have identity conditions. Questions about their instantial individuation, about their criteria for identity, do not appear to be well-formed. This makes it tempting to infer that the notion of a bare particular makes no sense. (There is, I recognize, a vortex of difficult issues here concerning identity and instantial individuation into which further discussion threatens to drag one.)

Perhaps this raises deep metaphysical issues that need not concern

7 As, indeed, Locke stressed in his discussion of identity in the *Essay,* Book ii, ch. xxvii. Cf. also Hobbes, *De Corpore,* Part II, ch. 11, §7.

us at all, and I do not mean to rest more weight on the instantial - taxonomic distinction than it can bear. The chief point to draw from this discussion is that on the view of individualism I am adopting, the debate over individualism falls squarely within the philosophy of science as an issue about the nature of taxonomy and explanation in psychology. Though we will discuss our fair share of metaphysical issues, particularly in Part II, such discussion will proceed with this broader view of the topic in mind.

## 8. AN OVERVIEW

The aim of Part I of this examination of individualism in psychology is to state and critically discuss three influential recent types of arguments for individualism: an a priori argument, an empirical argument, and a pair of methodological arguments. The details of each of these arguments are important, for I think that each has been generally accepted either as providing compelling reasons for thinking individualism to be true or as having identified an important way in which its denial is problematic or even incoherent. In Chapter 2, I consider what I call the *argument from causal powers,* an argument that develops many of the intuitions that motivate individualism discussed in this introductory chapter. In Chapter 3, I examine the *computational argument* for individualism, an argument that rests on the computational theory of mind. In Chapter 4, I consider an argument that claims that a non-individualistic psychology is methodologically incoherent and another argument that appeals to a pattern of explanatory success in support of individualism. I shall argue that each of these arguments is unsound and should be rejected.

In Part II, I consider puzzles about mental causation and psychological explanation that have led some to think of individualism as a minimal condition on the sciences of the mind. Much of the discussion in Part II focusses on *why* psychological kinds need not be individualistic in order to describe entities that feature in causal explanations, and involves developing a non-reductive view of both causal explanation in general and psychological explanation in particular. Chapter 5 extends the argument in Chapter 2 against the argument from causal powers in two ways. First, it examines two related appeals to causal powers and shows that they are subject to much the same objection to which the argument from causal powers is subject. This consolidates the view that the problem identified in the argument from causal powers is a *deep* problem rather than the result of carelessness in expression or a slip of the tongue. Second, it sketches the broader metaphysical conception that makes such appeals to causal powers so tempting and introduces reasons for thinking that this conception is mistaken. In Chapter 6, I respond to the charges that those who deny individualism are committed to implausible views, such as the 'violation of supervenience' and 'action at a distance' in psychology. Showing such charges to be mistaken is an important part of making sense of mental causation without individualism. Discussion here focusses on the significance for psychological taxonomy and explanation of the idea that causation is *local*.

In discussing the computational argument for individualism in Part I, I bracket the question of whether *folk psychological* states ought to be conceived of as computational in order to be viewed as causal. In Chapter 7, I return to this issue by discussing an influential version of the view that folk psychological states are to be understood in terms of the computational theory of mind. I argue that one does not need to accept this 'language of thought' view of folk psychology in order to make sense of the causal nature of folk psychological explanation. What one needs instead is a proper view of the differences between the many levels of description at which psychological explanations can be offered. I develop this often-invoked idea in a way that shows how it is possible to chart a middle course between language of thought realism and instrumentalism about folk psychology.

Part III develops a more direct case against individualism itself. In Chapter 8, I introduce the concepts of causal depth and theoretical appropriateness, concepts that form the basis for two a posteriori constraints on good causal explanations. I argue that non-individualistic or wide explanations of behavior may be causally deeper and more theoretically appropriate explanations than their narrow rivals by reflecting on the case of *evolutionary* explanations of behavior; I then adapt this argument to the case of real interest, that of *psychological* explanations of behavior. In Chapter 9, I examine individualistic proposals for both a content-free and an intentional psychology, arguing that neither looks very promising. In examining particular proposals for both syntactic and narrow content psychology, I draw on points emerging from the preceding four chapters and offer some general reasons for scepticism about the promise of an individualistic psychology.

Since arguments for individualism are unsound (Part I), since individualism itself is not a minimal commitment of any view of psychology attempting to make sense of mental causation and psychological explanation (Part II), and since a consideration of a posteriori constraints on explanation shows why wide psychological explanations should, in some cases, be preferred to their narrow rivals (Part III), individualism should be rejected. Or so I shall argue.

# Part I

*On arguments for individualism*

# 2

# *An a priori argument: the argument from causal powers*

In the Introduction we saw that much of the appeal of individualism derives from intuitive general views about explanation, causation, and causal powers. These views are the basis for an influential argument for individualism developed by Jerry Fodor (1987:ch. 2) that claims that individualism in psychology follows from the nature of scientific explanation. Its central claim is that scientific taxonomies satisfy a general constraint of which individualism in psychology is a particular instance.

## 1. STATING THE ARGUMENT

The argument can be summarized as follows. Sciences typically individuate their explanatory categories and kinds by causal powers, and the causal powers that anything has supervene on that thing's intrinsic physical properties. So, if psychology is to be a science, mental states must supervene on the intrinsic physical properties of individuals; thus individualism is a constraint on psychology.

Both those who have criticized this argument as unsound (Braun 1991; Egan 1991; van Gulick 1989) and those who have been more sympathetic to it (Crane 1991; McGinn 1991; Owens 1993; Williams 1990) have assumed that the argument is at least valid. I shall argue, by contrast, that this argument for individualism equivocates on 'causal powers', and that this equivocation is not simply inherent in a particular formulation of the argument. Rather, the equivocation points to a deep and recurrent problem for those who claim that individualism in psychology follows from generally acceptable claims about explanation, causation, and causal powers. The appeal to the notion of causal powers itself is at the heart of the problem. In terms I shall explain, there is a distinction between an *extended* and a *restricted* notion of causal powers that, once drawn, makes it difficult to see

31

how individualism could be a consequence of the purported scientific nature of psychology. This point about causal powers has implications for related arguments for individualism (see Chapter 5).

Let us be more precise. Consider the following explicit argument for individualism, which I shall refer to as the *argument from causal powers:*

(1) Taxonomic properties and entities in the sciences must be individuated by their causal powers.
(2) The cognitive sciences, particularly psychology, purport to identify taxonomic *mental* causes and formulate generalizations about those causes.
(3) In the cognitive sciences, both the mental causes of an individual's behavior and that behavior itself must be individuated in terms of the causal powers of that individual.

So, since

(4) The causal powers of anything are determined or fixed by that thing's intrinsic physical properties,
(5) Any causes of behavior that are to be taxonomic in the cognitive sciences must be determined or fixed by the intrinsic physical properties of the individual. Thus,
(6) The cognitive sciences, particularly psychology, should concern themselves only with states and processes that themselves are determined by the intrinsic physical properties of the individual.

Despite the argument's apparent validity, in §4 I argue that (1) and (4) require different notions of 'causal powers'; in §§5–7 I defend my claim that this equivocation in the argument constitutes a deep and recurrent problem.

As a grounding for these claims, I focus in the next two sections on Premise (1) and the reasons that have been given for accepting it. This premise articulates a form of *global individualism,* that is, a generalization of the constraint that individualism imposes on psychology. Fodor appeals to what he claims to be general facts about causation and causal explanation, particularly in the sciences, in arguing for global individualism. I make two points about Fodor's argument for (1). First, in the next section, I argue that (1) does not follow from such general facts about causal explanation. Second, in §3, I argue that the most plausible way of defending (1) is by invoking a general claim about the *revisability* of causal explanations and taxonomies. Far from following from uncontroversial claims about causation and causal explanation, (1) rests on an interesting but controversial claim about the nature of scientific explanation.

## 2. AN ARGUMENT FOR GLOBAL INDIVIDUALISM: POWERS AND PROPERTIES

Fodor makes two relatively uncontroversial general claims about causal explanation in support of global individualism. He says:

> We want science to give causal explanations of such things (events, whatever) in nature as can be causally explained. Giving such explanations essentially involves projecting and confirming causal generalizations. And causal generalizations subsume the things they apply to in virtue of the causal properties of the things they apply to. Of course.
>
> In short, what you need in order to do science is a taxonomic apparatus that distinguishes between things insofar as they have *different* causal properties, and that groups things together insofar as they have the *same* causal properties. (1987:34, footnote omitted)

The first claim is that scientific explanation is causal. The second is that the taxonomies that classify the *explanantia* in causal explanations must do so according to causal similarities and causal differences. Hence, Fodor argues, if we are to develop a scientific explanation for some phenomenon, we must taxonomize by causal similarities. The causal nature of scientific explanation *requires* individuation by causal powers.

This final conclusion does not follow, since individuation by sameness or similarity of causal *properties* is not the same thing as individuation by causal *powers*. The concept of a causal property is broader than the concept of a causal power: Powers are essentially forward-looking in a way that properties in general are not (cf. Chapter 1, §3). The relevant causal similarities between two phenomena in a given discipline may involve the *causes* of those phenomena or the causal relations they stand in, rather than what those phenomena are capable of causing. The historical and relational properties that two entities share may well explain why those entities share many other properties, and there is no reason to regard explanations citing such properties as non-causal. Entities taxonomized by historical and relational causal properties can feature as both *explanantia* and *explananda* in causal explanations, and, as I shall argue in some detail in §4, the taxonomy of entities by their historical and relational causal properties is pervasive across the sciences. The fact that sciences offer causal explanations and individuate by causal properties does not entail that they must always individuate by causal powers.

Although I assume a fairly broad notion of causal property in what follows, one that does not rule out a priori either relational or historical properties as causal properties, this does not imply that I take *any* relational or historical predicate to name a causal property. Even on a narrower notion of causal property, which allows only intrinsic and extrinsic causal powers to be causal properties, the distinction between intrinsic powers and properties more generally still points to what is wrong in Fodor's argument for (1), as well as to an inherent tension in the argument from causal powers. Since the notion of a causal property must include at least the extrinsic causal powers that an entity instantiates, and since these do not supervene on that entity's intrinsic physical properties, my reliance on the broad notion of causal property is inessential to the form of my argument.

To illustrate the invalidity of Fodor's inference in his argument for global individualism, consider a non-scientific case. If individuation in science is individuation by causal powers *because* scientific explanation is causal, then the causal nature of other types of explanation should entail that the entities they refer to must be individuated by their causal powers. Suppose we pick out a group of individuals with the predicate 'is a victim of the Hiroshima bombing'. What determines whether someone belongs to this group are facts about that person's history, or perhaps even facts about that person's parents' history, not facts about that person's causal powers; an individual's causal powers do not constitute the individuative criteria that determine whether she is a victim of the Hiroshima bombing. Still, this way of classifying people proceeds by identifying a causal *property* that certain people share, and I take it as obvious that all sorts of causal generalizations are true of people who are classified together by this predicate. In virtue of having been present in Hiroshima at a certain time (or of having had parents who were present), certain people suffered cell degeneration, cancerous growths, and genetic diseases that were caused by the American nuclear attack on Hiroshima. The various generalizations true of these people are systematic, and it is explanatory to point out that some individual was a victim of the Hiroshima bombing in response to a query about aspects of her current bodily state.

This sort of relational individuation is ubiquitous in talk about groups of people (e.g., university graduates, divorcees, pensioners) and the individuals constituting those groups. The existence of a causal explanation for a given phenomenon does not entail that either the entities constituting the phenomenon or those referred to in the causal explanation must be individuated by their causal powers. Therefore, the ubiquity of causal explanation and individuation by causal *properties* across the sciences does not entail a commitment to explanation and individuation by causal *powers*.

## 3. THE PRELIMINARY CHARACTER OF RELATIONAL TAXONOMIES

Despite the invalidity of Fodor's argument for (1), that argument rests on persistent intuitions about the nature of causation and causal explanation that warrant more careful consideration. Even granting some distinction between powers and properties, reflection on the nature of causal explanation brings out an intuitive distinction between relational and historical properties, on the one hand, and intrinsic properties, on the other. Though relational and historical kinds may feature in causal explanations, the properties that individuate such kinds do not play an appropriate explanatory role: Such kinds and properties are not *themselves* the ultimate bases of causal responsibility. If we are interested in entities qua causes or qua *explanantia,* there must be something about those entities themselves that our explanations strive to identify; a category can be genuinely taxonomic only insofar as it groups entities that share causal powers. Such intrinsic properties are causally responsible for the effects we ascribe in causal explanations, and therefore entities must be taxonomized in causal explanations in virtue of sharing them. Whether or not we insist on taxonomy being by causal 'powers', causal taxonomies must at least be by properties that supervene on the intrinsic properties that some entity instantiates.[1]

I have already said that the appeal to causal powers is at the core of the problem with the argument from causal powers; in this respect, what we call a 'causal power' is not a verbal issue, as the previous point perhaps suggests. However, I want to bracket discussion of this issue for a moment in order to point to a prior problem for a proponent of global individualism, even one who claims only that individuation in science must be 'by intrinsic causal properties' rather than 'by causal powers'. The problem stems from the fact that there

1 These intuitions about the characterization of an entity qua cause in a causal explanation have been expressed to me independently and in various forms by Carl Ginet, Terence Horgan, Terence Irwin, and Sydney Shoemaker. They will be focal in much of the remaining discussion in this chapter.

35

are many causal explanations that, like the one in the example I introduced in the previous section, *do* feature kinds individuated by relational and historical properties, and such explanations violate the constraint of global individualism. Given the prima facie conflict between the constraint of global individualism and our explanatory practices, how does the proponent of global individualism explain away the appearances?

A focus on the 'victim of the Hiroshima bombing' example might suggest the following response to this problem. Showing that there are *commonsense* causal explanations of human traits and actions that taxonomize people by something other than their intrinsic causal powers does not show anything about *scientific* causal explanation. After all, our everyday causal talk is not solely aimed at providing causal explanations, and one should expect such talk to be shaped by the other roles it plays in our lives. Perhaps because of this, common-sense causal explanations do not presuppose individuation by causal powers. By contrast, there is something special about the causal nature of *scientific* explanation that entails that scientific explanation presupposes individuation by causal powers.

If one thinks that (1) makes a point not about causal explanation in general but about scientific causal explanation, one needs some criterion distinguishing scientific from ordinary causal explanation. There are a number of closely related and familiar criteria that have been claimed to mark off scientific explanations from other types of explanations. For example, scientific explanations are projectible, law-instantiating, and quantify over natural kinds in a way that other explanations need not. If it is only explanations with these properties – scientific explanations – of which (1) is true, then the existence of ordinary causal explanations that feature relational and historical kinds is irrelevant.

One serious problem with this proposal is that it is notoriously difficult to articulate these notions in such a way that they serve as criteria that demarcate scientific explanations as a class from non-scientific explanations. For example, part of what it is for scientific explanations to be projectible is for them to be *counterfactually rigorous:* In nearby possible worlds, entities of the kinds specified in the explanation also have the properties ascribed in the explanation. However, ordinary causal explanations that form no part of any science are counterfactually rigorous in precisely the same way; much the same is true of the criteria, such as degree of naturalness, entrenchment, or simplicity, that have been offered for marking off projectible from non-projectible predicates. More pointedly, generalizations about historically or relationally individuated entities are no less projectible or scientific than any other types of causal generalizations. Indeed, as we will see in the next section, explanations that feature such kinds are widespread in existing sciences.[2]

Taking on the burden of demarcating scientific from ordinary causal explanation in order to defend global individualism is not a promising way for the proponent of global individualism to discount our liberal appeals to kinds individuated by historical and relational properties. More plausibly, such a proponent could concede that although both scientific and non-scientific causal explanations do feature relational and historical kinds, these are always *preliminary* to taxonomies that conform to global individualism. The preliminary character of relational and historical taxonomies reflects the fact that relational and historical properties are not *themselves* ultimately caus-ally responsible for what entities instantiating such properties do and can do. Relational individuation plays a *reference-fixing* rather than an *essence-identifying* role in causal explanation (*sensu* Kripke 1980). Although many causal taxonomies do not individuate entities by their causal powers, they correspond to taxonomies that do; relational kinds feature in causal explanations because the classification of enti-ties by readily observable, relational properties allows one to investi-gate further the intrinsic causal powers that these entities instantiate. And it is these causal powers that our scientific taxonomies aspire to identify.

A variation on our victim example illustrates what these claims about historical and relational kinds amount to. Suppose that the following generalization is true: that most victims of the Hiroshima bombing suffered from radiation effects of a specific type, say, some specific form of cancer. Though we might use the historical predicate 'is a victim of the Hiroshima bombing' to pick out a particular group of people, what determines whether the preceding generalization is true of *particular individuals* is something about those individuals themselves, not something about their causal histories. The general-ization applies to particular individuals in virtue of some intrinsic,

---

2 What I say about projectibility goes also for appeals to laws and natural kinds as criteria of demarcation. Thus, recent discussions of psychological laws (Fodor 1987:ch. 1, 1991b; Horgan and Tienson 1990; Schiffer 1991) are not really relevant to the argument from causal powers. See also Chapter 7.

physical feature, such as the mutation of a particular gene or the destruction of certain cells. What *really* explains why people with a historical, relational property – being in a certain spatio-temporal region – have a specific type of cancer is that these people now have the intrinsic physical property that *causes* the cancer. This claim about the causal (and thus explanatory) priority of such an intrinsic causal power is plausible because the possession of a certain gene or damage to certain cells partitions the class of people initially taxonomized as victims by the historical-relational property: Those with the gene (say) have the cancer, and those without it do not have the cancer. This allows us, at least in principle, to revise our initial taxonomic scheme. In the new taxonomy, people *are* taxonomized by some intrinsic causal power they have, and their sharing this causal power provides the basis for our causal generalizations about them. We thus arrive at an individualistic taxonomy that *does* form the basis for true causal generalizations; our historical classification is a preliminary guide to or approximation of this taxonomy. Relational taxonomies are sometimes revised in science in this way, as exemplified by the narrowing of the concept of *weight* to that of *mass* in Newtonian mechanics (Stalnaker 1989:291): We begin with an extrinsic property (weight) and decompose it into an intrinsic property (mass) plus a relation (gravitational force). Importantly, we arrive at a property, an intrinsic causal power of an entity, that itself is ultimately causally responsible.

The claim that relational scientific taxonomies have a preliminary and revisable character – a claim needed to defend Fodor's argument for global individualism – rests on some variation of the following view: *Any* category that features in a causal explanation must do so ultimately in virtue of the intrinsic causal powers of its instances. One could determine the plausibility of these general views of scientific taxonomy and explanation by examining a variety of accepted explanations in different sciences, and should some of these fail to taxonomize by intrinsic causal powers, one could determine whether such taxonomies are revisable in the appropriate way. I shall argue that there are such scientific explanations and taxonomies (§4) and that they are not revisable in the prescribed manner (§5). There are kinds and explanations in a variety of sciences for which global individualism is simply false. Or it is false if one gives 'causal powers' what I think is its usual sense. As I hope to show in the next section, however, the argument from causal powers relies on *more than* this sense of 'causal powers'.

## 4. CAUSAL POWERS AND SCIENTIFIC EXPLANATION

In summarizing his discussion of the sort of argument for individualism that we are considering, Fodor identifies two main points:

*Methodological point:* Categorization in science is characteristically taxonomy by causal powers. Identity of causal powers is identity of causal consequences across nomologically possible contexts.

*Metaphysical point:* Causal powers supervene on local microstructure. In the psychological case, they supervene on local neural structure. (1987:44)

There is no understanding of 'causal powers' that satisfies both of Fodor's points here; the same is true of (1) and (4) in the argument from causal powers.[3] If Fodor's methodological point is to be true of sciences as they are actually practiced, then causal powers do not always supervene on local microstructure. If his metaphysical point is to specify a truth about causal powers, then scientific taxonomies do not, as a matter of fact, always individuate in terms of causal powers (cf. Braun 1991:380; Egan 1991:187; van Gulick 1989:157).

To take this latter point first, assume that Fodor's metaphysical point, and so (4) in the argument from causal powers, are true. Burge (1986a:14–20, 1989:309–10) has claimed that when we examine patterns of individuation in a range of sciences, we find that individuation is not always solely or even primarily in terms of an individual entity's intrinsic causal powers. Burge's particular examples (battles, continents, plates, organs, species) are in no way special cases. Evolutionary paleontology offers reconstructive hypotheses about skeletal and other structures of past creatures based on the fossil record. In no real sense could it be said to taxonomize exclusively in terms of the causal powers of past creatures. Many of the geosciences are concerned with how certain formations, such as volcanos and mountains, came about, not with those entities' causal powers; volcanos and

---

3 These were, respectively: (1) Taxonomic properties and entities in the sciences must be individuated by their causal powers. (4) The causal powers of anything are determined or fixed by that thing's intrinsic physical properties.

mountains are not classified in these sciences by their causal powers. Epidemiology sometimes taxonomizes diseases by how they are caused. For example, viral diseases, though varied in their particular causal powers, are grouped together because they are caused by viruses. The same is true of many particular diseases: syphilis, lead poisoning, and birth trauma are diseases or conditions that are typed in terms of their respective causes, not by what they themselves have the power to cause. For example, syphilis is a disease caused by the *Treponema pallidum* bacterium, which infects the blood vessels. This is how it is distinguished from closely related diseases, such as yaws and pinta (Schofield 1979:ch. 5).

The revisability claim sketched in the previous section makes a point about entities insofar as they are to be considered *as causes* or *as explanantia* for a given phenomenon. It might be thought that the previous examples invoke entities only as *explananda* rather than as *explanantia;* although entities that are not taxonomized by their intrinsic causal powers may be cited in causal explanations, they feature only as the *explananda* to which the generalizations apply. There *are* causal generalizations about continents, volcanos, mountains, skeletal structures, and viruses, but, the objection goes, none of these generalizations feature such kinds as causes or *explanantia*. And it is only qua *explanantia* that scientific kinds must be taxonomized by intrinsic causal powers.

Although intuitive, this claim is difficult to maintain once one acknowledges the ubiquity of explanations in the sciences in which there are kinds that do not conform to the constraint of global individualism. For such explanations do not refer to these kinds only as *explananda,* and the claim that they do is at best the sort of reconstructive claim about the nature of scientific explanation of which one should be wary. Explanations of the form 'Because it is an *x*', and 'Because it has *x*', where *x* designates some non-individualistic kind or property, are common in the sciences. For example, the relational property of being highly specialized is causally responsible for the extinction of a species during rapid or catastrophic evolutionary change: 'Because it is specialized' or 'because it's a hedgehog' (i.e., a highly specialized organism) are both explanatory claims within evolutionary biology. Yet the property of being specialized and the properties that individuate species kinds are not individualistic. A particular virus can be cited as a cause of illness even though that kind of virus is taxonomized relationally. Entities taxonomized under historical or relational kinds themselves are often cited as causes in scientific explanations. Relationally individuated kinds play the role of both *explanans* and *explanandum* in explanatory practice, and such practice should be the ultimate arbiter for claims about constraints on scientific explanation.

Let me clarify this response and emphasize the importance of my methodological appeal to explanatory practice before moving on. The question of whether relational kinds can feature as causes in explanations, to which the answer is 'Yes', is one question. Whether the relational properties that individuate those kinds are themselves causally responsible for the events, processes, and states being explained is another question, a question whose answer depends in part on broader and more controversial metaphysical issues, such as whether relations themselves can be causally efficacious (see Chapter 5). My claim is that one *must* accept an affirmative answer to the first question in light of explanatory practice in the sciences. Given this, however, a negative answer to the second question becomes more difficult to maintain. The most plausible way in which the 'Yes–No' option can be defended is by accepting the view I described in the previous section, according to which relational taxonomies are always preliminary and lead to revised, individualistic taxonomies. As I shall argue *in passim,* this general revisability claim should also be rejected once one attends to explanations in the range of disciplines constituting the sciences. There may be a priori considerations that entail that historical and relational taxonomies are not 'properly scientific', but the focus on explanatory practice in science must function as a check on such claims about the nature of scientific explanation.

If the causal powers of an entity supervene on the local microstructure of that entity, then global individualism is false. The intrinsic causal powers of individual entities are not all that important in some types of scientific causal explanation. Many sciences are not primarily concerned with what a thing can do. In some cases, the relevant discipline concentrates not so much on abilities as on the *history* or the *structure* of the entity or phenomenon of interest. This is true particularly in the social and biological sciences, where there is significant interest in *processes* and *systems,* rather than in the individual things constituting those processes and systems. This does not make these sciences any less scientific or entail that they are not concerned with formulating causal explanations for the phenomena in their respective domains.

To consolidate the preceding claim about global individualism I shall discuss three particular examples of non-individualistic taxonomic kinds. The diversity of these examples together with those already mentioned suggests that it will be difficult for one simply to restrict the thesis of global individualism to some subset of scientific disciplines of which psychology is clearly a member. The details of the accompanying discussion not only address particular objections to my denial of global individualism, they also illustrate why there is an *inherent* tension in the use to which the notion of causal powers is put in the argument from causal powers.

Anthropologists are often interested in understanding a set of actions or practices in a particular culture. Those actions or practices are frequently taxonomized at a relatively abstract level by understanding the role of the practices in the larger social context. For example, incest is forbidden in many cultures and is often considered a paradigm *taboo*. The concept of a taboo is central to many explanations in anthropology, taboos being social attitudes or beliefs. Though different types of activities are considered taboo across cultures, practices are not taxonomized as taboos by their intrinsic causal powers. In classifying certain actions or practices as taboos, one is not concerned with the 'local microstructure' of those actions or practices. Rather, one locates the practice amongst a complex network of other social and moral practices. Taboos are non-individualistic; taxonomy in anthropology is not, or not *entirely,* individualistic.

The same is true of central categories in many other social sciences: gender and categories of sexual preference in various fields of sociology, class in economics and history, criminal in social psychology and sociology. To take one of these, consider the social kind *criminal*. Being a criminal is a relational property that some people instantiate: A person is a criminal if he or she breaks any of a number of laws in a certain class. Whether a particular individual can be properly classified as a criminal is a function of the relations that that person has entered into; it is not determined by that individual's intrinsic causal powers. Still, there are many generalizations in sociology (and perhaps even in social psychology) about criminals as a social kind, and it is explanatory to appeal to an individual's criminal status to explain some of her behavior.

In order to clarify what someone who denies global individualism must accept, consider two related objections to my claims about the category criminal. The first objection is that I must be supposing that certain types of theories about criminality (e.g., Lombroso's theory of criminal man; see Gould 1981:ch. 4) are false, since these theories *would* provide some intrinsic causal power of an individual that determined whether he or she was a criminal. Now, although there are various theories about why some people are criminals, it should be clear that these are primarily accounts of what is causally responsible for criminal behavior in particular individuals; they need not supply criteria for individuating the kind criminal. Of course, *some* such theories might purport to identify the 'underlying essence' of criminality. Yet it is compatible with the social kind criminal being a scientifically interesting kind that such theories be mistaken, or that they account for only some kinds of criminal behavior. So, although I do think that such theories are unlikely to be true, their truth is irrelevant to my claim about the taxonomic individuation of the category criminal.

The second objection is that without the existence of *some* intrinsic causal factor causally responsible for criminal behavior the category must be empty, like the category witch: Either there is some intrinsic property that criminals share *as* criminals, or the category can be of no theoretical interest at all. How else could being a criminal be an explanatory causal property of an individual? There are two problems with this objection. First, unlike being a witch, being a criminal is *not* a property deeply embedded in a theoretical framework in such a way that the falsity of the theory would render the corresponding category empty. Even if no theory could adequately explain criminal behavior, this would imply neither that there were no criminals nor that there were no theoretically interesting generalizations about criminals. Second, all that causation requires is that there be some causal factor that results in criminal behavior in each particular instance. Yet these factors may vary inter-personally and even intra-personally over time; they need not be shared by individuals instantiating the kind and so constitute criteria for the category criminal.

In both of these cases, taboo and criminal, the properties that make an entity the kind of thing it is are not intrinsic to that individual entity. An entity falls under either of these concepts because of the relations that entity enters into. Central taxonomic properties in the biological sciences are also, like taboo and criminal, relational. In evolutionary biology, the concept of *species* is a central (perhaps *the* central) taxonomic concept. There are various causal generalizations true of members of a particular species, some of these concerning genetic and morphological properties, properties that *are* individualistic. Yet a species is taxonomized relationally as 'a reproductive community of populations (reproductively isolated from others) that occupies a specific niche in nature' (Mayr 1982:273). Although there is some variation in the precise definition of the species concept in evolutionary biology,[4] the *essentialist* conception of species, whereby species are defined exclusively in terms of the intrinsic genetic or even morphological characteristics that their members possess, is inadequate for explanation in the discipline. Species are taxonomized relationally, not by the intrinsic causal powers of individuals.

In saying that species are not individuated by intrinsic causal powers but relationally, I mean two things. The first is that an individual organism's species membership is not fixed by that organism's intrinsic properties but rather by the relations it bears to other individuals. To take the most extreme case, two individual organisms could be physically identical (or, more pertinently, *biochemically* identical) in composition and structure and still belong to different species. This is because two organisms identical in their intrinsic causal powers could be reproductively isolated and have independent phylogenies. The pattern of individuation in evolutionary biology as it is practiced does not abstract away from actual history.

Second, as biological kinds, species are not individuated from one another by their intrinsic causal powers. This is because species are individuated from one another, in part, by their phylogenetic history. Furthermore, if Mayr is right in thinking of species as populations, it is difficult to make sense of the claim that the causal powers of a species, considered as a population, distinguish that species from some other species. As populations, species don't seem to be the right type of thing to be individuated by intrinsic causal powers.

As a related aside, note the common misconception that both an individual organism's species membership and the individuation of species from one another are determined by the genotypes and phenotypes that individuals possess. Coupled with the claim – equally

---

4 For example, this definition differs from Mayr's own earlier definition (1942); see Mayr (1982:ch. 6) for an overview. Note that even phenetic conceptions of species (Sokal and Crovello 1970) individuate species in terms of relational properties, such as behavioral and ecological properties. Richard Boyd's (1988, 1989, 1990) discussions of homeostatic property-cluster definitions indicate, I think, why species are not individuated by their intrinsic causal powers.

misleading, in my view – that an individual's genes fix her intrinsic causal powers, this view about taxonomy in evolutionary biology might be taken to support the claim that species *are* individuated by their intrinsic causal powers. Yet this view of species membership is mistaken. Both genotypes and phenotypes may vary across individuals belonging to the same species. Moreover, as Elliott Sober (1980, 1984:ch. 5) has convincingly argued, evolutionary thinking that recognizes the reality of populations and the inherent variability among their members offers explanations that are incompatible with what Sober calls the 'natural state' explanations that essentialists offer. The sort of essentialism we are considering should be rejected because it presupposes a type of explanation of variation that is implausible.

Assuming that causal powers supervene on an individual's intrinsic physical properties, taxonomy in science as it is actually practiced is not exclusively individuation by intrinsic causal powers. Consider, now, the other conditional that is part of my claim that (1) and (4) are incompatible: that if we assume (1) and so Fodor's 'methodological point' to be true, (4) and so Fodor's 'metaphysical point' must be false. That is, if categorization in science typically *is* taxonomy by causal powers, then causal powers do not always supervene on local microstructure.

One way of explaining how historical and relational individuation is compatible with individuation by causal powers would be to broaden the notion of a causal power so as to allow an individual's causal *properties* more generally to constitute causal powers. Such a conception of causal powers would be an extension of that which we have been considering thus far, and though we might reasonably question how inclusive such a notion of causal powers need be, note that it must include at least *some* historical and relational properties if (1) is to be true. If one were to reconsider each of the examples I have given, supposing some appropriately extended notion of causal powers, then none of them would constitute a counterexample to my claim that (1) is false. For example, if one considered the phylogenetic lineage of an organism, one of its historical causal properties, to be one of its causal powers, then the criteria used for taxonomizing species *would* be cast in terms of the causal powers of individual entities (or at least this would become a more plausible view to hold). However, this wouldn't do for the individualist, since clearly on this view (4) would be false. If 'causal power' is understood to mean causal *property,* then causal powers don't supervene on internal physical states. Some scientifically taxonomic, causal properties are historical and relational; such properties *can't* supervene on an individual's intrinsic physical state.

Here is a diagnosis of the problem in the argument from causal powers. For (1) to be true, 'causal powers of $x$' must refer to a notion of causal powers that includes not only the intrinsic and the extrinsic causal powers of $x$, but all the causal properties of $x$, including at least some of its historical and relational causal properties: 'causal powers' must be used in what I shall call its *extended sense*. For (4) to be true, 'causal powers' can refer only to an entity's intrinsic causal powers: 'Causal powers' must be used in what I shall call its *restricted sense*. The extended and restricted senses of 'causal powers' are different, and so (1) and (4) cannot both be true on a common understanding of causal powers. Hence, (5) cannot be concluded in the argument from causal powers. Whether there is or ought to be solely individuation by causal powers in psychology is not something to be decided by an appeal to the *causal* nature of psychological explanation.

Although I have been assuming a relatively broad notion of causal property throughout this section, the basic point I have made is true even assuming the more minimal notion of a causal property that I mentioned in §2, which counts only intrinsic and extrinsic powers as causal powers. An individual's extrinsic causal powers, in contrast to her intrinsic causal powers (but like causal properties in general), do not supervene on that individual's intrinsic physical properties. Kinds taxonomized in terms of forward-looking properties (powers) that are extrinsic are not globally individualistic. If extrinsic causal powers play taxonomic and explanatory roles in the sciences, as I believe they frequently do, then the conclusion I have drawn could be reached assuming the narrower notion of a causal property. The argument would proceed in much the same way that my argument has proceeded, namely, by focussing on taxonomic practice in a range of sciences. Though such an argument would warrant a somewhat stronger conclusion than the one I have drawn, and would allow one to see that it is the attention to actual taxonomic practice rather than an excessively broad notion of a causal property that provides the backbone of my argument, its articulation requires a careful discussion of the distinction between intrinsic and extrinsic causal powers, as well as an examination of a different set of examples from the sciences. It is, I think, sufficiently clear in outline how such an argument would proceed; I leave its development for others.

## 5. RELATIONAL TAXONOMIES AND INDIVIDUALISM

My argument in the previous section appealed to the relational nature of individuation in a variety of sciences to show that those sciences were not individualistic. This argument presupposes that there is an incompatibility between relational and individualistic taxonomies, a presupposition that a proponent of global individualism is likely to reject. Indeed, Fodor himself has claimed that the prevalence of relational taxonomies in science does not show global individualism, his 'methodological point', to be false. In this section I defend the claim that relational and individualistic taxonomies are incompatible. Here we will return to the revisability claim about relational taxonomies introduced in §3.

Consider, first, the following argument for the incompatibility of relational individuation and individuation by intrinsic causal powers. Relational individuation involves taxonomizing an entity at least partly in terms of the relations that entity enters into. The relations that any entity enters into are determined partly by properties extrinsic to that entity. To individuate by intrinsic causal powers, as the individualist has stressed, is to taxonomize an entity *wholly* in terms of that entity's intrinsic physical properties. But no one type of thing can be partly individuated by properties that are extrinsic to it and wholly individuated by properties intrinsic to it. Hence no one *type* of thing can be both relational and individualistic.

Fodor has challenged this incompatibilist view of relational and individualistic taxonomies:

Just as you'd expect, relational properties can count taxonomically whenever they affect causal powers. Thus 'being a planet' is a relational property par excellence, but it's one that individualism permits to operate in astronomical taxonomy. For whether you are a planet affects your trajectory, and your trajectory determines what you can bump into; so whether you're a planet affects your causal powers, which is all [that] individualism asks for. (1987:43)

This way of reconciling global individualism with the prevalence of relational taxonomies in the sciences is also manifest in Fodor's comments on the distinction between methodological *individualism* and methodological *solipsism:* 'Methodological individualism is the doctrine that psychological states are individuated *with respect to their causal powers*. Methodological solipsism is the doctrine that psychological states are individuated *without respect to their semantic evaluation*'

47

(1987:42). Having drawn this distinction and conceded that solipsistic individuation *is* incompatible with relational individuation, Fodor continues: 'there is nothing to stop principles of individuation from being simultaneously relational and individualistic. *Individualism does not prohibit the relational individuation of mental states;* it just says that no property of mental states, relational or otherwise, counts taxonomically unless it affects causal powers' (1987:42).

The claim here is this: The idea at the core of global individualism is that an entity's causal powers are crucial to ways in which that entity is taxonomized in science. Yet the claim that taxonomy in science is 'by causal powers' should not be construed too narrowly. One can preserve the core idea by taking global individualism to say that properties that *affect* an entity's causal powers in the same way can make no difference to scientific taxonomy. A relational property must make a difference to an entity's causal powers if it is to provide the basis for taxonomizing that entity scientifically.

Stalnaker (1989:307–8) has pointed out that the reformulation of individualism proposed by Fodor here contrasts in a non-trivial way with standard characterizations of that view. Individualism is the view that taxonomy is by causal powers, not, as Fodor implies here, by what *causally affects* causal powers. The fact that being a planet affects the causal powers that a large blob of matter has is simply not relevant to the question of whether individualism is true. As Stalnaker goes on to argue, were individualism the thesis that individuation in psychology must be individuation by what affects causal powers, individualism would be compatible with *wide* individuation in psychology, since environmental facts clearly causally affect the causal powers that objects have, including their *intrinsic* causal powers. Stalnaker's point is that Fodor's compatibilism requires a construal of global individualism that is too liberal for global individualism to be the basis for individualism in psychology. I want to defend Stalnaker's claim and show how it relates to my own criticisms of the argument from causal powers. Since talk of 'affecting' causal powers is somewhat vague and lumps together a variety of cases, let me first distinguish two different ways in which something can causally affect an entity's causal powers. (I am indebted to Sydney Shoemaker here.)

An entity's causal powers can be causally affected by the *relations* that that entity actually enters into: What that entity can do at a time is partially a function of what it is related to at that time. It is in this sense that a given entity's causal powers are affected by its being a planet and so by its having the relational property of orbiting a star. In this same sense, the causal powers that an organism has are causally affected by that organism's being a member of one species rather than another. Call this way in which an entity's relational properties affect its causal powers *contemporaneous* affecting: The relations that an entity stands in at a given time causally affect what powers it has at that time.

A second way in which the causal powers an entity has can be causally affected is historically: Events that form part of the history of the entity can be causally responsible for that entity's having certain causal powers rather than others. For example, the causal powers that a person has at a given time might be affected because she was present in Hiroshima in 1945, took a particular drug, or underwent special training. An event, process, relation, and so on *historically* affects an entity's causal powers only if that event made a difference to those causal powers at some earlier time.

I focus subsequently on contemporaneous affecting, partly because the case that Fodor considers is of this type but also because it is this case in which the problem with broadening global individualism to allow for properties that affect an entity's causal powers is most evident. Could we take global individualism to be the view that taxonomy in science must be either by causal powers or by what contemporaneously affects causal powers? I think not. Suppose that (1) in the argument from causal powers is extended in this way: This is how one should understand the claim that sciences taxonomize 'by causal powers'; I shall refer to (1) so extended as (1*). The problem is that on such an understanding of taxonomy being 'by causal powers,' those properties in terms of which one must taxonomize do not supervene on intrinsic physical properties, and the argument does not allow one to infer either (5) or (6); precisely the same is true of 'historical affecting', appealed to in this way. This is because either the fourth premise is false, if we modify it in the way we modified (1) to (1*), or although it is true [keeping it as (4) in the original argument], (1*) and (4) do not together allow one to infer (5). We thus arrive at the same conclusion I drew in §4: There is no single constraint on taxonomy, its having to be 'by causal powers', which is reflected in actual taxonomic practice in science *and* which specifies properties that supervene on the intrinsic physical properties of the entities in the extensions of the resulting kinds.

We can understand what is wrong-headed about the general idea

49

of modifying the argument from causal powers throughout to allow for taxonomy by what contemporaneously affects an entity's causal powers by considering what (5) and (6) in such an argument would have to say. Making the appropriate modifications would give us (5*) instead of (5):

(5*) Any causes of behavior that are to be taxonomic in the cognitive sciences must be determined or fixed by the intrinsic physical properties of the individual *or must contemporaneously affect those properties.*

Premise (6), the statement of individualism in psychology, would also need to be modified appropriately to include the emphasized disjunct. Yet an individualist should resist this modification of her view because individualism so construed would no longer imply that doppelgängers *must* be taxonomized under the same psychological kinds. Since molecularly identical individuals may be subject to different contemporaneous effects, they may be taxonomized differentially, even supposing these reformulated versions of global individualism and so individualism in psychology to be true. Recall that the intuition that a properly scientific psychology must treat doppelgängers in the same way motivates individualism in psychology in the first place; this same intuition gives the individualist a prima facie reason to think that the taxonomy of mental states offered by folk psychology is objectionable. The proposed reformulation of the argument from causal powers does not allow one to derive a version of individualism in psychology worth deriving.

So Fodor's attempt to account for relational individuation by weakening or extending global individualism fails for much the same reason that the initial argument from causal powers fails: No single sense of 'causal powers' makes both (1) and (4) true. Consider a second way in which an individualist could attempt to reconcile global individualism with the prevalence of relational taxonomies in science. The claim that historical and relational taxonomies have a *preliminary* character and the revisionary claim that often accompanies it are relevant here. Although an entity's history and its relations affect what causal powers it has at a time, this should not be taken to imply that its historical and relational properties are themselves taxonomic. Only causal powers (or properties that supervene on causal powers) can be taxonomic in science, even if historical and relational properties serve as a reliable guide to what causal powers it has. When an entity's history or its relations make a relevant differ-ence to that entity's behavior, the corresponding historical or rela-tional kinds are at best an approximation of or a proxy for taxonomic kinds individuated by causal powers.

To see how problematic these claims about relational taxonomies are, consider Fodor's own example of a putatively relational but individualistic concept, that of a *planet*. Something is a planet in virtue of facts about that thing's constitution (since comets are not planets) *and* facts about that thing's motion relative to a particular star (since meteors are not planets). The concept planet is relational. A physical duplicate of the Earth, say, that does not bear the relation to a star constitutive of being a planet is not a planet, even though that duplicate must, *ex hypothesi,* possess the same intrinsic causal powers as the Earth. Even a physical replica of the Earth that moved with exactly the same velocity as the Earth due to some complex combina-tion of forces would not be a planet unless it orbited a star. Neverthe-less, the concept of a planet *as it is* features in explanations in astron-omy. It at least appears to be a perfectly acceptable concept in itself and does not seem to be preliminary in any way. Moreover, one cannot simply abstract away from an entity's actual relations in de-termining whether or not that entity is a planet. Because of these facts about taxonomic practice in astronomy, it is implausible to think that the concept planet is in any way preliminary or must be revised in some way in order to form a proper scientific kind. In fact, the concept appears to be *essentially* relational in that if we attempt to revise the concept planet in the required way, we lose the concept of a planet altogether. This suggests that it is neither necessary nor even possible in general to offer an individualistic revision of relational, scientific kinds.

Likewise, it is implausible to view the concept of a *species* as preliminary or as being revisable in the specified way. Reproductive isolation and niche occupation in an actual environment are two relational features that are part of the species concept (see §4). Neither of these components of the species concept is or could be fixed by the intrinsic causal powers that an individual has; the relations that individual organisms instantiate play a crucial role in determining which species they belong to. Taxonomic practice in evolutionary biology does not appear to view the species concept as in any way preliminary, and as with the case of planet, I suggest taking the appearances at face value. Reflection on this example also suggests that it is neither necessary nor even possible in general to offer an individualistic revision of relational, scientific kinds.

The problems for the individualist's claim about the preliminary character of relational taxonomies and her subsequent revisability claim about the concepts of planet and species stem from two important differences between these cases and the paradigm case of a successful revision, that of the revision from weight to mass. In the latter case, there is a clear way in which the concept of weight can be factored into distinct internal and external components, and it is a trivial matter to show how these novel factors (mass and gravitational attraction, respectively) are to operate within Newtonian mechanics. The cases of planets and species have neither of these features. This is an a posteriori, contingent difference between the cases, depending as it does on how the concepts are embedded in the corresponding scientific theories. A more detailed discussion of the similarities and differences between these types of cases would, I think, help in determining whether *psychological* kinds are likely to be revisable in the required way. But to recognize that not all scientific kinds must be revisable is already to acknowledge the failure of the argument from causal powers as an argument based on global individualism.

## 6. CAUSAL POWERS, ONE MORE TIME[5]

Fodor (1991a) has offered a renewed and somewhat revised defence of his own position in *Psychosemantics* that is of interest not only because it expresses the tensions in the individualist's appeal to the notion of causal powers that I have identified, but also because it reflects more starkly the a priori character of Fodor's own commitment to global individualism. For these reasons and for the sake of completeness, I conclude my substantive discussion in this chapter by considering Fodor's more recent argument.

Fodor focusses on the ubiquity of relational individuation in the sciences, a fact that he takes to entail that certain relational properties, properties such as being a planet and being a member of a particular species, are causally and explanatorily adequate in themselves. In this

5 Even one more time will be one too many for some readers, who may prefer to go straight to the conclusion to this chapter. All quotations in this section are from Fodor's 'A Modal Argument for Narrow Content', as are all page number references.

respect, these relational kinds contrast with other relational properties, such as being a brother or having siblings. Even if there is some sense in which individuals have causal powers in virtue of instantiating this latter type of relational property, there is an intuitive sense in which an appeal to these causal powers is not truly explanatory. Given that properties like being a planet and being a member of a particular species are, as Fodor puts it, 'relational properties in good standing' (p. 12) but that not *all* ascriptions of relational properties are explanatory, what is needed is some criterion distinguishing the two. Fodor takes the intuitive differences between the examples he presents as reason to develop a necessary condition 'for when a difference in the properties of causes constitutes a difference in their causal powers' (p. 10). When is a relational property that an entity instantiates itself causally responsible for some effect?

Fodor thinks that there is an a priori answer to this question, an answer that provides a criterion for distinguishing two types of relational properties. Those concepts or kinds that satisfy this constraint or criterion can be taxonomic and so explanatory in the sciences; those that do not satisfy it cannot be taxonomic or explanatory. Fodor organizes his discussion around the claim that *wide* contents do not constitute causal powers satisfying the general condition he develops; hence, they are not to be taxonomic or explanatory in psychology. Fodor's argument for individualism in psychology here, like the argument from causal powers, utilizes a more general claim about scientific taxonomies.

Before examining Fodor's criterion itself, I want to express my doubts about Fodor's way of stating the problem that the prevalence of relational taxonomies poses for an individualist. For Fodor, the question that needs answering is this: When can the (relational) property of a cause count as what he calls a *real causal power,* where only real causal powers feature in scientific taxonomies and generalizations? Like the 'methodological point' that Fodor made in *Psychosemantics* discussed in §4, the relation that Fodor presumes to hold between causal powers and scientific explanation holds only if causal powers are conceived of as violating the constraint of supervenience specified in Fodor's 'metaphysical point'. Fodor relies on what I have called the *extended sense* of 'causal powers' even in stating the problem in the way that he does.

Fodor presupposes the extended sense of 'causal powers' throughout much of the paper. Consider the following two passages:

Taxonomy by relational properties is ubiquitous in the sciences, and it is not in dispute that properties like *being a meteor* or *being a planet* - properties which could, notice, distinguish molecularly identical chunks of rock - constitute causal powers. (p. 12)

And the intuition about features of causal history is that some of them *are* causal powers (e.g., having been dropped in transit; having been inoculated for smallpox) and some of them are not. . . . (p. 18; emphasis added)

If molecular duplicates can differ in some property, then that property cannot supervene on the internal physical properties that those duplicates share. Fodor is here abandoning the 'metaphysical point' he made in *Psychosemantics,* the claim that causal powers supervene on local microstructure. As I argued in §5, however, this metaphysical point is not an optional extra for an individualist defending the view that individualism in psychology follows from global individualism. In fact, elsewhere (e.g., pp. 16–17, 25), Fodor himself identifies the central claim of individualism as the claim that psychological kinds are locally supervenient.

Like Fodor's version of the argument from causal powers, his argument here shifts between two different and incompatible notions of causal powers. In accord with the first, the extended sense, taxonomy in science *is* taxonomy by causal powers; in accord with the second, the restricted sense, causal powers supervene on intrinsic physical properties. The dilemma here can be stated in the terms that Fodor uses in 'A Modal Argument'. If real causal powers must supervene on intrinsic physical properties, it is false that *only* real causal powers taxonomize scientific kinds. And if it is true that only real causal powers are used to taxonomize scientific kinds, then real causal powers do not supervene on intrinsic physical properties, and so there is no reason for the properties of a scientific *psychology* to be locally supervenient.

Consider, now, Fodor's criterion, which he states in terms of what he calls *cause properties* (CP), the properties that a cause has:

For the difference between being CP1 and being CP2 to be a difference of causal powers, it must at least be that the effects of being CP1 differ from the effects of being CP2. But, I claim, it is further required that this difference between the effects be *nonconceptually* related to the difference between the causes. (p. 24)

In keeping with the spirit of the original argument from causal powers, this general criterion applies to scientific taxonomies per se. Properties that, intuitively, do not seem to endow their bearers with real causal powers include being a brother, having siblings, being an

H-particle (defined in Fodor 1987:ch.2), and having water thoughts. Fodor claims that what the inadmissable cases have in common is that statements ascribing the effects that such powers have are conceptual truths. So, for example, if you are a sibling, you have the 'power' to have sons who are nephews. But this is true in virtue of the meanings of 'sibling', 'son,' and 'nephew'; it is a conceptual truth that siblings have the power to have sons who are nephews. This is not true of the causal powers used in scientific taxonomies. As Fodor says of one's real causal powers, 'to put it roughly, your causal powers are a function of your *contingent* connections, not of your conceptual connections' (p. 19). Relational taxonomies are genuinely explanatory kinds (i.e., they classify entities by their real causal powers) only if some of the statements that describe the effects that putative powers have are not conceptual truths.

Note that this criterion presupposes the analytic–synthetic distinction, since conceptual truths are just analytic truths, even if in some cases unobvious ones. The introduction of the notion of analyticity here to delineate real causal powers from what one might think of as *mere-Cambridge* causal powers (*sensu* Shoemaker 1980) would be enough for some of us to think that something had gone wrong. Whatever else one resurrects to save an argument for individualism, let it not be the analytic–synthetic distinction! Even those who disagree here about the general value of the analytic–synthetic distinction in the philosophy of science should have doubts about Fodor's reliance on it in this context, and not only because of Fodor's own explicit criticisms (Fodor 1987:ch. 3; Fodor and Lepore 1992) of views that, he claims, are committed to it. As I shall argue, the analytic–synthetic distinction simply cannot do the work that Fodor requires that it do in distinguishing real causal powers from mere-Cambridge causal powers. I shall focus specifically on the case of psychology, though the objection I want to make can be generalized unproblematically.

Fodor claims (pp. 23–4; cf. pp. 20–1) that each of the following statements is conceptually necessary:

If B is a property that water thoughts have, then if I am connected to water in the right way, then B is a property that my thoughts have.

If B is a property that water behaviors have, then if my thoughts are water thoughts, then my behaviors have B.

Being connected to water rather than twater leads to water thinking rather than twater thinking.

For these statements to be conceptually necessary, they must both be necessary truths and be true in virtue solely of the meanings of the words they contain. I think that the analytic status of even these three statements can be reasonably questioned, though I shall not defend this claim here. Even if these statements *are* analytic, this is not sufficient to show that the property of having a particular wide content is not a real causal power; to show that, *every* statement ascribing an effect to the wide content of a mental state must be analytic, and this is an extremely implausible claim *whatever* one thinks of this type of appeal to the analytic–synthetic distinction. For example, consider each of the following statements:

Stella turned on the tap because she wanted water.
Archie called his mother because he was worried about her.
Joan walked because she thought she needed the exercise.

Each of these statements offers a commonsense, psychological explanation of a behavioral effect, and none of them is analytic. There are *many* effects that having mental states with a particular content have, and it is implausible to see *every statement* reporting a causal effect of an agent's beliefs and desires as analytic. Even if intuitions about analyticity are shared to a large extent for some core cases, there is a potentially infinite number of cases to consider, and very few of them will be analytic.

There are more details to Fodor's argument than I have discussed here. But I do not intend this section to function as a comprehensive discussion of Fodor's paper, and rather than focus on the specifics, I want instead to return to the broader issue of why Fodor's general approach here is mistaken by relating my discussion in this section to that in §4 and §5.

In §5 I argued that the existence of relational taxonomies in the sciences constitutes a general problem for the argument from causal powers, since the properties in terms of which such taxonomies are individuated do not supervene on the intrinsic properties of an individual. Fodor does not seem to think that there is a *general* problem here, I think, because he primarily uses the extended sense of 'causal powers'. A central criticism of both the argument from causal powers and Fodor's defence of it in 'A Modal Argument' has been that the extended sense of 'causal powers' will not allow you to derive individualism in psychology.

Since Fodor does not consider there to be a general problem for global individualism concerning relational individuation, he formulates a weak necessary condition for being a real causal power. All that the condition needs to do is to rule out, in a principled way, mere-Cambridge causal powers as genuinely explanatory. Yet, general worries about the appeal to analyticity to one side, we have seen that it is doubtful whether *on its own terms* Fodor's criterion rules out an explanatory appeal to wide content in psychology. Because his criterion does not apply to kinds in themselves but rather to the causal generalizations that they feature in, it cannot rule out an appeal to a given relational kind unless *every* causal generalization that it features in is analytic.

At the end of §5 I suggested that the question of when relational properties are revisable into narrow properties has only an a posteriori answer: It depends on whether there is (or is likely to be) a theoretical framework for expressing the resulting narrow property. The same is true of the question that Fodor attempts to answer with his a priori criterion, the question of when a relational property is itself causally responsible for some effect. This is why his criterion *cannot* rule out appeals to wide content in psychological explanations.

The need for an a posteriori answer to this question is implicit in several places in Fodor's own discussion. For example, he says:

The question we are raising is not whether the difference between having CP1 and having CP2 is a difference in causal powers; rather, it is whether the difference between having CP1 and having CP2 is a difference in causal powers in virtue of its being responsible for a certain difference between E1 and E2 [effects], namely, in virtue of its being responsible for E1's having EP1 rather than EP2 and for E2's having EP2 rather than EP1. The point I am wanting to emphasize is that a cause property might fail to count as a causal power in virtue of its responsibility for one effect property, but still might constitute a causal power in virtue of its responsibility for some other effect property. (pp. 12–13)

Fodor illustrates his point here by considering the possibility of having *sibling's disease,* a disease that 'causes people who have siblings to break out in a rash' (p. 13). If there were such a disease, then having it would be instantiating a real causal power, since the effects it has are contingent, not conceptual. This implies that any of the properties that Fodor would like to place together under the heading 'relational properties not in good standing', properties like being a sibling, having a brother, being an H-particle, and having water thoughts, could be real causal powers were the world a certain way. All that one would have to do is to formulate some contingently true statement ascribing an effect that, say, having water thoughts has in order for water thoughts to count as real causal powers.

There is nothing about these relational properties *themselves* that makes them unsuitable for scientific taxonomies: Whether they are suitable or not depends on which effects you attribute to them *and* on how the world is. Precisely the same is true of the categories and kinds that feature in our existing sciences. There is no intrinsic difference between the relational properties of being a sibling and being a planet that makes only the latter suitable for scientific explanation. The relational properties of being a sibling and being a planet, as a matter of fact, do differ in the role that each plays in scientific taxonomies, but this is not because only one of them is of a special kind suitable for taxonomy in science. Determining an answer to the question Fodor has posed, the question of when a relational property that an entity instantiates is itself causally responsible for some effect, requires an a posteriori approach.

There is no *type* of relational property that plays an individuative role in scientific taxonomies, and so any a priori criterion attempting to capture what it is about certain relational properties that allows them to be taxonomic in science is not only mistaken but reflects a mistaken approach to issues concerning the nature of scientific taxonomies and explanations. This, in turn, brings us back to one of the key intuitions that motivates the argument from causal powers, the idea that it must be the intrinsic properties of entities that are taxonomic in science. For just as relational properties cannot be divided a priori into those that are and those that are not suitable for scientific taxonomy, neither can properties be divided into two groups, intrinsic and relational properties, only the first of which can be taxonomic in science.

## 7. CONCLUSION

The causal nature of psychology provides one with no reason to think that individuation in psychology, or indeed in any science concerned with developing causal generalizations, must abide by the constraint of individualism. It would be very interesting were some global analogue to individualism in psychology to function as a constraint on scientific explanation as it is practiced, or were there compelling arguments for thinking that it should serve as a regulative norm in science. The argument throughout this chapter has been that an examination of the patterns of individuation in sciences as they are practiced supports neither of these claims.

Central to my argument has been the claim that the individualist defending the argument from causal powers must employ an extended sense of 'causal powers' to make global individualism true, whereas she must use 'causal powers' in a restricted sense in order for causal powers to supervene on intrinsic physical properties. In §3 we saw that the proponent of the argument from causal powers might accept the view that any relational, scientific concept can be factored into one that individuates the entities in its extension by their intrinsic causal powers. Towards the end of §5, I suggested that the possibility of such revisions did not look plausible, but I have offered no *general* argument to show that this option is not defensible. Although I see no way that the ambitious revisability claim I have discussed can be successfully defended, a less ambitious claim about revisability might provide a suitable basis for a closely related argument for individualism. The argument I have in mind would require establishing what it is, if anything, about certain relational concepts in science that allows them to be revised narrowly and showing that relational concepts in psychology also have this property.

It would be a mistake to view my argument as showing (or even as trying to show) that causal powers have nothing to do with scientific taxonomy or that they are unimportant in scientific explanation. Many scientific taxonomies do individuate by causal powers, and in pointing out that there are many scientific taxonomies that do *not* individuate in this way, I do not mean to deny the interest that the former fact has. I have been concerned primarily with addressing a mistaken view about the consequences of adopting a 'scientifically respectable' view of psychology; a properly scientific psychology need not be individualistic.

Finally, I claimed in the introduction to this chapter that the argument from causal powers relied on a number of intuitions about explanation, causation, and causal powers. Although the argument from causal powers should be rejected, working out which of these intuitions should be rejected along with it, or which inferences from these intuitions to the premises of the argument are invalid, is a task I shall not undertake now. Those swayed both by the intuitions about causation and explanation and by my critique of the argument from causal powers need a positive view of causation and explanation that allows them to understand why psychology need not be individualistic in order to be properly scientific. I begin to articulate such a view in Part II, where I re-examine some of the persistent intuitions about causal powers and explanation more closely. Isn't there some *other* argument from the intuition that the notion of causal powers is central to explanation to the claim that individualism is a constraint on psychology? In Chapter 5 I consider two such arguments, one based on a view of the nature of *properties,* the other on a view of the nature of *causation,* and explore the metaphysical conception that underlies these arguments, as well as the argument from causal powers.

So, as extended as the discussion of the argument from causal powers in this chapter has been, we are not yet finished with the issues it raises. But let us not get ahead of the game. There are a number of other arguments for individualism that we must first examine. The first of these is the *computational* argument for individualism.

# 3

# *An empirical argument: the computational argument*

It has often been thought (Devitt 1990, 1991; Egan 1992; Fodor 1981a, 1987; Segal 1989a, 1991) that individualism in psychology receives support from the computational theory of mind, a view taken by many philosophers and cognitive scientists to be a foundational assumption of contemporary research in cognitive science (Cummins 1989; Pylyshyn 1984). The computational theory of mind, or computationalism, can be summarized as the view that psychological processes and states are essentially computational. It makes an empirical claim about the nature of cognitive processing and suggests to many a methodological claim about how cognitive psychology or the cognitive sciences more generally ought to proceed.

A question that arose in the conclusion to Chapter 2 was: Given that global individualism is not a general constraint on scientific explanation, what is different or special about *psychological* explanation that makes individualism a constraint on it? Computationalism provides the basis for an answer to this question: What is special about psychology is that it theorizes about mental processes qua computational processes, and computational processes must be individualistic. An appropriately refined version of this argument will be the focus of discussion in this chapter.

## 1. COMPUTATIONALISM IN PSYCHOLOGY

One could view the computational argument for individualism as having the same *form* as the argument from causal powers: The latter claims that mental processes are individualistic because of psychology's *scientific* nature, and the former claims that they are individualistic because of cognition's *computational* nature. Yet this view of the two arguments obscures an important contrast between them. The computational argument is an empirical argument for individualism,

61

one that turns on an a posteriori claim about the nature of mental processing; the grounds for computationalism (and so individualism) are the particular explanatory practices *in psychology,* not an a priori view about the nature of scientific or causal explanation.

More needs to be said here about the sense in which computationalism is an empirical claim about mental processing. Computationalism is not a claim that can be either falsified or confirmed by any particular experiment or finite set of experiments; rather, it is a proposal about cognition that structures a *paradigm* of research, in much the way that behaviorism structured a paradigm of research in psychology for much of this century. This view of computationalism has been defended by Alan Newell and Herbert Simon in proposing the *physical symbol system hypothesis,* the view that 'a physical symbol system has the necessary and sufficient means for general intelligent action' (1976:41), as a *law of qualitative structure* for the sciences studying cognition. Such 'laws' are general qualitative statements that determine the domain and, in some cases, the methodology that a field of inquiry encompasses; they can be thought of as structuring Kuhnian paradigms or disciplinary matrices. Other laws of qualitative structure include the doctrine that 'the basic building block of all living organisms is the cell' in biology and the view that 'the surface of the globe is a collection of huge plates' in geology (Newell and Simon 1976:38–9).

Since my primary interest in this chapter is in the argument from computationalism to *individualism,* not in computationalism itself, I shall discuss more general issues about computationalism only insofar as they are relevant to that argument. It may be worthwhile to mention explicitly two specific issues that I shall bracket.

The first concerns whether computationalism, as a law of qualitative structure, includes a specific claim about the nature of *folk psychology.* Jerry Fodor advocates a view that suggests that it does. Consider a representative quotation: 'having a propositional attitude is being in some relation to an internal representation. In particular, having a propositional attitude is being in some *computational* relation to an internal representation' (1975:198; cf. Fodor 1978a:198, 1978b:168, 1981b:26). According to Fodor, seeing the propositional attitudes as computational relations between an individual and mental sentences in that individual's 'language of thought' allows one to account for various features of the attitudes, including their intentionality, within a foundational paradigm in contemporary cognitive science. Fodor seeks to defend the integrity of folk psychology by placing the propositional attitudes in the domain of mental states to which computationalism is assumed to apply.

Fodor's view introduces claims about both cognition and computation that go beyond the minimal commitments of computationalism. For example, Fodor thinks that computationalism requires a systematic and productive language of thought, whose constituents are both the objects of the propositional attitudes and the theoretical entities of *subpersonal,* cognitive theories (cf. Stich 1978b). This view is controversial within the computational paradigm, and since the empirical research within the computational paradigm that I focus on in this chapter involves subpersonal cognitive states, not folk psychological states, I shall not discuss issues specifically concerning *folk* psychology and computationalism (see Chapter 7).

The second issue is whether computationalism entails a particular view of just what type of computational states psychological states are. In particular, does computationalism entail that they are computational in the *classic* (von Neumann) sense? Is the physical symbol system hypothesis the claim that cognitive processing involves only the systematic and productive manipulation of discrete symbols? Computationalism, as articulated by people like Newell and Simon, developed with the implicit assumption that the answer to this question is 'yes'. However, the much discussed distinction between classic and connectionist computational architectures raises the question of whether this answer is necessary for psychological states to be viewed as computational. I shall attempt to avoid the classic–connectionist debate altogether in this chapter; the points I shall be making draw on elements common to both 'classicists' and connectionists or points that can be conceded by either of them. Note that how one should view the distinction between classical and connectionist systems is a central issue of debate. For example, are connectionist systems simply implementations of a classical architecture (Fodor and Pylyshyn 1988; Smolensky 1988)? Can and do connectionist explanations of systematicity require an appeal to representations with constituent structure (Fodor and McLaughlin 1990; Smolensky 1991)? In what sense is connectionist processing non-symbolic (Clark 1993; Haugeland 1991)? I see no way of providing an answer to the question of precisely what computationalism entails that does not involve addressing such questions, amongst others, and the requisite discussion would take us far from the argument that is our focus here.

## 2. THE COMPUTATIONAL ARGUMENT
## FOR INDIVIDUALISM

An argument from computationalism to individualism is initially plausible, in part, because computationalism provides a theoretical grounding for many of the pre-theoretical intuitions that motivate individualism. Consider two such intuitions mentioned in Chapter 1. The first is that the *codes* our brains store, not *what* they code for, are relevant to cognitive behavior (McGinn 1982:210). Computationalism allows one to develop this intuition about mental codes in a particular way: Cognition is formal in that transitions from one mental state to another are mediated by formal rules governing possible concatenations of symbols in the mental code, so anything that affects an agent's cognitive processing must do so by changing the formal codes that constitute that agent's cognitive system. A second individualist intuition is that the organism is a *complete* and *natural* unit for the purposes of psychological theorizing (Devitt 1990:388). Computational states, like individualistic psychological states, are intrinsic to the system in which they are instantiated: They can be described solely in terms of their own intrinsic features and their relations to other internal computational states. Computational systems, like individuals, are complete and natural units.

Consider the following explicit argument, which I shall refer to as the *computational argument* for individualism:

(A) The sciences of cognition taxonomically individuate mental processes only qua computational processes.
(B) The computational states and processes that an individual instantiates supervene on the intrinsic physical states of that individual.

Therefore,

(C) The sciences of cognition individuate only states and processes that supervene on the intrinsic physical states of the individual who instantiates those states and processes.

This chapter challenges those who find this argument from computationalism to individualism plausible by identifying a possibility that has either been overlooked or not treated seriously by proponents of this type of argument. The possibility is that of *wide computationalism,* and I shall defend both the possibility and the plausibility of wide computationalism in the sciences of cognition.

My central objection to the computational argument is thus directed not at the argument's first premise, which some might object to as implausibly strong, but at its perhaps innocent-sounding second premise. For this reason, we could make (A) as weak or as qualified as we like and still reject the computational argument. Yet two brief comments are in order on why my expression of computationalism in (A) is so taxonomically imperialistic. First, such a strong view is required if we are to provide an argument for individualism as a general constraint on psychological taxonomy and explanation. Second, if the hypothesis that mental processes are essentially computational is to be a law of qualitative structure for the cognitive sciences, then it must have the generality expressed in (A). John Haugeland states that 'the guiding inspiration of cognitive science' is the view that 'at a suitable level of abstraction, a theory of "natural" intelligence should have the same basic form as the theories that explain sophisticated computer systems. It is this idea which makes *artificial* intelligence seem not only possible, but also a central and pure form of *psychological* research' (1981b:2). As this passage of Haugeland's suggests, computationalism has methodological implications for how the cognitive sciences ought to be done: Cognitive psychology and artificial intelligence are concerned with the same *domain* – namely, intelligent systems – and methods, techniques, and results from artificial intelligence form a central part of the cognitive sciences. This view about how one should investigate the mind is thought to hold for the study of cognition as such, not simply for parts of such a study. Individualism itself is rightly thought to have methodological implications for how the sciences of cognition ought to proceed (see Chapter 4); computationalism provides a framework for filling in the methodological details.

## 3. WIDE COMPUTATIONALISM

Suppose that cognitive processing is computational, at least from the point of view of those seeking systematic, scientific, psychological explanations. The states (and the processes that are the transitions between such states) over which a computational psychology quantifies need not be individualistic because the cognitive system to which they belong could be a *wide computational* system. That is, the corresponding cognitive system could transcend the boundary of the individual and include parts of that individual's environment. If this were so, then the computational states of such a cognitive system would not supervene on the intrinsic physical states of the individual; likewise, the resulting computational psychology would involve essential reference to the environment beyond the individual. The states and processes of a wide computational system are not taxonomized individualistically.

In this section I explain the coherence of the idea of wide computationalism, that is, defend the *possibility* of wide computationalism. I shall consolidate this defence in §6 by considering two objections to wide computationalism, going on in §7 to identify prima facie examples of existing research in computational psychology that can be plausibly understood as positing wide computational systems.

Wide computational systems are computational systems that are not fully instantiated in any individual. Since they literally extend beyond the boundary of the individual, not all of the states they contain can be taxonomized individualistically. Even though much of the processing that takes place in a wide computational system may well be instantiated fully within the boundary of the individual, not all of these computational processes are so instantiated. If there are computational (formal) descriptions of both an organism's environment and its mental states, and if causal transitions from the former to the latter can be thought of as computations, there is a process that begins in the environment and ends in the organism that can be thought of as a computation, a wide computation.

To some, the coherence of wide computationalism, its mere possibility, will seem unproblematic. For example, in responding to Martin Davies's claim that 'cognitive psychology treats information processing systems (modules) and whole creatures *qua* embedded in particular larger systems and ultimately particular environments' (Davies 1991:482), Gabriel Segal says:

The supervenience base of a representation's content is some larger system in which the representation is embedded. This could be: the whole creature plus its environment, the whole creature, the largest module in which the representation occurs, a sub-processor of that module, a sub-sub-processor of that module, a sub-sub-sub. . . . Individualism is the thesis that the representational states of a system are determined by intrinsic properties of that system. It seems likely that whole subjects (or whole brains) make up large, integrated, computational systems. Whole subjects plus embedding environments do not make up integrated, computational systems. That is one reason why individualists draw the line where they do: the whole subject is the largest acceptable candidate for the supervenience base because it is the largest integrated system available. (Segal 1991:492, ellipses in the original) [1]

Here Segal seems to concede the coherence of wide computationalism, claiming that, as a matter of fact, we don't find computational, cognitive systems larger than the individual. This passage identifies precisely where a proponent of wide computationalism disagrees with the proponent of the computational argument: She rejects the claim that the 'whole subject', the individual, is 'the largest integrated physical system available' for computational, psychological explanation.

Given the coherence of wide computationalism implicit in this passage, it is not surprising that in his surrounding discussion Segal notes that the disagreement here is properly resolved by an examination of empirical research in computational psychology. Segal himself thinks that the crucial claim that 'whole subjects plus embedding environments do not make up integrated, computational systems' can be defended on a posteriori grounds. One would expect, then, that an individualist of Segal's persuasion would also consider Premise (B) in the computational argument to have an a posteriori justification, one that, while allowing for the mere possibility of wide computational systems, shows why *our* computational, cognitive systems are individualistic.

Not all individualists adopt this view of (B). For example, Frances Egan (1992) has argued that computational taxonomies are individualistic of their nature: There is something general about taxonomy in computational psychology, or perhaps about computational theory more generally still, that entails that computational states and processes are individualistic. If Egan is right, then wide computationalism is inconsistent with some more general feature of computational psychology or computational theory, and (B) is not something that simply happens to be true of the computational systems that we instantiate; rather, (B) is a truth about computational systems per se.

To bring out the contrast between these two types of defence of (B), and to see why the latter, more a priori defence is problematic in this context, consider the details of Egan's argument. Egan's argument

---

1 Individualists actually adopt a more specific view of the subvenient base than Segal implies: It is constituted by the intrinsic physical properties of *the individual*. As we will see, one cannot simply equate individual and computational systems or assume that the latter will be a part of the former.

for her view begins with the claim that the goal of computational theories of cognition is 'to characterize the mechanisms underlying our various cognitive capacities' (pp. 444–5).[2] And such theories 'construe cognitive processes as formal operations defined over symbol structures' (p. 446). Now:

Symbols are just functionally characterized objects whose individuation conditions are specified by a *realization function* $f_R$ which maps equivalence classes of physical features of a system to what we might call 'symbolic' features. Formal operations are just those physical operations that are differentially sensitive to the aspects of symbolic expressions that under the realization function $f_R$ are specified as symbolic features. The mapping $f_R$ allows a causal sequence of physical state transitions to be interpreted as a *computation*.

Given this method of individuating computational states, two systems performing the same operations over the same symbol structures are computationally indistinguishable. (p. 446)

From this, claims Egan, it follows that 'if two systems are molecular duplicates then they are computational duplicates. Computational descriptions are individualistic – they type-individuate states without reference to the subject's environment or social context' (p. 446).

Egan's final conclusion here does not follow unless one equates computational systems with *subjects,* that is, with individuals. Yet doing so would beg the question against the wide computationalist, for the wide computationalist endorses precisely the claim that there can be computational systems that extend beyond the boundary of the individual. There is nothing in the method of computational individuation itself to which Egan points that implies that the class of physical features mapped by a realization function cannot include members that are part of the environment of the individual. This being so, Egan has not provided an argument for why individualism (about computational psychology) follows from the very nature of computational psychology, and so her view does not point to some internal incoherence in the idea of wide computationalism.

Wide computationalism is analogous to wide *functionalism,* the view that the conceptual role that mental states play extends into the world (Harman 1987, 1988). Yet wide computationalism is both

2 Egan continues: 'this goal is best served by theories which taxonomize states individualistically' (p. 445), suggesting that she sees computational psychology as individualistic for instrumental or pragmatic reasons. But, as I hope will be clear from what follows, her actual argument does not appeal to such reasons; rather, it claims that individualism is implied by the *method* by which computational states are individuated.

more modest and more radical than wide functionalism and provides the basis for a stronger case against individualism. It is more modest in that it concedes that individualism is true of at least some mental processes and rejects only its all-encompassing nature; it is more radical because it denies something about the notion of a formal or computational system – that it be instantiated in an individual – that is almost without exception taken for granted by individualists, and so undermines the computational argument in a fundamental way. And it is a more decisive objection to individualism, supposing the 'radical' claim, because it not only removes computationalism as one of the major supports of individualism without rejecting computationalism but also provides the basis for arguing from computationalism to a distinctly non-individualistic view of computational psychology itself.

The challenge to the computational argument for individualism is not posed by directly defending the claim that psychological states require a broad construal but, rather, by arguing that the *formal* or *computational systems* in which such states are instantiated (or of which they are a part) extend beyond the individual (cf. Kitcher 1985). The distinction between an individual and a cognitive, computational system is central to an understanding of wide computationalism. Even if one thinks that many computational, cognitive *systems* are fully instantiated in the individual, wide computationalism is a possibility because the boundaries of the individual and the cognitive or computational system need not be identical.

As an example of a possible wide computational process, consider the familiar process of multiplication (cf. Clark 1989:chh. 4, 7, 1993:ch. 6). Typically, apart from multiplication problems included in one's 'times table', one multiplies numbers by storing intermediate solutions in some written form, usually on paper, solving the next component of the problem, storing the result on paper, and so on. The actual process that one goes through in multiplying numbers together typically involves the storage of symbols *on paper*. The problem-solving activity need not and does not take place solely in one's head; it involves, rather, the use of symbols that are not stored exclusively in the head. A description of the process of multiplication must include a description of mathematical symbols, and for most human beings such a description presupposes a reference to something external to the individual organism. A crucial part of the process of multiplication, namely, the storage of mathematical symbols, extends beyond the boundary of the individual. Considered as multipliers, we are part of wide computational systems.

To show the coherence of wide computationalism, this need only be taken as an account of a possible cognitive, computational process, perhaps not one that *we* instantiate. Yet I have described the example in terms of *our* cognitive processing because I think that human mathematical problem solving, as well as much problem solving more generally, *essentially* involves the exploitation of representations in one's environment. The more complex the computational process we engage in – for example, non-trivial mathematical proofs – the more plausible this stronger claim is. For example, proofs of complex theorems in quantificational logic are rarely carried out entirely in one's head; at least *some* of the symbols are stored externally. What are stored are *pointers* to the symbols that one uses, and although such pointers may be stored in the head, the symbols to which they point are not stored internally at all: That's why one *needs* a blackboard or a pen and paper.

Not only can a case be made for conceiving of mathematical and logical processes as wide computational processes, the same is true of perceptual and behavioral processes. Wide computationalism is appropriate in cases in which the interaction between an individual and something extrinsic to that individual is a crucial part of the computational process being described as an *explanans* in psychology. In the case of perception, it is an intrinsic part of that process that the system accept input from the environment and process it so that that input is ready for further mental processing. The perceptual process involves an interaction between an individual and her environment. This is in no way incompatible with providing a *computational* account of perception (see §7). Since perception is a process that begins with environmental inputs, inputs that themselves may have a formal description and so may be accessible to a computational, cognitive system, all components of the perceptual process can be described as part of a wide computational system.

An individualist may object that this characterization of the process of perception simply begs the question. The relevant objects of perception are not external but internal to an individual; for example they are two-dimensional retinal images, not some type of environmental input. A wide computational account of perception presupposes a view of perception that an individualist should reject. This objection in effect concedes a weak or negative point I want to make in this section, namely, that the formal or computational nature of mental processing *itself* doesn't entail individualism: One also needs to make a substantial claim about, for example, the objects of perception in order to derive individualism from computationalism. The same is true, I think, for any area of cognition that is claimed to be computational. The formality of cognition itself does not entail individualism.

Insofar as this points to a gap between computationalism and individualism, it allows for the *possibility* of wide computationalism. But a stronger claim about wide computationalism can be formulated and, I think, ultimately defended. Psychological states are computational only insofar as they are part of an implemented formal *system*. (For those who find this controversial, see the discussion in the next section.) But the formal systems of which at least some mental states are a part are not fully instantiated in any natural individual, that is, in an organism. So, qua computational states, such psychological states are not instantiated in any individual. Stated in this way, the argument implies not only that a wide computational psychology is possible but also, assuming the truth of computationalism, that for at least some psychological states such a psychology is *necessary*.

Thus far I have said very little explicitly about the central notion of *formality;* to demystify wide computationalism further, I now discuss this notion more explicitly.

## 4. THE NOTION OF FORMALITY

Computationalism is sometimes expressed as the view that, since cognition is essentially *formal,* the cognitive sciences should be restricted to positing and quantifying over the formal properties of mental states. This expression of computationalism, what Fodor (1980a:226–8) has called the *formality condition,* may make the argument from computationalism to individualism in psychology appear compelling, for the formal properties that mental states have are often thought of as *intrinsic* properties of mental symbols, such as their *shape* and *size* (see Fodor 1980a:227, 1987:18).

This conception of computationalism depicts formal properties as a particular species of *causal powers* that mental states have, properties that supervene on the intrinsic physical properties of the individual, and makes it tempting to view computationalism as providing a general theoretical framework for further specifying the nature of such powers. On this conception of formality, the task of computational psychology is to discover the intrinsic properties of tokens in the language of thought. In senses that I shall explain later in this section, such properties are both *non-semantic* and *non-physical*. (The formality condition focusses, however, on only the first of these contrasts, the contrast between formal and semantic properties.)

It should be emphasized first that the formality condition is an *interpretation* of computationalism in psychology, a claim about what computationalism entails or involves, not simply a statement of computationalism itself. Although the notion of formality is often used in computational theory, talk of formal *properties* as intrinsic properties of the individual components of computational systems is, in certain respects, misleading. The conception of formality used in logic, mathematics, and computer science, the disciplines that provide the ultimate foundations for computationalism in psychology, is quite distinct from that expressed by the formality condition. In these disciplines, the focus is on the properties and behavior of formal *systems*. A formal system consists of primitives, formation rules, formulae, axioms, and rules of inference. The foundations of logic is concerned, in part, with the relationship between the notions of a formal system, an effective procedure, an algorithm, a computation, and the set of recursive functions. On this conception of formality, what I shall call the *systemic conception of formality,* a given formal system could be expressed in alternative notations and, in principle, could be realized by a nation of people related to each other as the rules of the system specify (cf. Block 1978; Searle 1980). In this sense, the intrinsic physical properties of symbols in a formal system are arbitrary (see also Devitt 1990, 1991; Rollins 1989:ch. 1).

On the systemic conception of formality, there is little talk of the formal properties that *particular* symbols have. The sorts of formal properties that are primarily discussed, properties such as being closed under *modus ponens,* being transitive, and being compact, are properties of formal *systems* or, derivatively, properties of symbols as elements of formal systems. Computational processes, operations, and instructions are often thought of as formal, but this is to say only that they can be adequately described as the result of the application of the rules or algorithms that constitute the system to which they belong. Insofar as particular symbols in a formal system have formal properties, it is not clear whether such properties are intrinsic or extrinsic properties of the symbols themselves. For example, an instance of the symbol $A$ will lead to an instance of the symbol $B$ and will do so in virtue of its 'shape' in a formal system containing only the rule $A \rightarrow B$. But since this formal property, having that particular shape, has that effect only in a formal system with a rule of that type, one should be wary of identifying such formal properties with intrinsic causal powers that symbols possess. In any case, such properties have the causal significance that they do only insofar as the symbols to which they are attributed are part of a formal system.

The systemic conception of formality, which I rely on in the remainder of this chapter, makes it natural to express computationalism as the view that the sciences of cognition ought to be pitched at a computational *level of description*. I said earlier that the formal properties of mental states are supposed to be both non-semantic and non-physical, and here I want to explain what these two contrasts imply about the (narrow) computationalist's conception of cognition by looking at the two different conditions that a computational level of description of psychological states and processes must satisfy.

In contrast to the *physical* level of description, the computational level is distinct from and irreducible to the levels of description that characterize the physical realizations of a particular formal system. The same computational program, the same formal system, can be instantiated in many physically distinct ways. Given computationalism, this is the sense in which psychology is autonomous of the physical sciences. It is this autonomy, and so the contrast between the formal and the physical, that I think underlies the first premise of the computational argument.

In contrast to the *semantic* or representational level of description, the computational level specifies the properties of mental symbols and the rules constituting the formal system of which those mental tokens are a part without reference to what, if anything, those symbols represent. A proponent of the computational argument for individualism claims that, unlike the semantic level of description, the computational level specifies properties that are determined by the intrinsic physical states of the organism. This feature of the properties specified at the formal level of description makes the second premise of the computational argument plausible.

I shall return in §8 to a discussion of the dual role that the computational level of description is supposed to play within a computational theory of cognition. But to clarify further the nature of the challenge that wide computationalism poses to the computational argument, I want to introduce an analogy between wide computationalism and a concept that Richard Dawkins has developed in evolutionary biology, that of the extended phenotype.[3]

## 5. AN ANALOGY: THE SELFISH GENE AND THE EXTENDED PHENOTYPE

Dawkins (1982, 1989) draws a distinction between *replicators* and *vehicles* in the process of evolution by natural selection. A replicator is 'anything in the universe of which copies are made' (1982:83), and a vehicle is any relatively discrete entity that houses replicators. Replicators are *active* if they can differentially influence their own replication and passive otherwise; they are *germ-line* if they are 'potentially the ancestor of an indefinitely long line of descendant replicators' (p. 83) and dead end otherwise.

Dawkins's view is that the active, germ–line replicators that are the survivors in natural selection are genes or small genetic fragments; these are, in his terms, *selfish genes*. On a fairly natural interpretation, this implies that genes, not individuals, are *the* fundamental units of selection; so interpreted, Dawkins's view displaces the individual from its central place in evolutionary biology. If we think of genes or small genetic fragments as the units of selection, and think of individual organisms as vehicles for the survival of these replicators, then the existence of organisms will simply be one phenotypic effect that replicators have. As Dawkins says:

Replicators are not, of course, selected directly, but by proxy; they are judged by their phenotypic effects. Although for some purposes it is convenient to think of these phenotypic effects as being packaged together in discrete 'vehicles' such as individual organisms, this is not fundamentally necessary. Rather, the replicator should be thought of as having *extended* phenotypic effects, consisting of all its effects on the world at large, not just its effects on the individual body in which it happens to be sitting. (1982:4)

Dawkins's main point here and throughout *The Extended Phenotype* is that if you accept the selfish gene view, then it is natural to think of the phenotypic effects that genes have as extending beyond the

---

3 As Dawkins himself acknowledges, the idea of the selfish gene is implicit in the work of earlier evolutionary biologists, such as Fisher (1930), and was made explicit in the work of Hamilton (1964) and Williams (1966). The fact that I point to parallels between Dawkins's advocacy of the extended phenotype and my defence of wide computationalism does not imply that I accept the selfish gene view.

individual organism. The clustering of genes into individual organisms is simply one (albeit important) phenotypic effect that genes have. Likewise, I want to suggest that a proper understanding of computationalism makes it natural to view the organism as simply a part, albeit an important part, of what instantiates psychological states qua computational states. There is also a parallel in the reasoning that leads to these similar conclusions.

Dawkins assumes the theory of natural selection as a framework for addressing the issue of how biological stability, diversity, and change are possible. Dawkins claims that the differential survival of replicators is essential to the process of natural selection. Since, he argues, genes or small genetic fragments are the most important replicators in evolution, we should see genes as the replicators that survive through natural selection: They are the units of selection. Furthermore, once one adopts the selfish gene view of the units of selection, one can see the individual organism as simply one of the extended phenotypes that these genes have.

I am assuming computationalism as a framework for addressing the question of how cognition is possible, and understand computationalism in terms of the systemic conception of formality, according to which computationalism is the view that we can conceive of systems of psychological states as formal systems. This conception makes it clear that there is nothing in the hypothesis of computationalism that requires that cognitive systems be completely instantiated in an individual organism, and so wide computationalism is possible. Furthermore, once one adopts wide computationalism, the individual organism is displaced from its focal role in the study of cognition: It is simply part of what computational, cognitive, systems are instantiated in.

In each of these cases, the adoption of a certain view of a law of qualitative structure suggests that the individual organism is an entity of less significance than is usually thought; in each case, the individual is displaced from its current privileged location in explanations of behavior. There is nothing about computationalism, properly understood, that implies that computational systems must be fully instantiated in individuals. Moreover, for some processes, namely, those in which environmental interaction is an intrinsic part of what a computational system does, wide computationalism is not only a possible but a necessary view.

## 6. TWO OBJECTIONS TO WIDE COMPUTATIONALISM

One prima facie strength of wide computationalism is that it is fairly non-committal regarding the precise computational character of cognition. For example, it would seem to be compatible with both classical and connectionist conceptions of computationalism in psychology. Yet this potential strength of the wide computationalist view may be seen as an Achilles heel by someone pressing the issue of the degree to which wide computationalism is a *realistic* view of computational psychology: To what extent does the plausibility or even the possibility of wide computationalism turn on a view of computationalism that is committed to little more than the utility of the computational *metaphor* in psychology? To put it slightly differently: Does wide computationalism presuppose that computational explanations in psychology only *model* the phenomena they purport to explain, in the same way that there are computational models of other phenomena, such as the motions of planetary systems? If so, then wide computationalism will be a view of little significance for computational *psychology*. Central to the computational paradigm in psychology is the idea that an individual's mind is not simply described or modelled by a computer program; cognition is *rule-guided*, not simply *regular* (Bennett 1964). Wide computationalism is possible only if one relies on a weak reading of the computational metaphor, a reading that does not do justice to computationalist commitments in contemporary cognitive sciences.

To understand how a wide computational system could produce rule-guided behavior, consider how a *narrow* computational system, a computational system that is individualistic, could do so. Since standard personal computers are paradigm cases of narrow computational systems, we can make our discussion more concrete by asking how they produce behavior by following rules. Computers follow rules by instantiating or implementing programs. So what does it mean to implement a program? A physical device is *capable* of implementing a given program if its physical states are configured in such a way that transitions between those states are isomorphic to transitions between states that the program specifies, that is, there is a mapping from equivalence classes of physical states to the symbolic states that constitute the program. (How fine-grained and extensive this isomorphism needs to be I take to be determined a posteriori, not a priori.) Since implementational power is characterized in terms of the mathematical notion of isomorphism, a given physical device can implement a large number of actual programs and an infinite number of possible programs. The gap between the power to implement and actual implementation is closed, however, by identifying the appropriate causal interaction between the physical storehouse for the program (e.g., a physical disk) and the computer itself. So, in response to the grand epistemological, scepticism-mongering question, 'Of the infinite number of programs that a computer could be implementing, how do we know that it is in fact implementing *this* program?', we say: 'It implements this one because it is this one that is encoded on the disk we inserted'. (And since a physical disk is simply one type of storehouse for a program, we could replace reference to it here by reference to anything else a program is stored on.)

This view of implementation may make the program sound *epiphenomenal* to the physical operation of the computer, raising doubts about the view as an account of rule-guided behavior: In what sense is the behavior the computer generates anything more than *regular* behavior, behavior that only appears to be rule-governed but in fact is not? I should make it clear that I think that the program *does* play a causal role in the behavior of the physical device, and that the behavior it produces is thus rule-governed and not merely regular. But although we may wish to say that the machine behaves the way it does *because* of the way it was programmed (i.e., because of the program it instantiates), we must be sure to distinguish this sort of 'downward' causation from that between the physical states themselves. Unless there is massive causal pre-emption 'from above', symbolic states can't be viewed as the efficient causes of later physical states. To understand how 'higher-level' states can play a causal role in the production of behavior, we need a broader conception of the notion of a causal role than is typically assumed (see Part II).

Although I have stated this view of how computers produce rule-guided behavior in terms of familiar, narrow computational systems, the narrowness of the system plays no significant role in the account; much the same story can be told of *wide* computational systems. The account of implementational power is precisely the same: A wide computational system has the power to implement just those programs for which there is an isomorphism between the system's physical states and the symbolic states the program specifies. The account of actual implementation is a generalization of that in the case of narrow computational systems: A wide computational system implements the 'program' physically stored in the environment with which it causally interacts. Determining the proper symbolic description of aspects of an organism's environment is very much an a posteriori matter, much as is doing so with respect to an organism's *internal* structure.

'Program' occurs in quotation marks here because of two important differences between the programs that run on standard computers and those that (narrow or wide) computationalists claim run on us: (a) Unlike the programs that we encode on physical disks, precisely what symbolic interpretations we can give either to aspects of an organism's environment or to its internal structure (or both) are things we must *discover;* (b) These interpretations may not turn out to be elaborate enough themselves to warrant the label 'program'. Significantly, (a) and (b) distinguish what we know (and love?) as actual computers from organisms. We simply are not in an appropriate epistemological position to claim either that our brains or our brains plus our environments instantiate programs in just the sense that computers do; that is, in part, why computationalism is a *proposed* law of qualitative structure for a research program and not a home truth about cognition. And in light of the similarities and differences between us and computers that emerge from empirical research, we will be able to decide whether 'programs' or 'languages' are appropriate categories with which to develop psychological explanations. None of this involves adopting a weak understanding of the computational metaphor in psychology, only some epistemic caution.

The idea that by going wide one is giving up on something basic to computationalism reflects a deeply Cartesian view of the mind, a vestige of thinking of the mind and body as distinct substances, which survives in contemporary materialist and naturalistic views of the mind. The vestige is the idea that there is something special about the mind, about what is 'in the head', that justifies the ascription of computational states to it, which is not shared with extra-cranial reality; there is a bifurcation between mind and mere matter that makes only narrow computationalism a serious option in the cognitive sciences (cf. Segal 1991:492, quoted in §3). I shall refer to this idea as *Cartesian computationalism* and will have more to say about it in the conclusion to this chapter (see also Chapter 9).

Let me turn to a second objection to wide computationalism, one that introduces broadly empirical grounds for doubting that *we* are wide computational systems. As Egan (1992:446, 457) notes, citing examples of research in early vision and in syntactic and morphological analysis in linguistics, the psychological processes for which there are the most satisfying computational accounts are *modular:* They are domain-specific and informationally encapsulated.[4] We have had our greatest empirical successes in computational psychology in explaining the character of psychological processes that function with relative independence from even much of the *internal* workings of the individual's cognitive system (let alone its external environment). If empirical success has come within computational psychology only or even predominantly with the correctness of the presumption of modularity, then that should cast doubt on the idea of developing an empirically adequate *wide* computational psychology.

Fodor (1983) makes this point about the relationship between modularity and computational psychology more poignantly by arguing that 'global systems are per se bad domains for computational models' (p. 128). Specifically, what he calls *central* processes, such as problem solving and belief fixation, are unlikely to have computational models precisely because they are, in his view, non-modular. The non-modularity of central processes gives one reason to be sceptical about the real (vs. mere) possibility of an adequate computational psychology explaining them. And what is true of central processes, which have access to a variety of representational inputs, is also true of wide computational processes, which access representations *outside* of the individual.

I discuss the issues that this argument from modularity to individualism raise in more detail in Chapter 4; here I simply want to note my general response to it. Suppose we agree that, by and large, empirical successes in the cognitive sciences thus far have involved highly modular systems, such as those employed in visual perception and phoneme recognition. Perhaps this is for a deep reason, such as that only highly modular systems *are* computational; alternatively, it could be due to a relatively shallow reason, such as that only highly modular computational processes can readily be understood by theo-

---

4 The notion of modularity I rely on here is that of Fodor (1983). Although these notions will be explored further in Chapter 4, here is an intuitive gloss on each for now. A *domain-specific* system is one that operates on some particular type of information (a domain); a cognitive system that is *informationally encapsulated* acts as an input–output function on a specific set of informational inputs and outputs and so is insensitive to other information.

rists as computational. In either case, there is nothing here that allows for the extension of a point about central processes to wide computational processes *since the latter can also be modular.* As I hope the discussion in the next section indicates, contemporary research in cognitive psychology that is properly considered as positing wide computational systems involves highly modular systems. The implicit premise in the argument from modularity to individualism – that modular systems are taxonomized individualistically – is false because modular systems may well encapsulate information that is in the individual's *environment,* not elsewhere in the individual; the module may be a part of a wide computational system.

## 7. WIDE COMPUTATIONALISM IN COGNITIVE PSYCHOLOGY[5]

Although the possibility of wide computationalism suffices to show that the second premise of the computational argument is false, for those antecedently disposed to think that wide computationalism is coherent the real interest in the computational argument lies in the claim that *we* are plausibly seen as wide computational systems. I think that wide computationalism *is* made plausible by some of the recent computational research in both human and animal cognition. Showing wide computationalism to be not only a coherent but also a plausible view of our cognitive processing would both consolidate and broaden my objection to the computational argument. I shall discuss two examples of recent research in cognitive psychology that show wide computationalism in action.

Sekuler and Blake (1990) devote a significant section of their chapter on spatial vision and form perception to a discussion of an approach to form perception pioneered in the work of Campbell and Robson (1968) known as *multiple spatial channels theory.* The basic idea of this approach is that there are specific stimuli that individual sets of neurons are sensitive to, these stimuli being decomposable into sinusoidal *gratings.* These gratings are relatively simple, having only four relevant parameters: spatial frequency, contrast, orientation, and spatial phase. Any figure composed of these gratings is definable formally in terms of these four parameters. The bold and controversial claim

---

5 Thanks to both David Field and Frank Keil for useful discussion of the material discussed in this section; they should not, however, be saddled with responsibility for the conclusions I draw here.

of this research program is that *any* natural scene in an organism's environment can be decomposed into its gratings, and this fact explains a great deal about human form perception, including its limitations.

On this conception of form perception, part of the task of the perceptual psychologist is to identify formal primitives that adequately describe the visual environment, and to specify algorithms that apply to these primitives to determine complete visual scenes. To see what this means, take a case simpler than human vision, that of a lens projecting an image of an object onto a piece of white paper. Figure 1 shows the *transfer function* for two lenses; it plots how contrast is transferred through the lens from object to image and is defined over a range of spatial frequencies. As input, this function takes contrast in an object, producing as output contrast in the image. We can likewise define a *contrast sensitivity function* for the human visual system, which takes the same inputs from the world to produce a visual output (see Figure 2). The formal system that perceptual psychologists working within this paradigm study is not instantiated in any individual: It includes but is not restricted to the intrinsic properties of an individual. This is reflected in the actual methodology employed by such psychologists, which involves the extensive and complex mathemati-

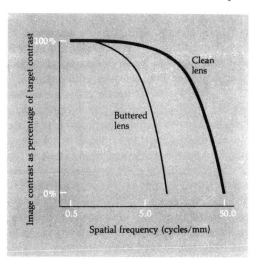

FIGURE 1 Two transfer functions for a lens. The curves specify how contrast in the image formed by the lens is related to contrast in the object.

81

cal analysis of natural scenes into their computational primitives. Such analysis appears to be an intrinsic part of the multiple spatial channels paradigm, not simply something preliminary to real perceptual psychology.

Gallistel (1989a) reports research on the conceptions of space, time, and number that a variety of animals have, including bees, rats, and ants. One of Gallistel's primary conclusions is that purely sensory-based models of a range of animal behavior are inadequate. Rather, the evidence overwhelmingly suggests that these animals construct quite complex representations of their environments and use these to guide their behavior. Gallistel argues that such representations are computational; that there is strong evidence that these animals in-

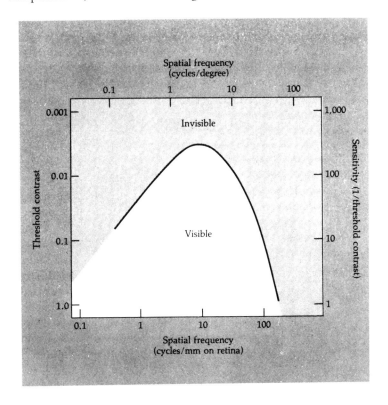

FIGURE 2 A contrast sensitivity function for an adult human. The upper horizontal axis is scaled in units specifying the number of pairs of light and dark bars of the grating falling within 1 degree of visual angle on the retina.

stantiate modules that are sensitive to the formal (e.g., the geometric) structure of their environments; and that this sensitivity is responsible for their navigation through their physical environments. For example, in ants and bees the computational process of *dead reckoning* (which integrates velocity with respect to time) takes as inputs the animal's solar heading, forward speed, and a representation of the solar azimuth, producing as output a representation of the creature's position relative to some landmark, such as a nest. The *ephemeris function,* which produces the third of these inputs, takes as its inputs a sighting of the sun and time on some endogenous clock (see Gallistel 1989b:70–6). In both of these cases, the computational process extends beyond the boundary of the individual.

Gallistel calls his view a *computational representational* perspective on animal cognition. Of animal navigation, Gallistel says:

Routine animal movements are governed by a navigational process closely analogous to everyday marine practice. This practice rests on an extensive isomorphism between the geometry of motion and position and the computational processes that underlie navigation. At the neurophysiological level of analysis, the hypothesis implies that the mathematical description of the processes in the animal brain that function during animal navigation parallels the mathematical description of the computations a human or computerized navigation system makes. (1989a:176–7)

This quotation suggests that Gallistel, like those working in the multi-channels paradigm in form perception, does not see anything mysterious in positing an extensive isomorphism between the formally described properties of an environment and those of mental processes.

Gallistel defends a general conception of learning that focusses on the claim that an animal attunes its behavior to the 'formal properties' of its environment. He says:

There is a rich formal correspondence between processes and relations in the environment and the operations the brain performs. Brain processes and relations recapitulate world processes and relations. The recapitulation is not fortuitous. To fit behavior to the environment, the brain creates models of the behavior-relevant aspects of the environment. The formal properties of the processes that realize these models reflect the formal properties of the corresponding external reality because these processes have been subject to evolution by natural selection. Selection has been based on the fidelity of these processes to the external reality. Evolution by natural selection creates rich functioning isomorphisms between brain processes and the environment, and learning is to be understood in terms of these isomorphisms. (1989b:27)

The isomorphism between computational processes instantiated in the head and certain 'formal properties' in the environment is responsible for the successful navigation behavior that many animals exhibit.

Two central postulates of these otherwise diverse research programs are that the environment of the organism has a certain formal structure to it, and that it is the organism's sensitivity to this structure that explains core parts of its cognitive performance. Characterizing the specific nature of the environment in computational terms appears to be a central part of the conception of cognitive explanation implicit in these research programs. Despite some of Gallistel's own claims about the view he advocates (see later), I see no way in which this is merely additional or peripheral to these research programs, and in the remainder of this section I defend the belief that both research programs support the view that we and our biological kin are parts of wide computational systems.

Recall Segal's view of the relationship between computationalism and individualism discussed in §3: that, as it turns out, our cognitive systems are narrow, not wide, computational systems. Thus, wide computationalism should be rejected because although it is a coherent view, there is *no* research that, in Segal's words, treats 'whole subjects plus embedding environments' as 'integrated, computational systems'. This is a strong empirical claim, one to which I have thus far in this section provided two prima facie counter-examples. The individualist who wishes to defend Segal's claim needs to explain away the appearances. Once the coherence of wide computationalism is conceded – its mere possibility – there are likely to be many such appearances to explain away, and so such an individualist faces a prima facie difficult task.

I think that the most promising way to defend the computational argument for individualism from the line of objection I have developed is to concede that even if one *can* view the individual as embedded within a wide computational system, there is no *explanatory* motivation for doing so. For we can also view the individual itself as a computational system, a narrow computational system, and *doing so is always sufficient for computational, psychological explanation.* Consider the two examples I have given of purportedly wide computational research. Even if the multi-channels paradigm does seem to posit a formal structure to the environment, it could also be viewed as claiming that the retinal image has such a structure. If this view of the paradigm is correct, then although one *could* view the paradigm as being computationally wide, there is no need to adopt this view of it. Likewise, although the computational representational view that Gallistel defends might seem to view an individual as part of a wide computational system, a system that includes features of that individual's environment, one could also see his view as positing an interesting isomorphism between *two* formal systems, one of which is fully instantiated in the individual (cf. Palmer 1978); crucially, the cognitive sciences study the *narrow* computational system. Since the form of this defence of the computational argument is the same in each of these cases, I shall develop and respond to it by focussing only on Gallistel's view.

Several comments that Gallistel makes about his own project offer support for an individualistic interpretation of it. Gallistel says that his 'agenda is a reductionist one: to understand learning as a neuronal phenomenon' (1989b:24), going on to say that studying the total computational system is simply a 'necessary prelude to understanding what the system does in terms of what its elements do' (1989b:24). This implies that figuring out the computational structure of an organism's environment, although methodologically necessary, is peripheral to an understanding of the nature of learning itself, and suggests that there is no deep sense in which Gallistel advocates a view of learning as a wide computational process. In addition, in the conclusion to his book, Gallistel says that '[t]he structure of the computational mechanisms is dictated by the formal structure of the representations to be computed and by the sensory or mnemonic data from which they are computed' (1989b:581), suggesting that he sees the *computational* system of interest to the psychologist as fully instantiated in the individual organism.

A general feature of Gallistel's view of animal cognition that might also be thought difficult to reconcile with a wide computational view of it is that much animal behavior is governed by internal maps and mathematical representations of the environment rather than by direct sensory input. This view ascribes to an animal a high degree of autonomy from its environment, and this aspect of Gallistel's view at least *seems* individualistic: Animals navigate by *internal maps,* not by sensory tracing, homing, or other environmentally interactive methods. In characterizing how an animal navigates, we abstract away from its actual environment and concentrate on the intrinsic features of its map or model of that environment.

One response to this claim corresponds to and reinforces the weak or negative claim I made in §3. Even if one *can* see Gallistel's view as a narrow computational approach, the fact that it also can be given a wide computational interpretation shows that computationalism itself does not entail individualism: Computational systems need not be individualistic. Yet this response does not address the issue of which interpretation of Gallistel's view, the wide computational interpretation or that of the individualist, has greater explanatory adequacy. A second response, corresponding to one of the stronger claims made in §3 – about the plausibility or even necessity of wide computationalism in psychology – addresses this issue.

The sorts of behavior that Gallistel explains involve a flow of information from the environment to the organism. One of Gallistel's main points is that this is not a constant flow of information, as we might have supposed. Yet it would be a mistake to think of his view as denying that formal properties of the environment play a significant role in a complete cognitive explanation of animal navigation. Even if an animal's behavior in navigation is *primarily* governed by internal maps, there are a number of ways in which the view of these maps as part of a wide computational process is explanatorily richer than the individualistic view of them.

First, these maps are updated by periodically acquired information about the organism's movement and the relative position of objects in the environment. These updates ('fix-taking', in Gallistel's terms) are a necessary part of a complete psychological explanation of the behavior. If one takes the computational representational view to provide a comprehensive paradigm for the investigation of animal learning and cognition, then fix-taking must be accommodated within that paradigm. Narrow computationalism allows that relations between psychological states can be computational. The wide computationalist proposes a natural extension of this view to allow for organism–environment interactions, such as fix-taking, to be subject to a computational approach. The individualist must explain processes such as fix-taking in some other way, since her claim is that computational systems are fully instantiated in individuals. The wide computationalist is able to offer a view of fix-taking that has greater explanatory unity than that available to the individualist.

Second, as shown by the previous examples of environmental inputs in Gallistel's account, characterizing cognitive computational states *as representations* sometimes requires non-individualistic descriptions. If a representational psychology may violate individualism in the descriptions it offers of psychological states, then why must a computational psychology be individualistic (especially if one accepts a computational representational perspective on cognition)? This question is not rhetorical, for (a) whether representational psychology violates individualism in particular cases is a substantial question, and (b) the width of representational content might be thought compatible with the narrowness of computational psychology because of the different functions that intentional and computational ascriptions serve. For example, Egan (1992) has argued that the role of semantics in computational psychology is to provide explanatory *models,* models that may be either narrow or wide, for individualistic computations (cf. Antony 1990; Kitcher 1985). If Egan is right about the different explanatory roles that content and computational ascriptions play, then this provides a principled reason for distinguishing between representational and computational aspects of psychology with respect to individualism.

In discussing this issue further, I shall examine an often invoked trichotomy, that between the physical, the syntactic or formal, and the semantic; doing so will also bring us back to a consideration of Premise (A) of the computational argument for individualism. But let me first briefly summarize our conclusions in this section. Wide computationalism is not only coherent but also the most plausible view of at least some existing research *within* the computational paradigm. Given that, the computational argument for individualism can be turned on its head: Individualism does not impose a constraint on how we individuate mental states precisely because, in at least some cases, psychological states are considered as (wide) computational states for the purposes of psychological explanation.

## 8. THE FIRST PREMISE: COMPUTATIONALISM RECONSIDERED

The first premise of the computational argument says, effectively, that the computational nature of psychological processing exhausts the interest that the cognitive sciences have in mental states. I shall argue that this claim is too strong and that an appropriate weakening of it is compatible with the acceptability of wide, intentional explanations in cognitive psychology. Even if wide computationalism were false or incoherent, one would have reason to reject the computational argument. Since in this section I am interested in offering an independent criticism of (A), the first premise of the computational argument, I shall ignore the discussion thus far of (B); I briefly discuss the relationship between my rejection of each of these premises in the conclusion to this chapter.

The first premise of the computational argument states a particular strong relationship between computationalism and the cognitive sciences, namely, that *all* of the research in the cognitive sciences presupposes that mental processes are computational (or that all of the current research worth pursuing is computational). Some philosophers have made this strong claim; as it is sometimes put, computationalism is 'the only game in town'. For example, Robert Cummins writes: 'Computationalism is hard to swallow . . . but it is equally hard to spit out. The only alternatives are dualism, which is not an alternative theory but the claim that theory is impossible, and 'neuronalism' – i.e., the doctrine that intentionally characterized capacities are realizable only as neurophysiological capacities' (1983:90; footnote omitted). There is no reason to think, however, that 'dualism' and 'neuronalism' are the only alternatives to accepting computationalism. The falsity of computationalism would not entail that scientific studies of cognition, apart from those provided by the neurosciences, are impossible any more than the falsity of *behaviorism* implies this. Cognitive psychology could be autonomous of the neurosciences without all (or even any) psychological states being computational. The fact that a significant proportion (perhaps even the majority) of research in experimental, *developmental,* cognitive psychology does not presuppose computationalism should remind us that the two alternatives that Cummins presents do not constitute a serious dilemma for the cognitive psychologist (see Carey 1985; Keil 1989; Leslie 1987; Spelke 1990). One reason, then, to reject the first premise is that the best research in some areas of the cognitive sciences is not computational at all. But even when the computational paradigm is adopted, there is no good reason to think that only the computational level of description is appropriate for the cognitive sciences.

In §4 I said that the claim that cognition is formal marks two contrasts: formal processes are, on the one hand, *non-semantic* and, on the other, *non-physical.* These two contrasts suggest that psychological states can be described at a physical, a computational, and a semantic level of description, but that only the computational level should constitute a developed and properly scientific study of cognition. I want to call this claim into question here. The core motivations for thinking that there is a computational level of description in psychology distinct from the physical level of description also give one a reason for thinking the same of the semantic level of description. Moreover, individualistic criticisms of the causal relevance of wide semantic properties for psychological explanation also apply to properties specified at the computational level. These two claims provide one with reasons to reject the view that *only* the physical and computational properties of psychological states are relevant to the cognitive sciences, not these *and* the wide semantic properties of psychological states.

One philosophical motivation for computationalism derives from its relationship to functionalism in the philosophy of mind. One of the chief reasons for rejecting a type-type identity theory of mental states in favor of functionalism was the *multiple realizability* of psychological states: Creatures made of very different material stuff could realize or instantiate the same psychological states, were these states to be described functionally. Computational psychology provides a systematic way of specifying distinctly functional psychological descriptions. As a functional level of description, the computational level is autonomous relative to any physical level of description.

Precisely the same relationship holds, however, between the representational and computational levels of description, and for just the same reasons. Intuitively, many *representational* functions that organisms instantiate are realized differently both in different individuals and in members of different species. To adapt an example that Kim Sterelny discusses (1990:98), both bats and owls instantiate psychological states with the content 'mouse down there', and this shared perceptual state explains their common subsequent behaviors. But since bats instantiate this state in an echolocation system, whereas owls instantiate it in a visual system, it is extremely unlikely that there is one *computational* description of their shared state. The fact that this function is instantiated, not precisely *how* it is instantiated, is relevant to some aspects of psychological explanation.

Causal relations between semantically described psychological processes are realized in organisms as computational (non-semantic) processes, at least if computationalism is true, much as computationally described (non-physical) processes are realized in organisms *as* physical processes. Since, in each case, the latter can vary while the former remains constant, there is precisely the same rationale for positing an autonomous *representational* level of description as there is for positing an autonomous computational level of description. Just as the neuro-physiological characterization of a psychological capacity is incomplete, the computational characterization of that capacity does not exhaust the interest that cognitive psychologists have in that capacity. There are questions of *psychological* interest that do not reduce to questions about how psychological states are realized in either computational or neurophysiological structures. We need to move beyond the computational level of description, much as we need to move *to* that level, in order to capture generalizations that we would otherwise miss.

One reason those interested in developing a scientific psychology have been wary of characterizing mental states by their (wide) content is that individuals instantiating different wide contents could behave identically. For this reason, differences in the content that two individuals instantiate are sometimes thought to make no *causal difference* to the psychology an individual possesses; wide contents are not causal powers. Yet formal systems as *non-physical* systems have constituents that have *no* causal powers; formal systems are constituted by abstract entities, such as numbers, sets, axioms, and theorems. By contrast, *implemented* formal systems *are* constituted by states that do have causal powers, and computationalism in psychology gains much of its plausibility from an individualistic perspective because the computational level is thought to describe the causal powers that psychological states have. However, implemented *semantic* systems, that is, systems of states characterized by their content, also have causal powers. Let me elaborate.

It is sometimes said that if the semantic properties of mental processes are to be available for causal explanations, it must be in virtue of their correlation with formal properties. The idea that there is some systematic correspondence between the syntax and semantics of the language of thought has been dubbed the *correlation thesis* (Stich 1983:186). The correlation thesis is misleading insofar as it implies that it is *merely* the correlation between semantic and syntactic properties that gives the former a role in psychological explanation. Rather, this correlation between syntax and semantics is evidence for positing an *instantial* relation between the two, and *this* explains how semantic properties can be causally relevant to explanations of behavior. This same relation holds between the computational and physical levels of description: It is in virtue of the instantiation of computational systems (e.g., programs) in physical devices (i.e., computers) that the properties of the former are causally efficacious. The systematic correspondence between, on the one hand, properties specified at the semantic and computational levels and, on the other, properties specified at the computational and physical levels of description is underpinned by an instantial relation. If computational properties can be said to be causally efficacious in virtue of this relation, then so too can *semantic* properties.

In virtue of the motivations and problems shared by the computational and representational levels of description, it is prima facie implausible to insist that only the former of these is *the* level at which psychology should be pitched. In light of this, it is tempting to draw the further conclusion that the computational and representational levels of description play the same explanatory roles within the cognitive sciences, and so reject a view, such as Egan's, that distinguishes their explanatory roles in some fundamental way.

## 9. CONCLUSION

The computational argument for individualism should be rejected because both of its premises are false. I have argued in §§3–7 that the second premise, which claims that computational processes in general are individualistic, is false because of the possibility and plausibility of wide computationalism in the cognitive sciences. I argued in §8 that the first premise, the hypothesis of computationalism in psychology, does not have the exclusionary consequence that it must have to support the constraint of individualism.

Much of my discussion aims to explain the coherence of wide computationalism, what I have been calling its mere possibility. I think, however, that the most significant issue concerns not the coherence of wide computationalism but the extent to which a wide computational research strategy is employed within the cognitive sciences. Given that, why have I concentrated on the mere possibility of wide computationalism, rather than its plausibility in the cognitive sciences?

The central idea behind wide computationalism is extremely simple. However, fleshing out the idea and being explicit about the implications it has for issues in philosophical psychology allow one to see the respects in which it represents a radical departure from the conception of the mind underlying much contemporary research in computational psychology, what I have called Cartesian computationalism. Precisely because Cartesian computationalism is typically unidentified and unexamined, even the basic idea behind wide computationalism is likely to produce knee-jerk puzzlement. It is for this reason that I have spent so much time demystifying wide computationalism by articulating what the mere possibility of wide computationalism amounts to.

Although my arguments for the rejection of each of the premises in the computational argument have been developed independently, note that assuming wide computationalism makes the idea that psychology should be cast only at a computational level of description somewhat less plausible. For, like the individuation of psychological states by their representational content, the individuation of computational states in a wide computational system requires going beyond the boundary of the individual. In a wide computational system, the distinction between 'syntax' and 'semantics' is blurred in the following sense: Psychological states have both computational and representational characterizations only insofar as those states stand in a particular relation or set of relations to entities and properties outside of the individual. One cannot, even in principle, inspect a mental state itself and see either what wide computational or representational powers it has.

In this respect, neither the computational nor the representational levels of description specify intrinsic causal powers that psychological states have. Having thus reached a conclusion about psychological taxonomy – that it is not by intrinsic causal powers – that parallels our conclusion in Chapter 2 about scientific taxonomy more generally, it would seem time to stop.

# 4

# *Methodological arguments*

In Chapter 2 I considered an a priori argument for individualism, the argument from causal powers; Chapter 3 focussed on an empirical argument for individualism, the computational argument; in this chapter I consider two methodological arguments for individualism. What is the methodological clout of individualism? More particularly, are there methodological reasons for adopting individualism as a constraint on the study of cognition?

## 1. A PRIORI, EMPIRICAL, AND METHODOLOGICAL ARGUMENTS

Methodological arguments have remained very much in the background of the debate over individualism, in part because such arguments rely less directly on general, intuitive considerations that support individualism, and because the distinction between individualistic and wide psychology has not typically been drawn in terms of methodology. If there are facts about how narrow and wide explanations operate or must be developed that imply the methodological coherence or the empirical fruitfulness of only the former, then there is reason to think that research in the cognitive sciences ought to be individualistic. Such arguments are *stronger* than either the a priori or empirical arguments we have examined in that, if sound, they leave no further room for an appeal to explanatory practice in psychology.

We can also view these three arguments – the a priori, the empirical, and the methodological – as forming a series of possible concessions to the anti-individualist; in this respect, each of these arguments is *weaker* than that which precedes it. If there were a general argument that showed that sciences had to individuate their kinds by the intrinsic causal powers of the entities those kinds subsume, then individualism in psychology would follow from what I have called *global* individualism; but global individualism is false. If the computational nature of psychological processing entailed that individuation in the cognitive sciences had to be individualistic, then individualism would constrain those sciences; but the computational argument for individualism also fails. Individualism in psychology could still be vindicated if it could be shown that the best methodologies available for research in psychology treat psychological states and processes *as if* they were individualistic or, conversely, that methodologies that are clearly non-individualistic suffer from an inherent methodological problem.

## 2. CONCEIVING OF INDIVIDUALISM IN METHODOLOGICAL TERMS

As a putative constraint on psychological taxonomy and explanation, individualism is not an abstract, metaphysical issue devoid of either methodological or normative import. But can we conceive of individualism as implying a methodological view of psychology, a view of how one ought to study cognition? Are there general methodological differences separating individualists and their opponents? Developing affirmative answers to both of these questions presupposes that we can empirically identify approaches to cognition – research paradigms in psychology – that express, respectively, narrow and wide perspectives on psychological theory; this, in turn, presupposes that we can conceptually distinguish two such perspectives in general terms.

One can draw such a conceptual distinction by considering two idealized philosophers who set out to put their respective individualistic and wide views of taxonomy and explanation into psychological practice. (Who knows, maybe they picked up a large grant from the NSF or NSERC to do so.) The two differ over their views of the significance of the *embeddedness* of the organism in a physical and social environment for theory construction in psychology (cf. Fodor 1980a:229, 1980b). For the individualist, psychology must abstract away from an organism's particular environment; the relation between an organism and its environment obscures rather than illuminates the nature of psychological kinds and explanations. In seeing the individual as the largest complete psychological unit, the individualist claims that for the purposes of psychology the environment can be bracketed from the individuals located in it: All of the information

94

strictly relevant for psychology is contained in the mental representations of individuals. The wide psychologist, by contrast, considers the embeddedness of an organism in a specific environment as intrinsic to the development of psychological taxonomy and explanation.

We can tease out some of the methodological implications of these differences, and move from the conceptual to the empirical presupposition, by supposing that our narrow and wide philosophers-cum-psychologists both endorse computationalism in psychology. The narrow computationalist claims that the character of the world is relevant only insofar as it affects the *formal* properties of mental representations (see Fodor 1980a:231). Psychology studies the intrinsic properties of mental representations and the computational relations between them. One may discover such properties and relations by examining their role in causing behavior, but one examines behavior only as a means to this end. (Thus, individualists do *not* think that psychological states are not connected to anything external to the individual instantiating them; rather, they hold that we ought to treat psychological states and processes *as if* they were such states. This is another respect in which individualism can be viewed as a form of *methodological* solipsism.) For the wide computationalist, by contrast, computational psychology is not concerned solely with what is 'in the head', but rather with the causes of an organism's behavior, where both behavior and its causes are considered *as* computational processes located in an environmental context.

As my discussion in Chapter 3 suggests, this general contrast is not a pure fiction. Much of the research done within the computational paradigm, particularly in central areas of artificial intelligence, such as planning, knowledge representation, and problem solving, has been conducted within a Cartesian computational framework; by contrast, I take both the multi-channels approach to form perception and the computational-representational perspective on animal learning to embody a wide perspective on psychological research within the computational paradigm. Individualism and wide psychology are more than fictional positions in some philosophical narrative; they are types of research perspectives active in psychology. Consider the following well-known exemplars of each type of approach.

Approaches to natural language inspired by Noam Chomsky (1957, 1965, 1980), particularly transformational grammar, have typically been highly individualistic in their methodology. Such approaches assume that sentences in natural languages have both surface and deep structures, and that the competence of speakers of natural languages consists of the representation of such structures and the rules that cause transformations between them. The central notion of linguistic competence is a property of individuals or, more specifically, of an individual's language acquisition device. In determining an individual's linguistic competence – syntactic, semantic, and phonological – one must abstract away from that individual's environment and consider instead the relationships that exist between internal linguistic representations of various types.

The perceptual psychology of J. J. Gibson, his ecological optics, is a paradigmatic example of wide psychology, striving as it does for an understanding of visually directed behavior in terms of the information contained in what Gibson calls the 'ambient optical array'. Central to the Gibsonian approach to visual perception is the view that perceivers are embedded in an environment. No small part of the task of the perceptual psychologist consists in adequately characterizing this environment at a level appropriate for a visual science. Gibson provides a clear statement of how his direct perception model is part of a wide research strategy:

When I assert that perception of the environment is direct, I mean that it is not mediated by *retinal* pictures, *neural* pictures, or *mental* pictures. *Direct perception* is the activity of getting information from the ambient array of light. I call this a process of *information pickup* that involves the exploratory activity of looking around, getting around, and looking at things. This is quite different from the supposed activity of getting information from the inputs of the optic nerves, whatever they may prove to be. (1979:147)

Gibson makes this statement at the beginning of Part Three of his book, having used the earlier parts to specify the environment that an organism perceives (Part One) and the information in the ambient optical array (Part Two).

Supposing that we can distinguish, broadly speaking, two research paradigms for psychology, consider a question that Fodor (1980a:233–4) has raised: What reason is there to think that we cannot accept *both* as appropriate for research in the discipline? Why not have one type of psychology that abides by the constraint of individualism – in Fodor's terms, a *rationalist* psychology – and another type of psychology that is not individualistic – a *naturalistic* psychology? Why not accept an ecumenical view of taxonomy and explanation in psychology, one encompassing both narrow and wide perspectives? In the present context, such a pluralistic conception of psychology is dualistic and suggests a certain type of division of labor within psychology. There are parts of psychology that explain cognitive processing that are individualistic (e.g., narrow computational psychology) and parts that explain how individuals with such processing mechanisms manage to represent and act in the world they inhabit; these latter parts constitute wide psychology.

This division of research labor corresponds to a distinction in Hartry Field's construal of the problem of intentionality. Taking belief as a paradigm example, Field divides the problem of intentionality into two subproblems:

*subproblem (a):* the problem of explaining what it is for a person to believe* a sentence (of his or her own language).
*subproblem (b):* the problem of explaining what it is for a sentence to mean that p. (1978:80)

where 'believe*' designates 'a relation between a person and a sentence in his own language' (1978:80). A generalization of these subproblems that applied Field's distinction to representational psychology in general, and not just to the propositional attitudes, would give us the division of labor implicit in the dualism about methodology sketched earlier. Subproblem (a), the problem of how representations interact causally and inferentially, could be solved within the individualistic paradigm of research, and subproblem (b), the problem of how our representations have the content they do, could be solved within a naturalistic paradigm.

Despite the possibility of such ecumenism, there are broadly methodological reasons for thinking that the individualistic option is the only feasible option in psychology. I shall consider two such lines of reasoning for this conclusion that stem from Fodor's work. The first owes its formulation to Fodor; the second is implicit in Fodor's claims about the modularity of much of cognition (see also Chapter 3, §6).

## 3. AN ARGUMENT AGAINST 'NATURALISM' IN PSYCHOLOGY

Fodor has argued that a naturalistic approach to psychology involves a research strategy that requires the completion of *all* of the rest of science in order for psychology to characterize its basic vocabulary adequately; such an approach is methodologically futile. Fodor's argument for this conclusion proceeds as follows (see Fodor 1980a:247–

52). A naturalistic psychology claims that one can make science out of the relations between an organism and its environment. Doing so requires law-instantiating descriptions of these relations, which presupposes that one has access to projectible descriptions of the relevant *relata*. But the sorts of things that organisms are related to in an environment are the subject matter of sciences *other* than psychology, the task of each of the various sciences being, in part, to provide projectible descriptions of the objects in its domain. Thus a naturalistic psychology must rely on other sciences for the descriptions it needs to state its laws. This relation of dependence between a naturalistic psychology and progress in other sciences implies that a naturalistic psychology requires a hopelessly *holistic* research strategy, one that presupposes the completion of sciences other than psychology before psychology itself can be completed. As Fodor says, 'the naturalistic psychologists will inherit the Earth, but only after everybody else is finished with it. No doubt it's all right to have a research strategy that says "wait awhile". But who wants to wait *forever?*' (1980a:248).

To gain a clearer understanding of Fodor's point, consider an example that Fodor discusses. If one wants to develop naturalistic psychological generalizations involving a person's thoughts *about salt,* then one needs a nomological description of salt. Such a description is provided by chemistry, and so psychology, conceived along naturalistic lines, presupposes that we possess the appropriate *chemical* descriptions. This reliance of naturalistic psychological descriptions on those offered by other sciences is, Fodor claims, quite general. If determining the appropriate level of description for a naturalistic psychology requires knowing the corresponding descriptions in other disciplines, then a naturalistic research strategy is methodologically flawed. Whatever other promise there might be for a naturalistic research strategy, because of its methodological dependence on other sciences, there is no practical hope of completing a naturalistic psychology, and, as Fodor says, 'for methodology, practical hope is *everything*' (1980a:252).

Fodor's chief claim is that characterizing organism–environment relations requires nomological descriptions of psychological states that can only be provided by other disciplines; thus, the methodological dependence of a naturalistic psychology on the rest of the sciences. In the next section, I shall argue, first, that a naturalistic or wide psychology need not be methodologically dependent on other sciences in the way that Fodor claims it must; second, even if it were so dependent, this would not constitute a deep methodological problem for wide approaches to psychology.

## 4. WIDE PSYCHOLOGY AND TAXONOMIC DEPENDENCE

There are two reasons to suspect that Fodor's argument against a naturalistic or wide psychology must be mistaken. First, by parity of reasoning, Fodor's argument should also apply to any new science that both refers to objects that are taxonomized in some existing science and cross-classifies those objects because this new science subsumes these objects under novel kinds. Were the argument sound, it could be applied at any stage in the *history* of science, and it would thus imply that most currently existing sciences are methodologically problematic in the way he claims a wide psychology is. (Also, Fodor's argument would seem to be applicable to *any* ecological study of organisms insofar as such a study involves establishing what relationships exist between organisms and their ecological environment. Thus, were the argument sound, the ecological sciences would be methodologically incoherent.)

Second, there are many examples of research conducted in the naturalistic tradition *in psychology,* and they do not appear to suffer from the particular problem that Fodor identifies. In Chapter 3 I introduced two different paradigms in psychology that seek to provide a formal description of the environment as part of a computational account of the relevant psychological processes. In this chapter I have also indicated that Gibsonian perceptual psychology adopts a naturalistic research paradigm. None of these theories or paradigms is troubled in practice by the problematic methodological dependence on other disciplines that Fodor claims plagues wide research strategies.

One problem in Fodor's argument is that it assumes that there is *a* nomological, physical description for each thing that an organism enters into a psychological relation with. These descriptions, so the argument goes, are provided by chemistry if you include entities (such as salt) that are subsumed under chemical kinds; physics provides such descriptions if you include those entities subsumed under physical kinds. Yet any given entity may be classified differently by different disciplines; something classified as a planet in astronomy is just a body with mass in physics. Importantly, each discipline finds a level of description at which its generalizations are pitched, and these descriptions need not be derived or adopted from another discipline. Emerging disciplines often develop *their own* kinds rather than adopt those of existing disciplines. There is no reason why a wide psychology will not construct taxonomic descriptions of its own rather than draw on those offered by other sciences; we should *expect* these descriptions to cross-classify entities that are already taxonomized in existing disciplines. The idea that the cognitive sciences should be pitched at a *computational level* of description presupposes this very point.

In short, Fodor's conclusion is aloof from actual taxonomic practice both in science in general and psychology in particular. His argument overlooks the fact that new theories or disciplines typically develop their own distinct taxonomic categories. Yet there is something *right* about Fodor's argument. Fodor's claim about the methodological dependence of a wide psychology on other sciences is more plausible when construed specifically as a claim about *folk* psychology. But − and here I part company with Fodor − I do not think that this dependence is in any way problematic for wide folk psychology. To unpack these points, we need to consider a version of Fodor's argument that applies specifically to the propositional attitudes.

An appropriately modified version of Fodor's argument turns on a point about the semantics of natural kind terms that follows from the causal theory of reference: The truth conditions for beliefs (and, more generally, the satisfaction conditions for propositional attitudes) about natural kinds are provided by the disciplines in which those natural kinds are individuated. Beliefs are taxonomically individuated, in part, by their content, and so knowing what beliefs someone has, that is, the kinds to which her beliefs belong, requires knowing what the content of the beliefs are. This information is provided by the disciplines in which the objects of belief are taxonomized. For example, since we have beliefs about chemical kinds, such as salt and water, individuating beliefs naturalistically requires knowledge from chemistry. A belief is individuated in part by the proposition that its that-clause expresses, and knowing just which proposition this is requires deferring to experts in other disciplines; it is not a matter of simply inspecting the individual who has the belief. This creates a problem of methodological dependence for those seeking to 'make science' out of propositional content.

To state this conclusion in Fodoresque terms, the semantics of the language of thought is not part of the job of the folk psychologist: Such a semantics requires knowledge of the taxonomies of other disciplines, knowledge that we won't have until the rest of science is completed. Thus, we can expect *at most* a computational, individualistic version of folk psychology, one that individuates folk psychological states, including beliefs, by the 'shape' of the corresponding sentence token, something that *can* be achieved systematically without the development of other sciences (Fodor 1980a:233–4, 244, 1987; cf. Field 1978, quoted earlier).

How should a proponent of a scientific, wide folk psychology respond? Again, one does well first to note that the methodological problem supposed to plague wide folk psychological taxonomy does not seem to hinder our *everyday* ascriptions of belief. We ordinary folk can and do ascribe wide contents to beliefs even though we don't know everything there is to know about these contents. That is, although we typically are able to report our own beliefs and the beliefs of others by identifying a specific proposition that is the content of the belief, we rarely (if ever) know all of the propositions that this proposition entails. In this respect, the knowledge we have of an agent's propositional attitudes is incomplete. For this reason, we defer to experts who have some of the knowledge that we lack. Importantly, our knowledge of the wide contents of beliefs need not be complete in order to individuate beliefs by those contents. We can specify belief contents with varying degrees of precision, allowing others, sometimes experts, to fill out the specification when necessary.

Consider the perhaps clearer case of language and how reference works *all the time*. The knowledge of the reference of the terms that *any* individual uses is, like her knowledge of everything else, necessarily incomplete. In the case of the reference of terms, this is because our knowledge of the *referents* of those terms is incomplete, and we rely on others to provide further information about these referents because of the incompleteness of our own knowledge. How incomplete this knowledge is varies with the particular terms and speakers in a given context (see Burge 1979). Just as it is implausible to suggest that a speaker must know everything (or even much) about the referent of a term in order to use that term reliably, so too is it implausible to suggest that ordinary folk must know everything about the wide content of a belief in order to report or explain an individual's behavior by appeal to that belief's wide content.

These points about everyday talk are particularly relevant to the modified version of Fodor's argument that we are now considering because they are also true of *scientific* inquiry. Scientists reliably and successfully use terms from one another's disciplines, and do so without knowing everything there is to know about the referents of those terms (cf. Gauker 1991; Hardwig 1985). In this respect, they are just like ordinary folk. This *mercenary reliance*[1] of scientists on one another's grasp of the terms and knowledge in their respective disciplines is an intrinsic part of scientific practice, manifest in scientists' reliance on instruments, methods, and mathematical techniques from scientific fields other than their own. The relations of (even mutual) epistemic dependence between scientific disciplines are no barrier to the development of explanatory taxonomies and scientific knowledge. Psychology, including refinements of folk psychology, is no exception. The fact that referents of terms used in the wide individuation of beliefs have their essences specified in disciplines other than psychology does not create a methodological problem for a wide psychology; rather, it reflects a more general reliance of our explanatory frameworks, including those offered by the sciences, on one another.

This account of how a wide folk psychology can depend on knowledge drawn from other scientific disciplines not only explains why our individuative knowledge in any scientific discipline is essentially incomplete; it also reflects the dependence present in our commonsense, general knowledge of the world. An intuitive consequence of this account is that it indicates why beliefs about things that are scientific kinds (e.g., water, salt) and those about things that are not (e.g., tables, fences) should be treated in a unified way. In each case, a definite reference for a term can be fixed without us as individuals having knowledge of the essence of the referent of that term. In the former case, this is because others (experts) have knowledge of the essences; in the latter case, this is because there are no essences to have knowledge of. Hence beliefs can be reported by using such terms without knowledge of essences present in either the attributer or the subject of the attribution.

So, Fodor's argument against naturalistic or wide psychology fails for two reasons. First, even if a wide psychology does require taxonomic

---

1 I borrow the term 'mercenary reliance' from Trout (1992), who has argued that this feature of scientific practice poses yet another insuperable problem for empiricist accounts of science. The reliance is *mercenary* in that scientists in one discipline use and rely on instruments, results, methods, and theories developed in disciplines in which they have no sustained professional interest.

descriptions of both organism and environment, these descriptions are likely to be developed *within* particular wide theories, not drawn from other disciplines. In this respect, a naturalistic approach to psychology is *not* methodologically dependent on the development of taxonomies in other sciences. Second, even though there is a sense in which wide taxonomies of *folk* psychological states do depend on other scientific knowledge, this simply reflects a mercenary reliance on reference and knowledge that is part of scientific practice in general.

## 5. MERCENARY RELIANCE AND LOAR ON PSYCHOLOGICAL EXPLANATION

Brian Loar (1988a) has introduced and discussed a number of intuitive examples that show that we can offer folk psychological explanations of an agent's behavior even though we have radically incomplete knowledge of that agent's *environment*. These examples, as well as Loar's conclusions about their significance, have received favorable further discussion and elaboration (Egan 1991; Patterson 1990). The mercenary reliance inherent in our folk psychological practice sheds some light on these examples and allows us to question Loar's own conclusions based on his discussion of them.

First, two of the examples. Consider a person, Bert, who writes in his diary, 'I fear I have arthritis, and so today I have made an appointment with a specialist'. Loar points out that we can explain Bert's action whether or not we know detailed facts about how 'arthritis' is used in Bert's linguistic community. Likewise, if we find a diary with the entry 'No swimming today; we think the water is too rough', the explanatory force of this report doesn't depend on our knowing whether the individual who wrote it was Rex or his Twin Earth doppelgänger, T-Rex. In at least these sorts of cases, folk psychological explanations of an individual's behavior do not presuppose an understanding of the specific truth conditions for that person's beliefs, for such an understanding involves knowledge of that person's physical and social environments, and we are able to offer psychological explanations even when our knowledge here is minimal.

What is the significance of these examples and this initial conclusion? Loar uses the examples to motivate an individualistic conception of content – what he calls *psychological content* – that is to be understood in terms not of truth conditions but in terms of *realization* conditions. The realization conditions for a belief are context-indeterminate and are fixed by the narrow conceptual role of that belief; they specify an agent's *conception* of how things are, a conception that can differ from how things really are. A grasp of such realizations conditions, conditions that apply to both Bert and Twin Bert, Rex and T-Rex, allows us, claims Loar, to offer a common folk psychological explanation for the behavior of individuals who share conceptions of perhaps different worlds. It is for this reason that our folk psychological explanations can operate independently of knowledge of an agent's physical and social environments.

I want to question these further conclusions by returning to our mercenary reliance in using folk psychology. Our ability and willingness to use and rely on attributions of belief and desire, even when our own knowledge of the precise contents of those states is incomplete, reflects not a commitment to an individualistic notion of content but a more general form of epistemic dependence and division of epistemic labor. Consider that we can also explain and predict an agent's behavior with very little knowledge of that agent's own particular conception of how things are. Here one can think of the standard Twin Earth cases, or even Loar's own examples, none of which articulate very much about *either* the nature of the agents' physical and social environments *or* their conceptions of how the world is. In my view, both sorts of cases should be understood in terms of folk psychology's mercenary reliance, which itself can be understood as a specific form of epistemic dependence prevalent in both common sense and science.

Let me make the import of this suggestion clearer by returning to Loar's examples. Take the case of Bert. We can understand and explain Bert's behavior because of our grasp of counterfactual-supporting, ceteris paribus generalizations such as (D):

(D) If an agent believes that she has a certain disease, and believes that by seeing a specialist she can get an accurate diagnosis of or treatment for the disease, then she will make an appointment to see a specialist,

and by assuming that Bert is such an agent. True enough, (D) does not itself tell us that Bert has a belief about arthritis in particular. But it also does not articulate much about Bert's conception of things, how the world seems to Bert. (D) allows us to taxonomize the actions of Bert and Twin Bert as actions of the same kind, but not by specifying some sort of narrow content, content that Bert must share with all of his doppelgängers. Rather, it does so by characterizing the ordinary wide contents of their beliefs in a less fine-grained way; 'a certain disease' is a more general, vaguer noun phrase than is 'arthritis'.

Similarly in the 'No swimming today' example. All we need to know in this case is something like (E):

(E) If an agent believes that some liquid stuff she could swim in is dangerous or likely to induce unpleasant experiences when she swims in it, then that agent will not swim in that stuff.

'Some liquid stuff' is a more general noun phrase than 'water', and so (E) allows us to treat Rex and T-Rex in the same way. Yet it does not express any sort of individualistic content, since one can construct a Twin Earth example in which Rex has the concept 'liquid' while one of his doppelgängers has the concept 'tw-liquid'. Our explanatory abilities hold in virtue of knowing general truths about the psychology and behavior of human agents, truths that pick out *wide* intentional contents with varying degrees of specificity. There is incompleteness in our specifications because of our practice of mercenary reliance.

The general challenge to Loar's conclusions should be clear; I hope to provide elsewhere a more complete comparison of this view of Loar's examples and Loar's own views of them. (Perhaps someone true to the spirit of mercenary reliance will beat me to it.)


## 6. FROM MODULARITY TO INDIVIDUALISM

Even if wide psychology is not methodologically problematic in the way suggested by the argument examined in §4, positive methodological considerations can also be adduced for developing the cognitive sciences individualistically. The particular feature of explanatory practice within the cognitive sciences that I shall focus on is the relative success of computational explanations of *modular* cognitive systems or faculties. To recapitulate a line of argument introduced in §6 of Chapter 3, since our greatest empirical successes in computational psychology have come in explaining psychological processes that function with relative independence of even much of the internal workings of the cognitive system, processes that are modular, the prospects for developing an empirically adequate *wide* (computational) psychology are bleak. By and large, it is the investigation of highly modular cognitive faculties that has led to robust theories with significant empirical confirmation. The taxonomies that emerge from such investigations are individualistic *because* the capacities they individuate are modular. Thus, individualistic taxonomies have tended to reflect empirical success, at least within computational cognitive psychology, and even if they are not the only game in town, they are our current best bet for future empirical success in the cognitive sciences (see Egan 1992; Fodor 1983).

This argument deserves to be developed and explored more fully by individualists, and to be directly addressed in its various manifestations by those who reject individualism. Discussion of such variations will raise questions about just what explanatory successes there have been in computational cognitive psychology; the place of computational explanations in psychology and their relationships to other psychological explanations; and the significance of the modularity of some cognitive processes. Let me begin with some clarification of the central notion in this methodological argument for individualism, that of modularity. Fodor (1983) has characterized modular systems in the mind by a cluster of concepts: Modular systems are domain-specific, mandatory, fast, innately specified, and informationally encapsulated. For our purposes, the most important of these concepts are the two that are less than self-explanatory: domain specificity and informational encapsulation.

A domain-specific system is one that operates on some particular type of information (a 'domain'). Domains vary along a continuum of grainedness, from coarse- to fine-grained. For example, we might think of *visual* inputs as constituting a domain (coarse-grained), or of *faces* or *colors,* as particular types of visual inputs, as doing so (fine-grained). Domain-specific systems contrast with cognitive systems that are *general-purpose.* Both long-term and short-term memories are typically considered examples of general-purpose systems: They store information from a variety of informational sources, information that does not constitute a domain.

Note that on this general characterization of domain specificity it makes sense to talk, as developmental psychologists are wont to do (Astington, Harris, and Olson 1988; Keil 1989; Leslie 1987), of domain-specific *conceptual* knowledge and abilities: for example, numerical, biological, and even folk psychological knowledge and abilities. The type of information constituting such domains has an *intentional* characterization: The domains are distinguished by what their

106

knowledge states are about. It should be clear that we can have domain-specific cognitive systems without such an intentional characterization; presumably modular input systems are not distinguished at such a level of description.

The intuitive idea of informational encapsulation is this: A cognitive system that is informationally encapsulated acts as an input–output function on a specifiable and specific set of informational inputs and outputs. It 'encapsulates' some kind or kinds of information and is insensitive to other information. Yet moving from this intuitive gloss on informational encapsulation to more explicit characterizations, although necessary, is problematic. Consider, briefly, two formulations of informational encapsulation, neither of which seems to me adequate.

First, Pylyshyn's (1984:133–4) characterization of *cognitively impenetrable* systems as those whose outputs are not a function of the goals and beliefs of some larger system won't do as a characterization of informationally encapsulated systems, because the latter are encapsulated not just from information 'from above', as it were, but also from information *from one another*. Second, to say that informational encapsulation is a matter of there being restricted access to information that an organism internally represents (Fodor 1983:69) is misleading, since this would make *all* cognitive processes informationally encapsulated to some extent or other, and we need to be more explicit about the nature of the restriction on informational access in encapsulated systems.

I think a more adequate expression of encapsulation is available. I shall say that a cognitive system (and thus the capacities it is causally responsible for) is informationally encapsulated when it is insensitive to information that falls outside of the domain of the system. On this characterization of encapsulation, being domain-specific is at least necessary for being informationally encapsulated, and it might even seem that the two concepts pick out one and the same property. The former of these consequences is actually desirable, the latter appearance misleading. Let us take these one at a time.

If domain specificity were not necessary for informational encapsulation, then it would be possible to have a cognitive system that was both encapsulated and general-purpose. Yet precisely the information precluded by a system's encapsulation (*whatever* information that is) will be information that this system cannot operate on. Hence no cognitive system can serve as a general processing device, operating on a range of informational inputs, and be informationally encapsulated with respect to any of those inputs. To make this point more graphically, consider a putative general-purpose system such as long-term memory that is capable of storing information from a variety of inputs. Whatever information such a system operates on must also be available to that system. Thus, it can only be encapsulated with respect to the range of informational inputs it operates on. If it were to encapsulate, say, only visual information, then it would not be a general-purpose device but one operating specifically in the visual domain.

If what I have said here is right, why not simply identify the properties of informational encapsulation and domain specificity? Doing so, however, would lead to the loss of an important distinction, that between what information a cognitive system or capacity is actually sensitive to (encapsulation) and what *it is supposed to be* sensitive to (its domain). Consider your favorite list of domain-specific capacities, which is likely to include some of the following: face recognition, phoneme recognition, syntactic parsing, color perception, shape perception, kinaesthetic feedback, and rhythmic sense. Suppose that each of these capacities is under the control of a particular domain-specific system. The domain over which each of these systems operates is the range of inputs to which each *ought to* respond. But it would certainly seem possible for information from outside of the corresponding domain to affect causally the operation of such systems. In fact, cases in which this happens would be cases in which these systems don't function as they are supposed to and errors are made. Moreover, I take it that it should be an *empirical* issue whether any (or many) of our domain-specific cognitive systems are actually sensitive to information that falls outside of their putative domain. That is, the informational encapsulation of domain-specific cognitive systems should be treated as an empirical hypothesis to be confirmed or falsified by psychological evidence. Informational encapsulation is thus a distinct property from domain specificity.

## 7. MODULARITY, WIDE PSYCHOLOGY, AND EVOLUTION

So much for putting some flesh on the concepts of domain specificity and informational encapsulation, and so on modularity. The method-ological argument from modularity to individualism makes two claims: that empirical success in computational cognitive psychology has tended to follow the presumption of modularity, and that modular systems are taxonomized in accord with individualism.

The first of these claims is plausible, and we can reflect on why we should expect this type of explanatory success. When we can identify a domain over which an informationally encapsulated system operates, the task of providing a computational account of how that system could be realized or implemented becomes much more tractable. This is because the assumption of modularity constrains the flow of information it is plausible to reconstruct in a computational explanation. To take an example, if we suppose that the perception of shape is informationally encapsulated with respect to the information contained in two-dimensional retinal images (Marr 1982), then any computational account of the process of shape perception will have a circumscribed range of inputs with which to work. This is not to imply that the computational details will be trivial or simple, only that the computational problem to be solved is more likely to be tractable on the assumption of modularity.

Modularity also makes for explanatory success in a more indirect way. Since it is typically presumed that modular systems are highly localized (and localized to the extent to which they are modular), the investigation of putative modular systems is facilitated by a consideration of clinical and induced departures from normal functioning, cases that typically involve particular cortical damage. For example, people with specific cognitive deficits, such as specific forms of aphasia and dyslexia, are known to have damage to particular areas of the cortex (Donald 1991:chh. 3, 9). Particular computational accounts of modular systems can more readily receive either falsifying or confirming evidence from neuropsychology than can accounts of other systems.

The second claim in the argument from modularity to individualism, that modular systems are taxonomized individualistically, is, in contrast to the first, false. Modular systems may well encapsulate information that is in the individual's *environment,* not elsewhere in the individual. Thus, the module may be part of a computational system all right, but a *wide* computational system, one that extends beyond the individual.[2] Neither of the chief two features of modular

---

2 A more subtle and independent reason why this inference fails is that one cannot infer individualism from claims about the instantial location of psychological states. I shall develop this claim in Chapter 6.

cognitive systems, their domain specificity and informational encapsulation, implies that such systems cannot be properly viewed as parts of wide computational systems. In fact, both of the examples of wide computational research I gave in Chapter 3 (from human form perception and animal navigation and learning) were of cognitive systems that are most likely modular. Being wide and being modular are compatible properties for a cognitive system to possess – and so modularity does not entail individualism – because the location of the information with respect to which that system is encapsulated does not affect that system's domain specificity. The issue that remains open is whether narrow computational accounts of given modular systems are always explanatorily richer than their wide rivals. And, as with my discussion of the parallel point in Chapter 3, I suggest that a starting point here is the existence of perfectly acceptable computational explanations that at least appear to be wide.

Adopting an evolutionary perspective on cognition is extremely apt for providing an understanding of why some cognitive systems, particularly modular systems, will be wide. The basic idea is that it makes evolutionary sense for organisms to exploit stable, environmental regularities and regularities between their environment and internal functioning, rather than attempt to build the entire informational processing task into their own cognitive systems. Andy Clark expresses this idea in what he calls the *007 Principle:*

In general, evolved creatures will neither store nor process information in costly ways when they can use the structure of the environment and their operations upon it as a convenient stand-in for the information-processing operations concerned. That is, know only as much as you need to know to get the job done. (1989:64; cf. Clark 1993:ch. 6).

The 007 Principle is one with particular application to cognitive modules that are sensitive to some specific type of information, since modular systems are more likely to develop over evolutionary time in response to world-mind constancies than are general-purpose systems. This is because, in light of their domain specificity and informational encapsulation, modular systems are *simpler* cognitive systems than are general-purpose cognitive systems.

As an aside, note that this evolutionary perspective raises a difficult question about how general-purpose cognitive systems could have evolved *at all,* as Dan Sperber (1994) has pointed out. Given stability over evolutionary time in the presence of some feature of the world, the evolutionary cheap, shortsighted thing for an organism to do is to develop, from the current tricks up its sleeve, a mechanism that selectively responds to that feature. If it already has general-purpose mechanisms that it can use to do so, fine. But the worry here is about the *original* evolution of such mechanisms: How did *they* evolve, given that they were preceded by modular systems, such as input systems, upon which they would seem to depend for at least some of their own inputs? One answer to this question has been provided by Sperber himself, who suggests an evolutionary path from modular input systems to simple integrating *conceptual* modules, to the sorts of central processing systems we have now, where the last of these are still modular to a significant extent. Another (perhaps complementary) answer is suggested by Merlin Donald's *The Origins of the Modern Mind:* We did not *evolve* general-purpose mechanisms, at least not in the usual sense, but developed them culturally through the informational structuring of our *external* environments. The transition from what Donald calls *mimetic* to theoretical culture involves not so much a change in *biological* hardware as one in *technological* hardware (1991:274): We can think as we do because we have developed *external storage systems,* which extend our cognitive systems beyond the individual (cf. Chapter 3, §3).

I want to use this evolutionary perspective on cognition to defend the view that central processes, such as inference, may also be modular. Consider the emerging field of *evolutionary psychology* (Barkow, Cosmides, and Tooby 1992), which is concerned with discovering the evolutionary basis for some of the particular cognitive biases and the corresponding psychological mechanisms that humans and other animals have. It proceeds by identifying the adaptive problems that the species has faced, considering what sorts of behaviors would have been required to solve those problems in the type of environment that existed at the time, and then proposing particular psychological mechanisms that could solve those problems by generating the posited behaviors. Consider an example of an evolutionary psychological research paradigm that is particularly pertinent to our discussion here.

Cosmides and Tooby (1987) argue that there are good reasons to think that we possess what they call *Darwinian algorithms* for performing certain cognitive tasks. These are automatic patterns of inference that evolved because they offered a solution to a specific evolutionary problem that our ancestors faced. Cosmides (1989) has also discussed in some detail the inference pattern underlying human

111

performance on the Wason–Johnson-Laird reasoning tasks from such an evolutionary psychological perspective, arguing that the standard errors (and successes) on these tasks reflect the operation of a module that evolved to draw inferences concerning *social exchange* and offering a computational model of how such a module functions (see also Cosmides and Tooby 1992). In terms we have been using, Cosmides's basic claim is that there is an inferential module whose domain is social exchange and that is pressed into service in the Wason–Johnson-Laird reasoning tasks. Although informational encapsulation here is partial and incomplete, information that this module tends to focus on and information that it tends to ignore in the Wason–Johnson-Laird tasks is to be understood in terms of the domain specificity of the module.

Cosmides and Tooby's general approach is one according to which the idea of modules that perform paradigmatic central processes not only makes sense but is well motivated. Independent of whether Cosmides is correct in her particular claims about the cognitive system underlying performance on the Wason–Johnson-Laird tasks, there is no conceptual or methodological barrier prohibiting at least some central processes from being modular. So, even on the strong assumption that modularity is a *precondition* to explanatory success in computational psychology, there is nothing that prohibits such success in a psychology of at least some central processes.

## 8. CONCLUSION: TAXONOMIC PLURALISM AND RECIPES FOR SUCCESS

The two methodological arguments scrutinized in this chapter, Fodor's argument for the methodological incoherence of a naturalistic psychology and the argument from modularity to individualism, should be rejected. In examining each of them, I have touched on a number of broader issues – concerning folk psychology, the relationship between cognitive psychology and other sciences, and the architecture of the mind – that I will discuss more explicitly in later chapters. To round off this discussion of methodological arguments for individualism, I want to step back from the particular details of each of the arguments and say something more general about individualism and methodology in psychology, and about the discussion in Part I as a whole.

One important feature of methodological arguments for individualism is that they attempt to make explicit the connection between what has been predominantly an abstract philosophical debate over individualism and explanatory practice in psychology. In §2 I said that we can conceive of the difference between individualistic and wide psychology methodologically in terms of the view that psychologists take of the *embeddedness* of the organism: Is it essential to psychological explanation to view the organism as embedded in its environment, or should one, by contrast, *abstract* away from mere environmental contingencies in attempting to specify psychological kinds? Having argued against two methodological arguments for taking the latter perspective, it might be thought that I am advocating the adoption of the former perspective, the 'embedded' view of organisms. Not so.

I think that psychology ought to be *methodologically pluralistic;* it ought to employ both the embedded and disembedded perspectives in developing its kinds and explanations. To think that only the latter, disembedded perspective will suffice would be to mistake partial explanatory successes (say, in narrow computational psychology) for a recipe for explanatory success; to think, conversely, that only the former, embedded perspective will suffice would be to fail to acknowledge some of the partial successes we have had in psychology already. More generally, proponents of either of these views deny a simple but important truth in the philosophy of science, namely, that *there are no recipes for explanatory success.* Precisely because of this, we need to embrace some form of methodological pluralism. Parallel general conclusions can be drawn from each of my more specific conclusions in Chapters 2 and 3.

Nothing in my rejection of the computational argument for individualism in Chapter 3 suggested that there were *no* cognitive capacities best explained by being viewed as the products of narrow computational systems. My argument for wide computationalism did not try to make an across-the-board case for wide computational explanation over other forms of explanation in psychology; likewise, my case for wide *representational* explanation over computational explanation in §8 of Chapter 3 did not attempt to derive a positive global conclusion. Narrow computational explanation has a place in psychology all right, but it is a place, not the whole goanna.

Turning to Chapter 2, the idea that we can express a truth, let alone an essential one, about scientific taxonomy in such a simple claim as 'Scientific taxonomy is taxonomy by (intrinsic) causal powers' strikes me as manifesting either an obvious disregard for taxonomic practice in science or as revealing a restrictive conception of science. Taxonomic practice in the sciences is so incredibly heterogeneous that it is unlikely that there are any single-sentence, general truths about it; moreover, I am sceptical that there are any substantive principles regulating scientific taxonomy at all. Yet in rejecting the argument from causal powers in Chapter 2, I was in no way rejecting the idea that, in some cases, only an entity's intrinsic causal powers are used in taxonomizing that entity. Again, the conception in the background here is one of taxonomic and so explanatory plurality.

So, although the primary conclusions of Chapters 2–4 have been negative insofar as they have denied that individualism follows from a priori, empirical, or methodological considerations, they have been drawn against an emerging positive conception of taxonomic, explanatory, and methodological plurality. It is to the development of this conception that I turn in Part II.

# Part II

*Psychological explanation
and mental causation*

# 5

## Rethinking the role of causal powers in taxonomy and explanation

A central part of my critique of the argument from causal powers examined in Chapter 2 was that it equivocates on 'causal powers', using that notion in both its extended and restricted senses. I claimed that this equivocation reflects a deep problem in this a priori argument for individualism, one that indicates a fundamental incompatibility in the claims that need to be true for any version of this argument to be sound. Less explicit in that chapter was my more general scepticism about the prospects for a priori arguments for individualism. In this chapter, I argue more directly for both the depth of the identified equivocation and this more general scepticism.

### 1. A PRIORI ARGUMENTS FOR INDIVIDUALISM

The intuition that causal powers occupy a special place in taxonomy and explanation was expressed in the argument from causal powers by the claim that sciences taxonomize by causal powers (global individualism). One reaction to my critique of the argument from causal powers that I have found common in discussion is to grant the basic points of the critique (e.g., concede that global individualism *is* false) but to suppose that there is some other, closely related argument from a premise about causal powers to individualism that is immune to the critique. The frequency of this reaction reflects the strength of the intuition that causal powers occupy a special place in scientific taxonomy and explanation.

In fact, there is a family of related arguments for individualism that appeal to this intuition about causal powers: Such arguments involve appeals to the nature of science (it taxonomizes 'by causal powers'), to the nature of properties (they *are* causal powers), and to the nature of causation (it operates *via* causal powers). To consolidate my claim about the depth of the equivocation in the argument from causal powers, which makes the first of these appeals, I argue that initially plausible arguments invoking the other two claims, about properties and causation, suffer from the sort of equivocation found in the argument from causal powers. My argument in this chapter provides reason to reconsider appeals to causal powers in arguments for individualism, and to rethink their role in taxonomy and explanation.

Each of these three arguments based on a claim about causal powers is an a priori argument for individualism in that each points to some quite general feature of the world or the nature of our explanatory practices that we should want psychology to respect, arguing that a psychology that does respect such a feature must be individualistic. General features appealed to in a priori arguments include the natures of causation, causal explanation, causal powers, scientific explanation, supervenience, and nomological behavior. The crucial claim in such arguments occurs in a general premise (e.g., All scientific explanation individuates by causal powers) with the minor premise about psychology (Psychology should individuate by causal powers) following from this major premise. The major premise, which makes no specific claim about psychology, bears the argumentative burden in a priori arguments for individualism. Even those who are ambivalent about individualism acknowledge the intuitiveness of such a priori arguments for individualism (see Crane 1991; Owens 1993; Williams 1990).

I have referred to arguments in which the argumentative burden falls on an empirical claim about psychology, one that might turn out to be false in light of empirical research in psychology, as a posteriori or *empirical* arguments. The most powerful of such arguments, examined in Chapter 3, make the claim that psychology is computational and thus individualistic; the methodological arguments discussed in Chapter 4 are also arguments of this general type. Such arguments pursue a more cautious strategy than do the a priori arguments in that they argue for individualism as a general constraint on psychology (or even on parts of psychology) in a piecemeal way: They argue from some particular feature of explanatory practice in psychology to a conclusion about psychological taxonomy.

I shall use my argument for rethinking the role that causal powers play in taxonomy and explanation to support my more sweeping claim about the prospects for a priori arguments for individualism. The a priori character of each of the arguments I shall discuss is responsible, in large part, for their failures. This conclusion about a

118

priori arguments for individualism has broader implications for the relationship between metaphysics and the philosophy of the special sciences that I shall take up in the concluding section to the chapter. The plausibility of the chief conclusions for which I shall be arguing in this chapter will depend, ultimately, on the adequacy of my alternative views of taxonomy, explanation, and the epistemology of science, which will be developed more fully throughout Parts II and III.

To work, to work. I begin with the first of our pair of arguments that appeals to the notion of causal powers.

## 2. DOES INDIVIDUALISM FOLLOW FROM THE CAUSAL THEORY OF PROPERTIES?

As I said in §1, the intuition that an entity's causal powers play a special role in explanations in which that entity features motivates the belief that there must be some sound a priori argument for individualism, even if such an argument has not yet been adequately formulated. One alternative way of deriving an appropriate general premise articulating this intuition invokes a view about the nature of *properties,* the causal theory of properties. Before stating this theory and the argument from it to individualism, I want to note an intuitive distinction that motivates the causal theory.

This is the distinction between what have been called *genuine* properties and *mere-Cambridge* properties.[1] Intuitively, not every property that we can refer to with a predicate is a causally efficacious property of the entity to which it is ascribed. For example, the properties of being 12,000 miles from Melbourne, of being admired by Paul Keating, and of being born during a particular space–time interval, although truly predicable of certain entities, are not themselves causally responsible for any effects that those entities bring about: They are mere-Cambridge properties of those entities. In this respect, they contrast with what are often thought of as paradigmatic

1 A note on terminology: Geach (1969:ch. 5) introduced the term 'Cambridge change' to refer to change that occurs whenever a statement of the form *Fx* is true at one time and false at another. Clearly, such a change need not involve a change in the object itself. Shoemaker (1979, 1980) introduced '*mere*-Cambridge' to refer to those Cambridge changes that are not, intuitively, changes in the object predicated. Mere-Cambridge properties are those properties acquired or lost only in mere-Cambridge change.

properties. Both *microstructural properties,* such as having a particular chemical structure and having a certain number of protons, and *primary qualities,* such as having a specific shape or size, are properties that, when coinstantiated with other properties in objects, give those objects causal powers to bring about particular effects. Much of the suspicion directed at talk of an object's mere-Cambridge properties is due, I think, to the intuition that such properties have no causal efficacy. Whatever sense we can make of conceptual schemes that employ the corresponding predicates, these properties themselves play, at best, only a background causal role in sustaining processes and bringing about events and changes in the world; at worst, the corresponding predicates are merely ways, perhaps even misleading ways, of talking about the world.

Proponents of the causal theory of properties, accepting the intuitive distinction between genuine and mere-Cambridge properties, claim that it is essential to a particular *genuine* property that it have the causal powers it has. The causal theory of properties says that properties, *genuine* properties, are identical just if they make the same causal contribution to an entity's causal powers, where an entity's causal powers are the total causal contribution that entity makes to its effects across possible situations. According to the causal theory of properties:

What makes a property the property it is, what determines its identity, is its potential for contributing to the causal powers of the things that have it. This means, among other things, that if under all possible circumstances, properties X and Y make the same contribution to the causal powers of the things that have them, X and Y are the same property. (Shoemaker 1980:212)[2]

The causal theory provides a sufficient condition for property identity. Distinguishing properties from their *instantiating circumstances,* we can express the causal theory as follows: For any properties, *A* and *B,* if *A* has the same effects as *B* in all of the same types of instantiating circumstances, then *A* and *B* are identical properties. According to

2 Although Shoemaker uses this formulation of the causal theory throughout his paper, in a postscript he offers a more restrictive version of the causal theory of properties that adds the conjunction 'and whatever set of circumstances is sufficient to cause the instantiation of [X] is sufficient to cause the instantiation of [Y], and vice-versa' (p. 233). I shall not be concerned here with the implications (particularly for how we are to think of wide content and causal powers) of the differences between these two formulations.

the causal theory of properties, there is a conceptual connection between properties, causal powers, and effects. Following Shoemaker (1980:212), we can view properties as second-order functions: They are functions from coinstantiating properties to causal powers, causal powers being functions from instantiating circumstances to effects.

The distinction between properties and their instantiating circumstances is integral to the causal theory of properties, which, expressed as the view that properties are second-order functions, implies that the causal powers used to individuate genuine properties must be *intrinsic* rather than extrinsic. An example that Robert Boyle introduces in 'The Origins and Forms of Qualities' serves as a good illustration of the difference between intrinsic and extrinsic powers that objects can possess in virtue of instantiating a given set of intrinsic properties. In virtue of its size, shape, and composition, a given key has the intrinsic power to open any lock of a specific size and shape or set of sizes and shapes. There is no way for that key to lose *that* power, as Boyle would say, 'without the intervention of any physical change in the body itself' (1744, vol. ii, p. 463). A key also has many extrinsic powers in virtue of having the size, shape, and composition that it does, including the power to open a particular door. Such extrinsic powers *can* be lost without changing the key itself. For example, simply change the lock on the door and the key loses the extrinsic power it had to open the door (see also Shoemaker 1980:221).

One of Boyle's main points in 'The Origins' is that it would be absurd to regard every name for a quality as a real power of the entity concerned, and it seems clear that for Boyle, real powers are intrinsic rather than extrinsic. We can express the necessity to restrict 'power' to mean 'intrinsic power' as a reductio, using the idea that properties are second-order functions. An object's extrinsic powers are not completely abstracted from their instantiating circumstances; and so, were they to be considered as the powers in terms of which the causal theory is stated, causal powers could not be complete functions from instantiating circumstances to effects. Stating the causal theory in terms of an entity's extrinsic powers would not provide an account of an object's genuine properties, for these are functions from one another to powers, and so must completely determine what those powers are. Yet an entity's extrinsic powers are not completely determined by its genuine properties.

Consider the property of being made of a particular type of glass.

When coinstantiated with other properties, this property has a variety of causal powers. For example, when coinstantiated with the properties of being circular and having a certain size, it gives an object the causal power to magnify objects; when coinstantiated with the property of being struck by light of a certain intensity, it gives an object the power to burn paper. Each of these powers is intrinsic in that an entity with such a power can lose that power only if some change is made to the entity itself. The power inheres in the entity in which it is instantiated; having the power to do something is compatible with not and, indeed, never being in the position to do it. According to the causal theory, what makes the property of being made of glass *that* property is its contribution to the intrinsic causal powers of the entities in which it is instantiated, where all possible instantiating circumstances are considered.

If one makes the prima facie modest assumption that taxonomic and explanatory properties in science must be genuine properties, the causal theory of properties might be thought to provide a general metaphysical view from which individualism follows. For if we assume that taxonomic properties must be genuine properties, and if genuine properties are defined in terms of the intrinsic causal powers they give rise to, then the properties used for taxonomy and explanation in science must be defined in terms of causal powers. In particular, scientific taxonomies cannot differ unless the corresponding entities taxonomized differ in their intrinsic causal powers. The individualist's claim about psychology – that the entities posited by a scientific psychology must be taxonomized by their intrinsic causal powers – would seem to follow trivially. If genuine properties are powers to give rise to causal powers in the objects in which they are instantiated, then in proposing that *psychology* individuate by causal powers, the individualist is simply claiming that psychology, like the rest of science, should taxonomize only by genuine properties, not by mere-Cambridge properties.

Note how this argument draws on one of the core intuitions motivating individualism. Individualists claim that wide content *itself* makes no causal difference to the mental states that instantiate it; doppelgängers, recall, can instantiate mental states with different wide contents even though they are *ex hypothesi* physically identical. Rex has thoughts *about water* because he is on a planet where there is *water,* whereas his molecular twin, T-Rex, has thoughts *about twater* because he is on a planet where there is only *twater,* not water. Yet intuitively the property of being in a world in which there is water, like that of being 12 000 miles from Melbourne, is a mere-Cambridge property – not a genuine property – that an entity instantiates. Instantiating *that* property makes no difference to the intrinsic causal powers that an individual has, and so that property should not be taxonomic in a scientific psychology. Such a property is not a genuine property at all.

One problem with this argument for individualism is that it pre-supposes that all genuine properties are intrinsic properties; this is a presupposition because individualism claims that psychological states must be taxonomized by properties that supervene on the intrinsic physical properties of individuals. Yet if we presuppose that all genuine properties are intrinsic, the assumption that taxonomic properties in science must be genuine properties loses the modest status that we had, prima facie, attributed to it; it becomes a claim that is false of actual scientific taxonomies. In many cases, scientific taxonomies are constituted by relational properties, not intrinsic properties, and as I have argued (Chapter 2, §5), this fact about scientific taxonomies is, pace Fodor, incompatible with the claim that taxonomies and explanations in science individuate their kinds 'by causal powers'. Two entities identical in their intrinsic physical properties can be taxonomized differently if they are individuated relationally, and such differential individuation will often be reflected in the different explanations that may apply to such entities. (Entities taxonomized relationally *need not* be subject to different explanations, however; differential taxonomy is not sufficient for differential explanation.)

Although nothing in the causal theory of properties strictly entails that the genuine properties an entity has must be intrinsic properties, the distinction between genuine and mere-Cambridge properties, on the one hand, and intrinsic and relational properties, on the other, is often collapsed in expressions of the causal theory (e.g., Shoemaker 1979, 1980, esp. §VI of each). There is significant motivation for doing so within the framework in which the causal theory is often discussed. The causal theory is motivated, in part, by the intuition that a *genuine* change in an entity's properties must involve a change in that entity itself. This motivation leads to the equation of the two distinctions, since a change in an entity itself involves the acquisition or loss of *intrinsic* properties.

There is a second reason for the equation of 'genuine' and 'intrinsic', and 'mere-Cambridge' and 'relational,' in discussions of mere-Cambridge properties and mere-Cambridge changes: the focus on relational properties that could have been different without making any significant causal difference to the entity itself. Consider Geach's example (1969:72): Socrates acquired the property of being shorter than Theaetatus in virtue of the latter's growth. Such properties themselves are not causally efficacious in that they do not endow their bearers with any intrinsic powers to bring about particular effects. (Note also the converse tendency to concentrate exclusively on those intrinsic properties that are explanatory within some science and so ignore the many intrinsic properties that *don't* make a significant causal difference to their bearers. For example, having 12 765 345 cells is an intrinsic property that some organisms instantiate, but not one that endows its bearers with powers to bring about effects likely to be of explanatory and so taxonomic interest to the biologist.)

Many relational properties, however, *are* causally efficacious in a way that the paradigmatic cases of mere-Cambridge properties are not. For example, being a mother, being unemployed, being a member of a particular species, being a planet, being located in a magnetic field, and occupying a relatively specific ecological niche are all relational properties that different entities can have in particular instantiating circumstances, each of which, when coinstantiated with the appropriate properties, enables an entity to bring about particular effects. With respect to causal efficacy, some relational properties are *just like* paradigmatic intrinsic properties, and this is a reason for counting those relational properties as genuine properties. Like the claim that there is something about relational and historical properties that makes them unsuitable for, say, *scientific* taxonomies, the claim that genuine properties *cannot* be relational should be evaluated by attending to our taxonomic and explanatory practices.

To illustrate how relational properties can be causally efficacious, consider a generalization from evolutionary biology mentioned in Chapter 2: Highly specialized species tend to extinction in times of ecological catastrophe. Roughly, a species is highly specialized if it adopts a limited range of survival strategies relative to other competing species. Hedgehogs are highly specialized organisms, whereas raccoons are not, and this difference between the two species explains why the latter but not the former have survived our encroachment on their natural habitats. Being highly specialized is a property whose possession is causally responsible for species-wide extinction in certain circumstances: *It* is a causally efficacious property.

I shall discuss this example in more detail in §4, where I argue that the property of being highly specialized is *essentially* relational: In contrast to a property like *weight,* which is not essentially relational, one cannot abstract away from the relations constituting the property of being highly specialized in a theoretically motivated way. There is no reason to think that every explanatory, relational kind must be factorable into an intrinsic kind plus a non-explanatory remainder, and the problem of seeing just what the factorization could be in particular cases is good reason to think that many cannot.

If the causal theory itself does not require the equation of 'genuine' with 'intrinsic', it might be thought that one can simply reformulate the argument I have given from the causal theory of properties to individualism, supposing that both intrinsic and relational properties can count as genuine properties. However, such a reformulation is not possible. The basic problem is that an entity's relational properties do not supervene on that entity's intrinsic physical properties. An entity's relational properties can change without a change in the thing itself, that is, without a change in the entity's intrinsic properties. If one were to reformulate the argument we are considering, using a conception of genuine properties that includes both intrinsic and relational properties, the intermediate conclusion in the argument, the general premise that bears the argumentative burden in this sort of a priori argument, would employ a notion of causal powers according to which 'causal powers' do not supervene on intrinsic physical properties. Such a notion of causal powers does not allow one to arrive at individualism. We saw just this sort of problem arise in discussing the argument from causal powers in Chapter 2, and we can be more explicit about why the problems are of the same kind. Assuming a *restricted* sense of 'genuine properties', which entails that all genuine properties are intrinsic properties, the major premise in the argument is false of science as it is actually practiced; by contrast, assuming an *extended* sense of 'genuine properties', which counts both intrinsic and relational properties as genuine properties, is incompatible with the supervenience of an entity's genuine properties and so its causal powers on its intrinsic properties.

I have not argued against the causal theory of properties here, but against the inference from this general view about properties to individualism in psychology. I shall focus more explicitly on the causal theory of properties itself in the next section, with two purposes in mind. The first is to uncover some of the intuitions that drive the argument we have just examined; as we will see, they are also intuitions that lie behind the more general idea that causal powers have a special role to play in taxonomy and explanation in science. The second is to explain why one should expect relational taxonomies to feature in a variety of sciences, and so to provide some reason for thinking that they may be perfectly suitable in themselves for explanation *in psychology*. Here we begin to develop a view of taxonomy and explanation, particularly in the special sciences, that is at odds with individualism.

### 3. EXPLANATION AND THE CAUSAL THEORY OF PROPERTIES

The causal theory takes for granted the intuitive distinction between genuine properties and mere-Cambridge properties, proposing an account of the former that attempts to remain fairly neutral about what sorts of properties count as genuine properties. A minimal but important conclusion to draw from §2 is that the causal theory must be combined with more substantive views about both causation and explanation if it is to be the basis for the constraint that individualism imposes on individuation in psychology.

There is, I think, a broader metaphysical conception that provides such substantive views. The causal theory naturally complements a certain view about the *comprehensiveness* of the explanatory framework provided by the corpuscular philosophy of the seventeenth century. The world is material; matter is made up of atomic components; it is the properties of these basic components that are ultimately causally responsible for the phenomena that we observe in the world. These sorts of properties themselves *are* the causal powers that things have, or at least are ultimately responsible for all such powers, and so should be what our sciences seek to discover. This corpuscular worldview, vague as I have left its expression here, could take on either a reductionist or a non-reductionist character, and it expresses a reason for holding that causal powers should play a special role in taxonomy and explanation in science. It is a view made more attractive by a certain claim about the nature of causation, that causation is *local* or *proximal,* where this expresses the idea that only the intrinsic properties of a cause, properties that are 'right there', are relevant to the role that cause plays qua cause. Only properties at the physical location of the effects brought about do the causal work in the world (see Chapter 6).

There is a positive view of causal explanation, the core of which is familiar and widely accepted, that requires the rejection of the metaphysical comprehensiveness of the corpuscular framework. This rejection is in no way a rejection of the centrality of causal explanation in science. The causal nature of scientific explanation itself, properly understood, gives one reason to doubt that the corpuscular view does provide an all-embracing framework for scientific explanation. Scientific explanations are causal in a very broad sense: They identify, in Wesley Salmon's (1984) phrase, parts of 'the causal structure of the world'. This general view of scientific explanation is one that individualists can accept: The reason that *sciences* ought to individuate by causal powers is that they offer causal explanations for the phenomena in the world. Yet this view of the nature of scientific explanation does not imply that the world has a *single* causal structure that, in principle, some complete science could describe with a single complex theory. The idea of there being a causal structure to the world is compatible with the various sciences offering many distinct levels of description, not all of which depict the causal structure in terms of the intrinsic causal properties of entities. There are causal truths about particles, atoms, cells, organs, organisms, and species, some of which do not presuppose the truth of *particular* causal truths or laws at any 'lower' level. Some underlying explanations *merely happen to* make higher-level explanations true in the actual world.

To take a standard and clear example of Fodor's (1974), consider the institution of monetary exchange. The particular forms of money – for example, coins, notes, and gold – are to a large extent arbitrary, depending very much on contingencies concerning, amongst other things, the availability of suitable materials. The exchange of money can be described in physical terms, and one can explain what happens in particular cases by describing the physical transactions that take place. Yet there is only a weak dependence relation between exchange explanations and the corresponding physical explanations of particular transactions. The truth of a given exchange explanation is compatible with the falsity of the physical explanation that *happens* to underlie its truth in the actual world. More pointedly, and in the language of possible worlds: There are nearby worlds accessible to ours in which the exchange explanation is true and the physical explanation false.

The same is true of a wide range of what I shall call *instantiating explanations,* explanations whose truth accounts for the truth of some higher-level explanation in the actual world. An explanation is instantiating, relative to some higher-level explanation, just in case it provides more of the details about the causal mechanisms or processes specified or implicit in that higher-level explanation. Examples of familiar instantiating explanations include explanations identifying DNA as the means by which genetic information is transferred (relative to explanations that identify genes as the causal agents in phenotypic transfer across generations); explanations of the behavior and properties of gases in terms of the properties of their constituent atoms; and explanations of the structural properties of buildings in terms of the tensile strengths of their constituent materials. Sometimes an instantiating explanation, while specifying details about the actual causal processes by which an event occurred or identifying the intrinsic properties of some cause, is not essential to a broader understanding of *why* that event occurred. In the spirit of the Cambridge–mere-Cambridge distinction, I shall refer to instantiating explanations that are inessential to a broader understanding of the *explanandum* as *merely instantiating* explanations. Sometimes lower-level explanations are merely instantiating explanations, and, when they are, corresponding higher-level explanations provide the causal information relevant for explanation.

Since higher-level explanations themselves often specify some of the details on how the relevant causal mechanisms operate, I am not implying that there are cases in which one offers a better causal explanation for a given phenomenon by *avoiding* talk of causal mechanisms altogether. Rather, the claim is that the most informative level of description at which an explanation can be pitched need not be the one that provides the greatest amount of causal detail. In explanation, sometimes less is more. After all, were this not the case, the best explanations that one could offer for *any* phenomenon involving material objects would be microphysical (or quantum mechanical?), and that is absurd. Not only are there no microphysical explanations for some phenomena, but even when there is a sense in which there are microphysical explanations, these may be wildly disjunctive, as are the 'kinds' they invoke. By contrast, individuating entities by their relational properties often allows one to offer explanations that are more *unified*.

These reflections on causal explanation begin to explain why corpuscularism is not a comprehensive metaphysical view, for they suggest why better causal explanations may well ignore microphysical or corpuscular properties; what is sometimes dismissively called the *pragmatics* of explanation has implications for our metaphysics. Yet we can put this point more metaphysically to make it clear that a reliance on relational taxonomies is not simply heuristic. *Because* of the complexity of the causal structure of the world, scientific explanations need to appeal to more than an object's intrinsic properties in explaining phenomena for which that object is causally responsible. The very reasoning that supports this conclusion also begins to explain *why* causal powers do not enjoy an explanatory privilege over other types of causal properties, that is, properties that play a genuine explanatory role in causal explanations. It is this sort of account that is needed – together with the corresponding focus on *explanation* – to show why the identity of the causal powers that two individuals instantiate need not imply that those individuals have the same explanatory *psychological* properties.

To conclude this section, a final point must be made about the causal theory of properties. One conclusion implicit in §2 is that there is a tension within the causal theory of properties that derives from two different motivations for that theory. It is entailed by one of the motivations for the theory – the idea that it is only a change in a thing itself that counts as a genuine change in its properties – that genuine properties be intrinsic properties. Yet the identification of genuine and intrinsic properties is inconsistent with another motivation for the view, namely, the idea that genuine properties are to be identified as those properties that are causally efficacious. Some relational properties are causally efficacious, just as intrinsic properties are. So, on the one hand, if an object's genuine properties just are properties that involve a change in the object itself, one can identify these with a subset of that object's intrinsic properties; on the other hand, if genuine properties just are properties that are causally efficacious, then since relational properties can be causally efficacious when coinstantiated with other properties, genuine properties need not be intrinsic.

One might wonder about the depth of this tension within the causal theory of properties, particularly about whether it can be resolved in a way that preserves the spirit of the causal theory. This is not an issue that I shall address here in any detail, though taking the ideas about explanation I have articulated in this section seriously appears to involve rejecting the claim that an object's genuine properties are a subset of its intrinsic properties: Some relational properties are genuine properties. How damaging such a concession would be to the coherence of the causal theory of properties itself I leave as an open question. The point I want to reiterate is that such a concession would be fatal to the argument from the causal theory of properties to individualism that we have examined.

One final note on this. It might be thought possible to maintain both of the motivations for the causal theory by acknowledging that an adequate causal theory of *properties* must be supplemented by a causal theory of *relations,* which would identify a relation, a *genuine* relation, by the causal effects that instantiations of that relation have across possible worlds. Expressing this view of relations as second-order functions, relations would be functions from coinstantiating properties and relations to causal powers, which themselves are functions from instantiating circumstances to effects. Whether this idea can be adequately developed or defended is not clear. But unless there is some way in which genuine relations can be reduced to genuine properties, on this view there remain properties, relational properties, that are genuine but not intrinsic, for some relational properties are instantiated in genuine relations. So, although this possibility allows one to say that there is a sense in which only intrinsic properties are genuine properties, it does not adequately preserve both motivations for the causal theory. More important for my purposes here, such a view would not allow one to derive individualism in psychology from a causal theory of properties and relations.

## 4. THE POWERS AND PARAMETERS ANALYSIS OF CAUSATION

The discussion thus far also sheds some light on a proposal that Colin McGinn (1991) has made about causation that appeals to the notion of causal powers. McGinn's proposal could be viewed as making either a specific claim about our ordinary, folk psychological concepts or a more general claim about causation. Since my principal interest here is in a priori arguments for individualism, I shall understand McGinn's claim in the latter way, for so construed, it can be seen to constitute the general premise in such an a priori argument. McGinn himself says: 'I intend my treatment of this subject to complement Fodor (1991) ['A Modal Argument for Narrow Content']. My aim, in effect, is to derive Fodor's position on causal powers and content from a more general conception of causation' (p. 576, fn. 4). This suggests not only that McGinn's direction of argument is from the more general to the more specific of the claims I list here, but also that he takes himself to be offering the basis for an a priori argument for some form of individualism.

McGinn says that 'for any particular causal transaction there must exist a power involved in that transaction that is abstractable and identifiable across contexts' (1991:578), taking this to be a variant of what he refers to as Hume's principle of the generality of causality. The basic idea here is that what we might loosely call 'causal factors' can be decomposed into their respective *powers* and *parameters*. Causal statements may run together these two distinct types of causal factors, but it is at least in principle possible to untangle them, and doing so makes the way causation works more perspicuous. As McGinn goes on to say, 'Powers drive nature's motor: parameters are just points on nature's map' (1991:578). Causality should be viewed as operating through the causal powers that objects possess, with the surrounding environment supplying the causal parameters. Although we might say that both types of causal factors, both powers and parameters, are causally relevant features of a given situation, it is in virtue of its powers that an object instantiates causally efficacious properties.

The example McGinn uses to illustrate the sort of decomposition he has in mind is that of a knife being sharp in New York on Halloween in 1990, where the *sharpness* of the knife is the power one can factor out of this causal property and being in New York on Halloween in 1990 is a parameter. Although much of what McGinn says (right down to this example) echoes ideas expressed in the causal theory of properties, McGinn himself does not draw any explicit connection between his view and that theory. But we can understand McGinn as making a parallel claim about causation to that made about properties by a proponent of the causal theory of properties. The causal theory holds that properties are to be analyzed in terms of a pair of notions, namely, causal powers and instantiating circumstances; McGinn argues that causation is to be analyzed in terms of a pair of notions, namely, causal powers and parameters. In addition, McGinn is explicit that not only is this an appropriate analysis for the concept of causation, but that causal powers are, in his words, what *drive nature's motor:* They are the means through which causation operates.

Like the causal theory of properties, the broad outlines of

McGinn's view of causation give that view an air of metaphysical innocence in that the pair of principal notions in terms of which the view is couched (powers and parameters in McGinn's case) seems to be acceptable independent of many broader metaphysical commitments. For example, nothing in the distinction between powers and parameters itself implies that all powers must be intrinsic or that all parameters must be relational. This metaphysical innocence makes the view intuitive; McGinn himself presents the powers/parameters analysis as a 'rather elementary' (p. 578) point about causation. But again, as with the causal theory of properties, this metaphysical innocence is lost once one pads out the view in terms of its motivations and the uses to which it is put.

There are many instances of causation for which a powers/parameters analysis is certainly correct: one can often identify a power that an object has in virtue of which it effects change in the world, and consign to contingencies of instantiation the value of parameters. Such powers are often properly cited as the cause for some particular effect, the aspect of the causal nexus that can be regarded as causally responsible for that effect. Yet the claim that this tells us something about how causation works in general – something that allows us to derive the general premise needed for an a priori argument for individualism – is not plausible.

Let us return to consider our example of a true, causal generalization from evolutionary biology – highly specialized species tend to extinction in times of ecological catastrophe – to see how this view of causation fares in a more complex case. A detailed examination of such a case is instructive, for it is too easy to mistake the vividness conveyed by a simple example (such as that involving the property of sharpness) for a sign of generality and depth. I have said that this generalization about highly specialized species reflects the causal efficacy of a relational property, that of being highly specialized. It might seem that such a generalization is perfectly suited to McGinn's powers/parameters analysis. The property of being highly specialized, it might be thought, contains hidden parameters that can be abstracted away from the real causal factors, the causal powers that a species has. After all, to be highly specialized is to be highly specialized *in a particular environment*. In this respect, being highly specialized would be like being the best player: It is a property that is implicitly relative. We might then suppose that to be highly specialized is to have physical capabilities $a \ldots n$ in environment $E_1$, or physical capabilities $c \ldots g$ in environment $E_2$, or $p \ldots \gamma$ in $E_3$, or $\ldots$. Such abilities can be properly regarded as causal powers: They are determined by the intrinsic physical properties that individuals instantiate. Thus, this sort of case is amenable to just the sort of powers/parameters analysis that applies to properties like being sharp. In order to abstract particular powers from the properties they constitute, we make the environmental circumstances parameters. The property of being highly specialized is thus analyzed into a set of ordered pairs, the first member of each pair denoting a range of physical capacities (a power) and the second denoting an environmental circumstance (a parameter).

One problem with this analysis is that being highly specialized – rather than engaging in certain physical behaviors in certain environments (and other behaviors in other environments), for example – is the explanatorily appropriate property to focus on if we are interested in identifying the property in virtue of which certain organisms, but not others, do not survive periods of ecological catastrophe. This is because it is this property that abstracts away from differences between organisms who are affected in the same way (i.e., extinguished), allowing one to arrive at a common, unifying explanation. Explanations for the fact of differential extinction that appeal to the particular behaviors that individuals engage in are, in terms I introduced in §3, *merely instantiating* explanations relative to those that appeal to the property of being highly specialized. If one insists that only intrinsic powers can be causally efficacious, then one breaks the connection between causal efficacy and causal explanation. But in §3 I suggested that our best causal explanations provide the best guide to what properties in the world are causally efficacious, and such explanations often posit relational properties, such as being highly specialized.

This problem does not derive simply from having given the wrong analysis of being highly specialized. Suppose that one decomposes being highly specialized not into particular behaviors (plus environmental parameters), but into something like having highly *inflexible* behavior, where this means having few behavioral dispositions in one's repertoire. It is, after all, an organism's having a *variety* of behavioral strategies in its phenotypic kit that enables it to survive once the niches for which it has actually adapted disappear. Applying the powers/parameters analysis in this way, to be highly specialized is to have highly inflexible behavior, where the particular behaviors

133

that come to be identified as inflexible vary from circumstance to circumstance. Explanations that appeal to the property of being highly specialized can thus be factored, without loss of explanatory generality, into explanations in terms of causal powers, namely, those quantifying over highly inflexible behavior.

This suggestion suffers from a closely related problem. The problem in this version of how to apply the powers/parameters analysis to our example is that the power cited, that of having highly inflexible behavior, is not a causal power in the relevant sense. That is, it is not a power that supervenes on the intrinsic physical properties of the entity to which it belongs. For to have highly inflexible behavior, if this is to be understood as the causal property in virtue of which the initial generalization holds, is to be unable to adapt to alternative ecological niches: Organisms or species that can't do *that* perish. But, so understood, having highly inflexible behavior is at best an *extrinsic* causal power that an organism or species possesses, for it is a power that an organism or species could gain or lose without any change in its intrinsic properties. For example, an organism or species could lose this property if it were rapidly surrounded by other organisms or species that are even more highly specialized. A highly specialized species that finds itself amongst even more highly specialized species will tend to survive for precisely the reason that its competitors will not: They have highly *flexible* behavior relative to the competing species they will eventually replace.

Our discussion of each of these examples brings out a general point about McGinn's powers/parameters analysis. The first is that even though there are cases in which one can abstract a power from its parameters to identify a part of the causal nexus that has some claim to being *the* cause, there are other cases in which the resultant 'power-based' explanations have less explanatory unity. Although I have concentrated on the details of one example in this section, the same is true of the examples of relationally taxonomized kinds given in Chapter 2 and in §2. Relationally individuated kinds have been developed in the biological and social sciences (and elsewhere) precisely to allow one to offer more unified explanations, explanations that tell us what causal factors are most significant for the sorts of phenomena that those disciplines seek to understand.

The second point is that there is an implicit constraint on the powers/parameters analysis: that powers must supervene on the intrinsic physical properties of the entity to which it is ascribed. This is a constraint on what counts as a power only insofar as the powers/parameters analysis is supposed to provide some general reason for thinking individualism to be true, and it *is* such a constraint because individualism can be construed as making the same supervenience claim about *psychological* states and properties. The powers/parameters analysis initially looks promising as the basis for a major premise in an a priori argument for individualism only because one fails to restrict 'power' to mean 'intrinsic power'.

It will not be lost on some that one could express these two points in terms that bring out something very much like the problem we have seen plague other appeals to the notion of causal powers. Just as it is implausible to hold that taxonomy in science is taxonomy by causal powers if one assumes a restricted notion of causal powers, so too is it implausible to think that the powers/parameters analysis applies to all properties that are taxonomic or explanatory, assuming such a notion. Yet if we broaden or extend the notion of a power in a way that allows us to address this first problem, we do so at the cost of failing to have specified an analysis from which we can derive individualism in psychology, for such 'causal powers' do not supervene on the intrinsic physical properties of the entities in which they are instantiated. It is just this type of problem that arose with the notion of 'genuine properties' in §2.

## 5. CONCLUSION: AGAINST A PRIORI ARGUMENTS FOR INDIVIDUALISM

The discussion of a priori arguments for individualism in this chapter and in Chapter 2 provides us with a basis for some more general conclusions. Each of the three a priori arguments for individualism examined – the argument from causal powers, that from the causal theory of properties, and that from the powers/parameters analysis of causation – makes its central claims in terms of the notion of causal powers. It is not part of my argument to suggest that the notion of a causal power is not important to the philosophy of science. My concern, rather, is with a range of appeals that individualists have made to the idea that an entity's causal powers play some crucial role in taxonomy and explanation. One way of looking at the problem with such appeals is that there is *too much* in the concepts they use for the arguments that flow from them to be sound. In particular, the crucial notion of a causal power has at least two distinct senses, neither of which will allow us to derive individualism in psychology *via* these a priori paths.

With this substantive point in mind, consider the problem for these a priori arguments posed by the fact that some of our paradigmatic explanatory frameworks taxonomize relationally: relational kinds do not individuate by causal powers. One way of resolving this problem would be to soften or liberalize the meaning given to the phrase 'by causal powers' so as to allow certain relational taxonomies to count as taxonomies that individuate 'by causal powers' (cf. Chapter 2, §5 and §6). I have no argument to suggest that such a strategy cannot work, but I take it to be no coincidence that the particular proposals that have been made are incompatible with one of two required claims. Either they account for our intuitions about when relational taxonomies are permissible, but do so at the expense of failing to connect suitably with individualism in psychology; or they allow one to derive individualism in psychology from an a priori claim about science, properties, or causation, but fail to explain why relational taxonomies are permissible when they are.

Suppose that one concedes that there is a conflict between the taxonomy of entities by their intrinsic causal powers and their relational individuation. What of the claim that relational taxonomies, *when they are genuinely explanatory,* can be factored into taxonomies that are individuated by the intrinsic causal powers of the entities they subsume? This claim, like McGinn's claim about the generality of the powers/parameters analysis of causation, should be assessed by examining relational kinds in the sciences and seeing whether they can, as a matter of fact, be factored in the way proposed. In this chapter and in Chapter 2, we have seen examples (species, planets, being highly specialized) that seem resistant to such a treatment, and in §3 I attempted to explain why we should expect them and other examples mentioned (continent, virus, taboo, criminal, volcano, mountain, class, mother, unemployed) to be resistant.

This brings me to a more *methodological* moral concerning how one goes about doing the philosophy of science, particularly the philosophy of the special sciences, such as psychology: The way in which these arguments proceed, what I've called their a priori character, is mistaken. The general premise bearing the argumentative burden in a priori arguments for individualism must meet two requirements. First, to have the generality it purports to have, it must say something metaphysically innocent; second, to play a role in an argument *for individualism,* it must lead one to a restrictive view of taxonomy in psychology. The difficulty of meeting both requirements does not make a priori arguments for individualism impossible, but it does exert a pressure on them that, as we have seen, is often relieved through equivocation.

This sort of difficulty was also manifest in one version of the computational argument discussed in Chapter 3. Although the computational argument makes a particular empirical claim about psychological processing, I said that we can discern a more a priori version of the argument by considering the status of Premise (B), the claim that computational individuation is individualistic. If one takes (B) to express a truth about *computational* individuation in general, rather than about computational individuation as it has developed within psychology, then one is adopting an a priori view of (B). Such an a priori version of the computational argument derives it metaphysical innocence (and so generality) from implicitly equating 'computational system' and 'individual', precisely what a proponent of wide computationalism will reject. Yet without this assumption the argument does not allow one to derive individualism. Moreover, in turning to computational taxonomy and explanation, one can see the requisite metaphysical innocence lost.

Sciences, particularly the special sciences, develop their own taxonomies, theories, and explanations in response to very different research interests and problems, and with very different methodologies. Because of the often unappreciated, rich diversity within the sciences, any argument that relies on a premise about scientific taxonomies and explanations having some essential feature is unlikely to be sound; more so any argument that relies on a general premise about the notions of causation, property, or explanation, notions at least some of whose principal instances are found by turning to the sciences. The pragmatics of scientific explanation cannot be separated from its metaphysics, at least not if the metaphysics one proposes for science is to be taken seriously as an account of the metaphysics that science actually traffics in. Scientific practice is not simply the ultimate arbiter for claims about the nature of science; its examination is the way to do the philosophy of science. Although this conclusion may strike some as trite, we do well here to remember that philosophers, including philosophers of science, tend to crave the general.

(Perhaps my own 'methodological' conclusion is a manifestation of this tendency.) Insofar as this is a craving satisfied only by a priori argumentation, it should be resisted.

In thinking about broad questions in philosophical methodology and argumentation, there is never a time when all the evidence is in. But we have enough evidence to suggest that a priori arguments for individualism are unlikely to be any good. They should be given up.

# 6

# *Making sense of mental causation*

Implicit in a number of views we have already discussed is the idea that a proper understanding of the nature of causation leads one to individualism. For example, Fodor claims that global individualism follows from relatively uncontroversial claims about causal explanation (Chapter 2); McGinn considers his analysis of causal factors into powers and parameters to be a 'rather elementary' point about causation (Chapter 5). But thus far we have not focussed on the intuition behind such views: that making sense of *mental causation* requires accepting individualism.

There are two complementary parts to this intuition. One part is the idea that denying individualism commits one to unacceptable views about mental causation. For example, it has been said that denying individualism is tantamount to positing 'action at a distance' in psychology, commits one to the existence of 'crazy causal mechanisms,' and 'violates supervenience'. These claims have found their way into the philosophical subconscious and contribute to the intuitive pull that individualism has for many philosophers. If denying individualism committed one to any of these views, individualism would be compelling, if only by default, in much the way that it is often held that *some* version of materialism about the mind must be true because the various forms of dualism are metaphysically unacceptable. In §1 I state the arguments for and in §2 offer responses to each of these three related objections to the denial of individualism.

The flip side to these objections is the idea that individualism itself follows from a basic and unobjectionable claim about causation: that causation is *local*. This claim, and the inference from it to individualism, are the focus in §4 and §5. Although the metaphysics of mental causation has been and continues to be puzzling, those of us who are puzzled have no reason to accept individualism. Instead, we need to make sense of mental causation without individualism, and in §§5–7 I offer a push in the direction to take here.

## 1. ACTION AT A DISTANCE, CRAZY CAUSAL MECHANISMS, AND THE VIOLATION OF SUPERVENIENCE

The claim that a denial of individualism commits one to some kind of psychological action at a distance is made in Ned Block's (1986) discussion of a Twin-Earth-styled example. Imagining a tour bus half full of Earthlings and half full of Twin Earthlings, Block says:

> Suppose that the Earthlings and Twin Earthlings do not differ in relevant ways in genes or in the surface stimulation that has impinged on their bodies over their whole lives. Hence, in this population [i.e., those on the tour bus], differences in propositional attitudes cannot be attributed to environment (in the sense of surface stimulation) and genes (and their interactions): the differences in water attitudes are due to something that has nothing to do with differences in the genes or surface stimulations that have affected these people. An analysis of variance would have to attribute a large component of variance to differences in a factor that does not cause any differences in proteins, synaptic connections, or any other physicochemical feature of the body, as do differences in genes and surface stimulations. This would amount to a kind of action at a distance. . . . (1986:625)

Block's point is that if we suppose that the propositional attitudes are individuated relationally, two individuals might be identical in their intrinsic physical properties over their entire life histories and yet differ in their propositional attitudes. Yet what *causal* difference is there between the mental states that such individuals instantiate? There would seem to be no causal factors that *could be* responsible for such a purported difference. Denying individualism, then, commits one to some type of spooky action at a distance in psychology.

Jerry Fodor claims that those who deny individualism are committed to crazy causal mechanisms. In discussing the psychological difference between doppelgängers, Oscar and Oscar$_2$, that exists if we taxonomize their mental states by wide content, Fodor says that

> there must be some difference in the causal powers of their mental states - psychological taxonomy is taxonomy *by* causal powers. But if there is such a difference, then there must be some mechanism which can connect the causal powers of Oscar's mental states with the character of his linguistic affiliation *without affecting his physiological constitution*. But there is no such mechanism; the causal powers of Oscar's mental states supervene on his

140

physiology, just like the causal powers of your mental states and mine. (1987:40)

Although Fodor employs the notion of a causal power here, this is not a crucial feature of his (largely implicit) *reductio* argument, which we can spell out as the *argument from crazy causal mechanisms:*

(a) Intrinsic physical identity is sufficient for instantiation of the same physical mechanisms.
(b) Psychological mechanisms must supervene on physical mechanisms (so individuals with the same physical mechanisms must have identical psychological mechanisms).
(c) Individuals with the same psychological mechanisms must instantiate states of the same psychological kinds. But,
(d) To deny individualism is to allow individuals who are identical in their intrinsic physical properties to instantiate states of different psychological kinds. So,
(e) To deny individualism is to be committed to 'crazy causal mechanisms', that is, psychological mechanisms that don't supervene on physical mechanisms.

The idea that one must respect supervenience in order to provide an account of mental causation is the basis for a third claim about the denial of individualism, one that, although often appealed to in discussion, is less often found explicitly stated in print. But Fodor comes close. Noting that the propositional attitudes don't supervene on molecular structure, Fodor says:

Any scientifically useful notion of psychological state ought to respect supervenience; mind/brain supervenience (and/or mind/brain identity) is, after all, the best idea that anyone has had so far about how mental causation is possible. The moral would appear to be that you can't make respectable science out of the attitudes as commonsensically individuated. (1987:30)

We can, I think, be more explicit about how failing to 'respect supervenience' makes a mystery of mental causation. To be clear on terminology from the outset: A set of properties, $S$, supervenes on some set of properties, $B$, only if there can be no difference in two objects with respect to possession of members of $S$ without a corresponding difference with respect to the possession of some member of $B$. Call $S$ the set of *supervenient* properties and $B$ the set of *subvenient* or *base* properties. *Ex hypothesi,* doppelgängers have identical sets of intrinsic physical properties. Thus, any properties that are supervenient on these intrinsic physical properties must also be shared by doppelgängers. Taxonomizing psychological states by their wide content violates supervenience in that it allows the psychological states of two individuals to differ even though there need be no difference in their intrinsic physical properties. But states so taxonomized are not causally efficacious states precisely because they do not causally affect the intrinsic physical properties of individuals. Hence, psychological taxonomies that violate supervenience do not individuate types of psychological states that are causally efficacious.

## 2. THREE THINGS THAT THE DENIAL OF INDIVIDUALISM DOES NOT ENTAIL

Let us briefly consider each of these claims. In claiming that the denial of individualism commits one to action at a distance in psychology, Block is objecting to the idea that *causally remote* factors themselves could make any causal difference to the psychology of physically identical individuals. Wide taxonomies reflect historical, causal differences between individuals, but cases of doppelgängers show that such differences may fail to 'leave their mark' on individuals. Differences between doppelgängers can't be manifested as differences in their current internal physical states, and unless they are manifested in this way, they cannot make any causal difference to cognition and the behavior it causes. The claim being made here about *mental* causation derives from a claim about causation in general: that properties and events whose instantiation doesn't supervene on the intrinsic physical properties of a given entity can make a causal difference to the behavior of that entity only by affecting properties that do so supervene. I shall address Block's claim with this more general claim in mind. There are at least three different ways of thinking of properties (including relational and historical properties) as 'making a causal difference' to an entity: to its *causal efficacy,* to the causal *taxonomies* we use to individuate it, and to the causal *explanations* we offer for its behavior. Once these are distinguished, Block's claim should be rejected.

The first two of these ways have been distinguished, in effect, by Tyler Burge. Burge says, 'Causation is local. Individuation may presuppose facts about the specific nature of a subject's environment' (1986a:17), supporting this distinction between causation and individuation by discussion of two examples from the sciences, continents (in geology) and respiration (in biology). In saying that causation is local, Burge implies that historical and relational properties *themselves* do not have causal effects; rather, they have their effects by causally affecting an individual's intrinsic properties. Yet taxonomies of mental causes may well be non-individualistic. Burge is distinguishing between what it is to make a causal difference in the sense of being causal efficacious – which in his view, historical and relational properties are *not* – and making a causal difference in the sense of determining what taxonomies are appropriate for causal explanation. He concludes: 'Local causation does not make more plausible local individuation, or individualistic supervenience' (1986a:16). Although I have doubts about Burge's implicit concession that wide content is causally inefficacious (see §5 and §6), what needs further elaboration is the justification for distinguishing causation and taxonomy in this way, particularly when one is concerned with *causal* taxonomies (see Fodor 1987:41–2). To do so, one must say something more about how historical and relational properties can make a difference to the causal *explanations* that one offers.

Even if historical and relational properties are not themselves causally efficacious, this does not imply that differential effects must be explained in terms of differences between intrinsic physical properties. Consider two particles identical in their intrinsic physical properties (e.g., mass, charge) that move with different velocities because they are located in magnetic fields of different strengths. There is nothing causally mysterious in saying that they move with different velocities *because* of their locations in different magnetic fields, even though being so located does not supervene on the intrinsic physical properties that each instantiates. These relations have the efficacy that they do *via* their effects on intrinsic properties, such as mass and charge, but it is the non-supervenient, relational properties, not these intrinsic properties, that causally explain the differential behavior. (Recall, *ex hypothesi,* that the particles share intrinsic properties, such as mass and charge.) Historical properties are no different here.

Causal explanations that appeal to an entity's historical and relational properties are commonplace. They can be offered even when the differential behavior of two entities identical in their intrinsic physical properties is our *explanandum* (as in the preceding example) and even if we consider such behavior in a given context (think of two qualitatively identical billiard balls moving with different velocities in a given context). Precisely because an entity's historical and

143

relational properties can make a difference to the causal explanations we give for its behavior, they can make a difference to how that entity is taxonomized for causal explanation.

So, we sometimes explain the differential behavior of two entities by appealing to their different historical and relational properties. (I think this makes it plausible to see historical and relational properties as affecting an entity's causal path through the world, and so as causally efficacious, but put this to one side for now; see §5.) There is no action at a distance in such cases in general or in psychology in particular. In general, wide taxonomies presuppose extrinsic causal connections that in part constitute an entity's causal trajectory through the world; it is no different in the particular case of psychology. One path to the rejection of individualism consistently extends a causal theory of reference to mental representations; the causal theory considers the *causal location* of the individual in the world to be the primary determinant of the content of that individual's linguistic terms.

Consider the second claim about the denial of individualism: that psychological mechanisms that do not operate *via* the intrinsic physical states that individuals instantiate are crazy causal mechanisms. We can now see why those denying individualism need not also deny this. The wide psychological differences between doppelgängers with different histories derive from the fact that such doppelgängers are causally related to different kinds of stuff (or have grown up in different linguistic communities). There is no special type of causal relation or causal mechanism required to make sense of wide psychological differences between individuals, even individuals who are doppelgängers. All that we need to remember is that causal mechanisms can bring about different causal effects because of differences in their historical or relational properties.

The argument for this second claim – the argument from crazy causal mechanisms – suffers from a (perhaps by now) familiar-sounding slide between two senses of 'psychological mechanism'.[1] On a *restricted* sense of psychological mechanism, it is true (by definition) that psychological mechanisms supervene on physical mechanisms, and so Premise (b) is true. But then individuals with the same

---

1 The relevant premises of that argument are: (b) Psychological mechanisms must supervene on physical mechanisms; and (c) individuals with the same psychological mechanisms must instantiate states of the same psychological kinds.

psychological mechanisms need not instantiate states of the same psychological kinds, and so Premise (c) is false. By contrast, an *extended* sense of psychological mechanism, according to which psychological mechanisms make a causal difference to the effects that one's mental states have, makes Premise (c) at least plausible. Yet this same sense makes Premise (b) false.

Finally, what of the claim that individualism is required to respect mind–brain supervenience? The argument here can be summarized in a single (albeit long) sentence as follows: Since wide semantic properties don't supervene on the intrinsic physical properties of individuals, and so, as putative properties of those individuals, violate supervenience, they should not be included within a scientific psychology that purports to identify causally efficacious mental states. This argument should be rejected because it proposes a subvenience base that is unacceptably restrictive. Consider the following parody of the argument: Since being a planet doesn't supervene on the intrinsic physical properties of planets, and so being a planet violates supervenience, the property of being a planet should not be included within a respectable scientific discipline purporting to identify causally efficacious states. No astronomer faced with such an argument should take it seriously. Likewise, those who deny individualism in psychology should not be moved by the original argument.

Part of what is at issue between individualists and their opponents is whether the intrinsic physical properties *of an individual* fully constitute a subvenience base for psychological kinds. What is in effect assumed in this argument from supervenience is that the base properties must be the intrinsic physical properties of the organism. Thus the argument assumes the truth of individualism and so cannot be an argument for that view.

Any substantive argument relying on the notion of supervenience must specify the set of base properties. I think that any such argument for individualism will be faced with the following dilemma: Either the base is (plausibly) broad, in which case the argument offers no support for individualism, or it is (implausibly) narrow, in which case the argument will beg the question at issue. Individualists and their opponents can agree on the truth of *global* supervenience, the view that two worlds that agree in all the physical properties they instantiate agree in all other respects. Denials of individualism violate only *local* supervenience, for differences in the wide content of two individuals' mental states *require* a global physical difference. Far from being incompatible with global supervenience, wide taxonomies are a *consequence* of the global supervenience of the mental on the physical.

## 3. SUPERVENIENCE AND WIDTH: SOME OPTIONS

Given the prevalence of the concept of supervenience in characterizing and defending various versions of materialism (Davidson 1970; Horgan 1987; Kim 1982), let me be clear that those denying individualism need not avoid such characterizations. I have suggested that they can (indeed, ought to) accept global supervenience. However, a non-individualist can rest more or less weight on the concept of supervenience in making sense of mental causation in a physical world than is entailed by an acceptance of global supervenience.

Resting more weight on supervenience is likely to be an attractive option for those persuaded that the individualist's appeal to the supervenience of the mental on the physical is almost right. Those denying individualism could opt for a supervenience claim whose strength is intermediate between local and global supervenience. Such a supervenience claim would be *local* (vs. global), in that the supervening and base properties would be properties of individual entities, not whole worlds, but *non-individualistic* in that it allowed at least some of an individual's relational properties to count as both supervenient and subvenient properties. On one version of such a view, an individual's relational properties would form part of the subvenient base for psychological properties, but historical properties would not. Thus one could opt for a set of subvenient properties for psychology broader than that proposed by individualists without having to settle for what some may see as an unduly weak version of supervenience, global supervenience. (Thanks to John Heil for the thought expressed in this paragraph; cf. Heil 1992:ch. 3.)

Alternatively, those who reject individualism may be more pessimistic about the role that the notion of supervenience should play in a materialist account of mental causation because of how little either local or global supervenience tell us about mental causation. Let me begin with global supervenience. The global supervenience of the mental on the physical is *incompatible* with there being two possible worlds identical in their physical properties, only one of which contains immaterial mental substance and so mental properties. Yet as Kim (1987) has pointed out, the global supervenience of the mental

146

on the physical *is* compatible with there being two worlds that differ in some prima facie insignificant physical feature (Kim's example is the number of ammonia molecules in the rings of Saturn), yet only one of the pair had *any* mental properties at all. Provided that there is some physical difference between two worlds, those worlds can be as different as you like mentally, no matter how intuitively irrelevant to mentality this physical difference is; they could even differ in that just one of them has immaterial substances (provided that they do not have the property of interacting with material substance essentially). The problem with global supervenience that Kim identifies is that the set of base properties is so large, both in number and in range, that it is difficult to see how to draw any significant conclusions about the mental causation that goes on *in individuals*. I am suggesting, in addition, that global supervenience is not a sufficiently constraining *materialist* view of mental causation.

The implications of the acceptance of even *local* supervenience for views of mental causation are not clear until more is said about the character of an individual's intrinsic physical properties, about the properties that are supervenient on these, and about other properties of the supervenience relation itself. Arguably, even local supervenience leaves the most difficult puzzles about mental causation untouched. For starters, a version of the problem for global supervenience that Kim identifies exists for local supervenience, too. Suppose that two individuals differ only in that one has an extra cell in her big toe. The local supervenience of mental properties on intrinsic physical properties is compatible with only one of these individuals having *any* mental properties at all; more radically, local supervenience is compatible with just one of these individuals being composed of both material and immaterial substance. Also, why does local supervenience explain the causal efficacy of psychological states rather than explain such efficacy away? That is, why assume that locally supervenient properties, as opposed to the properties on which they supervene, have *any* causal efficacy at all? Supervenience, like identity before it, can be developed within a reductive or eliminative metaphysics, one that accords *no* significant causal place to supervening properties (see Horgan 1993).

Although I have endorsed global supervenience as an acceptable non-individualistic, materialist view, I share the general concern that motivates this more sceptical view of appeals to supervenience. Philosophical discussions of supervenience – and what other discussions of supervenience are there? – in recent philosophy of mind arose from and focus on the intuition that 'the mental' and 'the physical' are neither independent nor identical. The adequacy of the concept of supervenience for articulating this intuition and providing the basis for an account of mental causation is not an issue I wish to take up here. But I find it telling that advocates of the importance of particular supervenience claims – say, of the mental on the physical (e.g., Kim 1982:68) – although stating the plausibility of those claims in light of empirical advances in the neurosciences, seldom engage in a sustained examination of just *how* particular empirical findings support those claims. Metaphysical views that claim support from science need to be guided by scientific practice itself; we have some reason to be sceptical about the concept of supervenience.

But let us not lose sight of the forest for the trees. The general point about respecting supervenience is that there is ample conceptual space to make sense of mental causation without respecting local, individualistic supervenience.

## 4. LOCAL CAUSATION AND INDIVIDUALISM

Complementing the three objections we examined in §1 and §2 is the claim that individualism follows from an intuitively positive idea about the nature of causation. The idea, shared by many friends and foes of individualism (e.g., Burge 1986a, 1989; Fodor 1987:ch. 2), is that causation is *local* in that only the intrinsic properties of a cause, properties that are 'right there', are relevant to the role that that cause plays qua cause. Only properties instantiated at the physical location of a given effect can be causally responsible for that effect. Given that, what causal difference *could* the wide content of an individual's mental states make to the mental life of that individual? And *how* could wide content be causally efficacious?

Colin McGinn provides a tidy summary of the problem in terms of a puzzle about the causal relevance of a symbol's *reference*:

The reference relation, as between symbol and object, does not contribute to the causal powers of the symbol - it is not what empowers the symbol to bring about its effects. The causal mechanism whereby the symbol has an impact on the world does not somehow incorporate the relation of reference. The relation of reference is to the symbol what the country of origin of a car is to its engine, i.e., not part of the causal machinery. Intentionality is not what makes the world go from one state to the next. Content is not a *mechanistic* feature of the world. (1989:133, fn.)

148

We can state McGinn's' point as a dilemma facing those who think that the wide content a mental state has is causally efficacious. If, as McGinn says in the accompanying text, '[c]ausation is the same with brains and minds as it is with billiard balls', how *could* a state's having wide content empower that state with any causal efficacy? How could wide content *itself* be causally relevant to the effects that mental states have? And if content is causally efficacious only through its instantiation in non-intentional properties, properties that *are* capable of bringing about effects, then why think that wide content is causally relevant at all? That is, what reason is there to think that wide content is not simply *epiphenomenal?*

Epiphenomenalism about mental properties, states, events, and processes, where these are construed as distinct from physical properties, states, events, and processes, has received renewed attention of late.[2] Wide content, as a type of mental property, will be subject to general arguments that imply that the mental is epiphenomenal. But I am focussing here on motivations for epiphenomenalism *about content* in particular, and I think that the special problem about the causal efficacy of wide content derives from the idea that causation is local. There may be some principle that governs causation or some other characteristic of causation with which the very existence of mental properties in general may be incompatible, but it is the existence of mental states with *wide content* in particular that is incompatible with the local nature of causation.

How does *individualism* ensure that mental causation respects the local nature of causation? Given individualism, any difference in the mental must be reflected in a difference in the intrinsic physical properties of the individual, so mental causation would presuppose some sort of physical causation involving a change in the physical properties that were right there, the intrinsic physical properties of the individual. We might well have *other* concerns about the concept of mental causation, but at least by insisting that mental causes be individualistic, we satisfy a necessary condition for making sense of mental causation.

To mention one such concern from the previous section, what we say about the causal efficacy of supervenient properties in general

2  For recent discussions of epiphenomenalism, see Block (1990), Fodor (1989), Heil (1992:ch. 4), Heil and Mele (1991), Kim (1984, 1989a), Lepore and Loewer (1987, 1989), McLaughlin (1989), Robinson (1992), and Yablo (1992). The epiphenomenalism to which I refer here is what McLaughlin has called *type* epiphenomenalism.

(and so about supervenient mental properties in particular) is not an issue that the adoption of individualism resolves. Perhaps the right thing to say about local supervenience is that it is a reductive and eliminative relation; perhaps we ought to say different things about different sorts of cases of local supervenience, depending on the details of the case. But, claims the individualist, the acceptance of local supervenience is logically prior to such further articulation of the concept of mental causation, and we should not mistake incompleteness for falsity.

In the next section, I concentrate on the *inference* from local causation to individualism. There is a tendency to shift between two conceptions of the nature of individualistic mental states that makes this inference appear compelling when in fact it is not. This diagnosis of what is mistaken about appeals to the local nature of causation helps us to see how to make sense of mental causation.

## 5. TWO CONCEPTIONS OF MENTAL STATES

Individualistic mental states are often thought of as *internal* states of an organism or individual. The individualist who views mental states in this way considers those denying individualism as thinking of mental states as, in some sense, *external* to an individual: Meanings are somewhere other than *in* the head. Individualism is often expressed in terms of this spatial metaphor.[3] If one thinks of individualism as a view about the nature of the causes of behavior, this conception distinguishes causes that occur inside the boundary of an individual from those that occur outside of that individual, where these sets of causes are mutually exclusive and it is only the former over which psychological theory ought to quantify. This conception of individualism draws on an intuitive distinction between what I'll refer to as *local* and *non-local* causal factors.

An alternative conception of what individualistic mental states are views them as *intrinsic* rather than extrinsic to an individual. On this

---

3 For example, to remind you of some quotations given in Chapter 1: The individualist thinks that 'what is outside a person's mind is irrelevant to psychology' (Bach 1982:123) and allows 'only properties of representations that can be characterized without adverting to matters lying outside the agent's head' (McGinn 1982:208) to be referred to in theory construction in psychology. Cf. also Putnam's ' "meanings" just ain't in the *head*' (1975:227), often cited as an expression of the denial of individualism.

view, individualism is a constraint on the types of *descriptions* that can be offered of the mental causes of behavior. This conception differs from the 'internal' conception of mental states in that it is clear that it is mental states in the head that are being individuated in different ways by the individualist and the non-individualist: 'Intrinsic' and 'extrinsic' are labels for different descriptions of mental states instantiated in individuals. When Stich says (1983:ch. 8) that cognitive psychology should be concerned with behavior autonomously described, he is proposing a constraint on the description of an *explanandum* of psychology. The same constraint also applies to psychology's *explanans,* the mental states cited as the causes of behavior. The *autonomous description* of a mental state specifies what the individual contributes to her being in a broadly contentful mental state. As such, it provides the basis for an individualistic psychology, the idea being that folk psychological descriptions can be factored into descriptions that are autonomous and so explanatory in psychology.

Consider an analogy that brings out the difference between these two conceptions of mental states, the internal and the intrinsic conceptions (cf. Child 1994:145; Davidson 1987). People who remain in the sun for too long without adequate clothing often get sunburned; being sunburnt typically results in a number of modifications in a person's behavior. If we view the bodily state of being burnt in accord with the first, internal conception of individualism, then one can distinguish the internal cause of behavior, the state of being sunburnt, from the external cause, the relation between the sun and the person, which was causally responsible for this state. Alternatively, if we adopt the second, intrinsic conception of what individualistic states are, then the relevant distinction is one between two descriptions that we can attach to the one internal bodily state. 'Sunburn' would be an extrinsic description of an individual's internal bodily state: Only an internal state with the right type of causal history could be a sunburn. By contrast, 'inflammation', say, would be an intrinsic description of the same internal bodily state, that is, a description of an internal state *whatever* its history.

If one were to adopt the internal conception of a state of our skin, one could offer either 'sunburn' or 'inflammation' as a description of that state. The internal conception tells us where to look for causes of behavior – *on the skin* – but it does not itself impose a constraint on how we can taxonomize or individuate those causes. On the internal conception, advocating *dermatological individualism* would hardly cause the blink of an eyelid, let alone the raising of an eyebrow; on the intrinsic conception, however, such a view would be more controversial.

It should be clear that since the debate over individualism in psychology concerns how one should taxonomize mental states – states that *are* instantiated in an individual – individualism is more accurately construed by the intrinsic conception than by the internal conception of mental states. Individualists and non-individualists agree that mental states are in the head, but disagree about whether the *kinds* recognized by psychology must be individuated purely in terms of the intrinsic properties of individuals.

In suggesting that non-individualists can accept the view that mental states are in the head, that is, that the denial of individualism is compatible with the *internal* conception of mental states, I might be thought to misconstrue the position of at least some of those who deny individualism. Consider the position of someone who thinks that mental states and properties are not the sort of thing that can be *either* inside or outside of the head, someone who thinks that it is something like a category mistake to either accept or reject the internal conception of mental states (see Baker 1993a; Child 1994:ch. 2; Hornsby 1986; McDowell 1985). Such a person could still reject the intrinsic conception of mental states (and so deny individualism) and would be likely to think that my acceptance of the internal conception of mental states itself suffers from a residual Cartesianism about the mind that sees it as a place where mental entities are located.

This more radical abandonment of putatively Cartesian or individualistic ways of conceiving of mental states is most plausible, I think, if we fix on a 'language of thought' view of the propositional attitudes. To state the most graphic version of such a view, beliefs are tokens stored in one's belief box and desires are tokens stored in one's desire box, whose contents are inscribed on them in mentalese, the language of thought (Schiffer 1981:212). According to it, we can understand the claim that mental states are in the head quite literally: Beliefs and desires are physical particulars, tokens of mentalese, located in particular places in the head. They are in the head in the same way that the *brain* is in the head. The proponent of what I am calling the *radical view* may be simply advocating the rejection of this conception of the propositional attitudes. Yet it is important to see that the language of thought view of the attitudes does not provide the only way of understanding the 'in the head' metaphor. Because there are alternatives here for both individualists and non-individualists, the radical view is too rash in its rejection of the internal conception of mental states.

A focus on states of *believing,* rather than on *beliefs* as mental entities, provides a way of understanding the internal conception of mental states that is clearly not committed to the language of thought hypothesis about the propositional attitudes. Agents believe particular things in virtue of instantiating belief states, just as they can be sunburnt in virtue of instantiating a particular bodily state. The 'in virtue of' here is to be understood *conceptually* or *logically,* not causally. On this view, believing is a state of a particular individual because it is that individual in whom that state is instantiated. This is how we ought to understand the idea that beliefs are in the head; believing is literally in the mind of the believer. It is not, like the state of the economy or the city's financial state, either located in some entity larger than the individual or not located at all. This view weakens the grip of the reifying, locational metaphor by making it natural to see individuals as *in* states of believing, rather than those states as in the individual.

A nice feature of this view is that it provides us with a natural way of talking about beliefs in two ways. (This is a *nice* feature because we do talk about belief in these two ways.) Beliefs are specific to an agent – *my* beliefs – because belief states are individuated by attitude, content, *and agent.* If we abstract away from this third parameter, we can also talk of agents as believing the same thing or as sharing beliefs. And neither of these ways of talking presupposes that there is a language of thought.

Whether non-individualists defend either the internal conception of belief or the conception of believing as a state (or both), accepting at least the first of these conceptions is powerful dialectically. First, it enables someone who denies individualism to explain what is *right* about the individualist's conception of mental states, and to do so in a way that makes it clear how to make sense of mental causation: Individualists are right that mental states are internal states. Second, it provides the basis for seeing what is *wrong* in the individualist's claim that one needs individualism in order to make sense of mental causation: Individualists are wrong in thinking of mental states as *intrinsic* states.

Individualists hold that there is an individualistic (autonomous) description for every non-individualistic description that is taxonomic and explanatory in psychology, even if it is a further question whether such individualistic descriptions are syntactic (Stich 1983), express a notion of narrow content (Field 1978; Fodor 1987:ch. 2), or are actually part of folk psychology (Loar 1988a). Insofar as individualists think that such narrow descriptions of mental states are necessary *because* local causal factors are necessary, they slide between thinking of individualism in the first way (internal–external) and thinking of it in the second way (intrinsic–extrinsic). Block's claim that a rejection of individualism involves some type of action at a distance and Fodor's objection to the denial of individualism on the grounds that it requires the existence of crazy causal mechanisms, both claims discussed in §2, are clear examples in which the necessity of narrow descriptions of mental states is inferred on the basis of the necessity of local causal factors; the claim that denying individualism violates supervenience, also discussed in §2, less obviously makes this same inference in moving from a claim about the causal efficacy of super-venient properties (internal conception) to one about taxonomy (in-trinsic conception). The necessity of local causal factors would trivi-ally entail individualism, conceived as the view that only local causal factors should be cited in psychological explanations. It would be a mistake, however, to draw the further *required* conclusion that only descriptions of local causal factors supervening on the intrinsic physi-cal states of individuals may be used for taxonomy in psychology. So long as local causal factors exist, how we are to describe these factors remains an open question; in my view, it can be answered properly only by philosophical reflection on particular empirical research pro-grams, not by a priori philosophical analysis.

Consider how the dilemma argument for the causal inefficacy of wide content stated in §4 involves a shift from the internal to the intrinsic conception of mental states. Beginning with the internal conception, we note that *non-local* causal factors are causally effica-cious only when they act through corresponding local causal factors. Where there are no local causal factors for a putative non-local causal factor, there is reason to doubt the causal relevance of that non-local cause. In the case of psychology, the local causal factors are neurologi-cal events, states, or processes. So, any putative non-local causal factor is either a fake (if there is no local causal factor), or the explanatory work *it* is claimed to do is done by some local causal factor (if there is such a local causal factor). This is why wide taxonomies are not themselves explanatory in psychology.

This final conclusion about explanation requires a shift to the second, intrinsic conception of individualism. Explanations range over *kinds* of entities: It is not simply neurological events and processes that are explained and that, in turn, themselves explain, but these entities taxonomically individuated one way rather than another. Even were this argument assumed to show the dispensability (in principle) of non-local causal factors, it would imply nothing about how one should taxonomize, individuate, or describe the local causal factors that psychology studies.

Finally, the distinction between the internal and intrinsic conceptions of psychological states provides us with a new perspective from which to view wide computationalism, discussed in Chapter 3. Wide computational systems, recall, are computational systems that are not fully instantiated within the boundary of the individual; they literally *extend* into an individual's environment. Now the *psychological* states that an individual instantiates are *internal* states: They are located entirely within the individual. This is true even of psychological states that are part of a wide computational, cognitive system. However, when we view such states as computational states, when they are taxonomized qua wide computational states, they are not states that are *intrinsic* to the individuals in whom they are instantiated. They are, rather, intrinsic to the computational system to which they belong. Thus, although psychological states are internal to individuals, when they are taxonomized as parts of wide computational systems (or wide *modular* systems; see Chapter 4, §7), they are not individualistic states. To see that wide computationalism does not involve any sort of psychological action at a distance and is compatible with our intuitions about the locality of mental causation, adopt the (true) internal conception of psychological states; to avoid problems in conceiving of the possibility that we are wide computational systems, reject the (false) intrinsic conception of psychological states.


## 6. MENTAL CAUSATION, IDENTITY THEORIES, AND MATERIALISM

Tyler Burge (1979) has argued that the Twin Earth thought experiments showing that folk psychology is not individualistic also show a range of materialist accounts of the ontology of the mind, including functionalism and both type- and token-identity theories, to be mistaken. Since a combination of functionalism (as a view of mental state types) and a token-identity thesis has been perhaps the dominant materialist solution to the mind–body problem in recent philosophy of mind (see Dennett 1978b; Fodor 1981b), Burge's claim has sometimes been taken as a rejection of materialism; Burge's own qualms about contemporary materialism also suggest this interpretation of his view (see Burge 1986a:fn.7, 1992:38). Burge's claim is relevant to the account of mental causation developed in the previous section because that account may seem committed to a token-identity theory of the mental. We make sense of mental causation by accepting the *internal* conception of mental states; we do so without also accepting individualism by rejecting the *intrinsic* conception of mental states. An agent's mental state tokens are internal to her even though her mental state types are not intrinsic to her; doppelgängers have the same internal mental states. But if the rejection of individualism implies the falsity of token-identity theories, then the metaphysics underlying this account of mental causation is untenable.

The general view I am advocating can be developed in ways that avoid this conclusion. Before briefly indicating what these are, I want to note that materialists have often given themselves a restrictive set of 'theories' and 'isms' to choose from. In particular, materialists have continued to think of the solution to the mind–body problem as consisting of an *identity* theory of some kind, and in so doing have neglected alternatives that posit *realization* or *instantiation* as the appropriate relationship between mental and physical states (see also Chapter 3, §8). (For what it's worth, I think that this fixation on identity has as much to do with a preoccupation with conceptual analysis and the search for necessary and sufficient conditions as anything else.) Even when multiple realization arguments are taken to show the chauvinism of type-type physicalism, they typically lead to the further conclusion that mental states must be token-identical with physical states, indicating that the relation of realization itself isn't considered metaphysically robust enough to solve the mind–body problem.

As these comments suggest, I think that identity theories, including token-identity theories, are problematic; however, since they represent only a restricted range of the options open to a materialist, this poses no problem for materialism per se. Psychological states are in no way special here. Identity theories that attempt to provide identity

conditions for entities and states posited outside of physics are inadequate expressions of a materialist worldview, which is perhaps why
they have not been seriously entertained about the ontological status
of such entities (genes, knots, coughs) and states (of compression, of
good health, of excitement). So, even if Burge is right to claim
that individualism and materialist identity theories should be rejected
together, that is no reason to reject materialism.

Coming back to the account of mental causation I have sketched,
why isn't *it* a form of the token-identity theory? One *could* construe
the internal conception of mental states is such a way so as to entail a
token-identity theory; those less sceptical of identity theories could
do so and then either challenge Burge's claim about the relationship
between the rejection of individualism and identity theories or defend
individualism itself. This would be one way to develop the internal
conception of belief within a materialist framework. But the internal
conception of mental states is not committed to a token-identity
theory, since, as I suggested in §5, it may be developed in terms of
states of *believing* (rather than *beliefs*), which would remove much of
the temptation to think of beliefs as entities that can be identified
with particular physical entities in the head. Such states can be instantiated in individuals, but since their type identity is determined in
part by their *content,* even doppelgängers may fail to instantiate the
same states of believing.

## 7. CONCLUSION

The core questions about mental causation are metaphysical: What is
mental causation? How is mental causation possible? Is the existence
of mental causation compatible with physicalism? Yet the metaphysical nature of the cluster of issues that constitute the problem of mental
causation should not be taken to imply that understanding mental
causation requires a *focus* on the metaphysics, any more than the fact
that there is a shortage of food in a given situation (a food problem)
implies that the solution to this problem requires focussing on the
absence of food. We might insist (in the formal mode and with
mutterings under our breaths about analyticity, if we like) that the
solution to a 'food problem' must be a 'food solution'. But this does
not tell us anything about *how* to go about reaching that solution.
The way to solve a food problem might well be to address the
political conflicts that give rise to the problem in the first place.

157

If two of the central puzzles about mental causation are what it is and how it is possible, then one ought to consider how psychological explanations function, since it is in at least some such explanations that mental states and properties function qua causes (cf. Baker 1993b; Burge 1993). This will bring us back to our commonsense, ordinary folk psychological explanations of behavior; to types of psychological explanations that are conservative extensions of folk psychology (e.g., much of developmental cognitive psychology); and to types of psychological explanation that at least appear to abandon our folk psychological categories altogether (e.g., much of subpersonal computational psychology). In the next chapter, I focus on *folk psychological* explanation. As we saw in Chapter 1, the apparent conflict between folk psychology and the constraint of individualism generated much of the initial interest in individualism. Our folk psychological explanations are a good testing ground for whether one can think of mental states with wide content as causally efficacious without accepting individualism.

I have argued in this chapter that the denial of individualism does not require absurd views of mental causation and that the inference from causation's local nature to individualism is unsound. But a proper understanding of our best causal explanations of cognition and cognitive behavior may show individualism to be necessary for understanding mental causation after all.

# 7

## *The place of folk psychology: computationalism, individualism, and narrow content*

'Folk psychology' designates our commonsense knowledge about the mental causes of the behavior of agents who are rational in much the way that we ourselves are. We use this knowledge to predict and (especially) to explain the behavior of both ourselves and others by attributing beliefs and desires to such agents. Jane went to the refrigerator because she wanted a golden throat charmer and believed that the refrigerator was a conveniently close repository for such a drink. Peter doesn't drive when it snows because he thinks that under those conditions the roads are dangerous, and he wants to avoid harm both to himself and to others. In this chapter I focus on the *place* that folk psychology has in explaining human behavior, with three questions signifying the parameters of my discussion.

### 1. THREE QUESTIONS

First, **how is folk psychology related to *computationalism* in psychology?** Part of the motivation for discussing this first question comes from an interest in a more general question: What is the relationship between folk psychology and the cognitive sciences? The computational paradigm dominates much contemporary psychology and has served as an impetus for the cognitive sciences more generally. As a guide to the relationship between folk psychology and the cognitive sciences, I focus on the question about computationalism; such a focus has served as a surrogate for discussion of the more general question in much of the philosophical literature.

Second, **what is the significance of our views of the place of folk psychology for *individualism* in psychology?** We have seen that there has typically been thought to be a prima facie conflict between accepting individualism and viewing folk psychological categories as providing the basis for genuine causal explanations of human

159

and perhaps other animal behavior. Given this common perception, should we view folk psychology or individualism itself with suspicion? Or can one resolve this prima facie conflict?

Third, **what is the proper role of the notion of** *narrow content* **within folk psychology?** Narrow content is a type of content that respects individualism, and there are competing accounts of how it is best understood. Precisely how does the notion of narrow content resolve the prima facie conflict between folk psychology and individualism? And, perhaps more important, what is the preferred account of such a notion of content? To begin to approach the third of our three questions, we will look more closely at the notion of content itself in the next section. But, first, a reminder about my use of the term *folk psychology*.

In Chapter 1, I adopted a minimalist view of the conception of folk psychology as a theory, one presupposing only that folk psychology is systematic and predictive. Certainly, one might think that this conception entails much more. As a theory, folk psychology might be thought to contain *laws,* to be *reducible* in principle to existing or future sciences, or to be ultimately *defeasible* in light of developing theories in the neurosciences. I have not presumed any of these purported implications of conceiving of folk psychology as a theory, as they turn on more controversial views about the nature of theories. In fact, I argue in this chapter that these claims about laws, reducibility, and defeasibility are *false.*

## 2. PROPOSITIONAL CONTENT AND REVISIONISM

There is universal agreement that folk psychology uses a notion of *propositional content:* This is what is specified in the 'that' clause of, say, a belief attribution (e.g., Peter believes that *the roads are dangerous when it snows*). There is also widespread (though not universal) agreement that this ordinary, intuitive notion of content is *wide:* It does not supervene on the intrinsic physical properties of the individuals in whom those states are instantiated. How should we view this claim that propositional content is wide? I think it is both an obvious *and* a surprising claim.

It is obvious in that our commonsense mental states are *intentional;* they are about aspects of the world, including ourselves, and propositional contents tell us what they are about. Moreover, since the intentionality of folk psychological states is essential to their type identity, beliefs with different propositional contents are different belief types. Beliefs about different things in the world have different contents and so are of different kinds. As intentional kinds, beliefs are individuated by what they are about, and they are typically about the world beyond the individual. Thus content does not supervene on properties intrinsic to individuals. In another respect, this claim is surprising – indeed, deeply counterintuitive: How can some crucial individuating feature of *my* folk psychological states not supervene on *my* intrinsic physical properties? The claim implies that my beliefs don't supervene on the physical properties I instantiate and appears to clash with deep intuitions about mental causation (though see Chapter 6).

Whether obvious, surprising, or both, the claim that propositional content is wide implies that folk psychology itself is not individualistic. If we view individualism as a constraint on a properly scientific psychology, as do individualists themselves, then we would expect individualists to claim that folk psychology cannot be part of a scientific psychology; accompanied by the not uncommon view that science is the measure of all things, this claim of incompatibility should also lead to *eliminativism* about folk psychology. Few (if any) individualists, however, endorse an eliminativist conclusion about folk psychology, and very few are even incompatibilists; most opt, instead, to diffuse the prima facie conflict between folk psychology and individualism by appeal to a concept of narrow content.

Although narrow content defences of folk psychology have often been *revisionist,* some (e.g., Jackson and Pettit 1993; Loar 1988a, 1988b) have argued that folk psychological explanations employ a notion of narrow content, implying that folk psychology itself is individualistic. Unless the non-revisionist, individualistic line on folk psychology claims either that *all* of folk psychology is narrow, as it is, or that the parts that are not narrow are not genuinely explanatory (and so could be factored out or dropped without explanatory loss), there remains a variation on the prima facie conflict between folk psychology and individualism identified earlier. Thus a non-revisionist would need to be something like what Block (1986:625) refers to as a *pan-individualist,* an individualist about *all* propositional attitude individuation, in order to avoid such a conflict altogether

161

and thus defend folk psychology *as is* as part of an individualistic psychology.

Although in this section I have located our questions about individualism and narrow content, less has been said on our first question about computationalism and folk psychology; I turn next to a popular defence of the integrity of folk psychology that draws on computationalism.

## 3. FOLK PSYCHOLOGICAL COMPUTATIONALISM

One way to defend the integrity of (wide) folk psychology is by developing that idea that beliefs and desires are mental representations whose causal interactions with one another, as well as those with perception and behavior, can be understood as computations. One can conceive of an individual's propositional attitudes as relations between that individual and tokens in her language of thought, the nature of these relations being specified by particular computational theories of cognition. As Fodor says, 'having a propositional attitude is being in some relation to an internal representation. In particular, having a propositional attitude is being in some computational relation to an internal representation' (1975:198). I shall call this view *folk psychological computationalism.*[1] On such a view, mental representations 'function both as the immediate objects of propositional attitudes and as the domains of mental processes' (Fodor 1987:17). That is, both believing and desiring, on the one hand, and edge detection and subdoxastic inference, on the other, are processes that have appropriate descriptions as part of a computational system. This suggests a general conception of cognition as *internal representation crunching,* whether those representations are subpersonal states or the immediate objects of the propositional attitudes. Cognition is representation crunching, and the cognitive sciences explain how mental representations get crunched.

Fodor has been the leading advocate of this computational, language of thought conception of the propositional attitudes for some twenty years, the tidiest summary of which is contained in his introduction to *Representations:*

---

1 This view has had many adherents. For example, Field (1978) and Harman (1973:chh. 4, 5) are two early defenders of the language of thought view of the attitudes; Lycan (1981), Maloney (1989), and Schiffer (1981) are proponents who are more explicitly computationalist in their approaches.

(a) Propositional attitude states are relational.
(b) Among the relata are mental representations (often called 'Ideas' in the older literature).
(c) Mental representations are symbols: they have both formal and semantic properties.
(d) Mental representations have their causal roles in virtue of their formal properties.
(e) Propositional attitudes inherit their semantic properties from those of the mental representations that function as their objects.      (1981b:26)

Extending computationalism to the states posited by folk psychology provides the basis for explaining away the paradoxical claim that folk psychological explanations are both causal (and so narrow) and semantic (and so wide). We get the causal and the semantic together by endorsing the *correlation thesis* (Stich 1983:188), the view that there is a law-like correlation between the syntactic properties that a particular mental state has and its semantic properties. Let us unpack this view a little more.

Symbol tokens in the language of thought have their causal powers in virtue of their syntactic or formal properties, whether these tokens be the objects of folk psychological states or those of subpersonal psychological states. Yet because of the correlation between the syntactic and semantic properties of symbols in the language of thought, this computationalist view is compatible with ascribing an explanatory role to the semantic properties of psychological states. More pointedly, computationalism provides a way of understanding *how* such an ascription could be explanatory: It proposes that the semantic properties of psychological states are causally relevant to behavior *because* they correlate with the formal properties responsible for mental causation. And what is true of psychological states in general is true of propositional attitudes in particular.

There is one large problem with this defence of folk psychology: The correlation thesis is false (Stich 1983:188–90; 1991). The falsity of the correlation thesis should occasion no real surprise here, for its falsity is implicit in the very Twin Earth thought experiments that highlight the prima facie conflict between folk psychology and individualism. Individualists are often keen on computationalism because the computational properties that mental states instantiate are typically thought to supervene on the intrinsic physical properties of individuals. But the standard Twin Earth cases provide reason to think that content does not supervene on such intrinsic physical properties. Hence, even if there is some sort of de facto correlation between syntactic and semantic properties, this relation is not strong enough to explain how the content of mental states is causally relevant to the effects those states have; such an explanation requires a law-like, necessary connection between syntax and semantics. If content merely coincides with causally efficacious properties of mental states (so-called syntactic properties), then explaining behavior by an appeal to mental content would be like explaining why a key opens a lock by appealing to the color of the key. Even if there happens to be a correlation between key color and key shape, the color is not causally relevant to the opening of the lock.

Stich is right: The correlation thesis *is* false. He is also correct in implying that endorsing both the *formality condition* and the representational theory of mind is inconsistent. The formality condition (Fodor 1980a; see Chapter 3, §4) says that the cognitive sciences should be restricted to quantifying over the formal properties of mental states. The representational theory of mind, of which the language of thought hypothesis is a particular version, entails that the representational properties of mental states, properties that are *not* formal, are part of the ontology of the cognitive sciences. As Stich says (1983:188), Fodor cannot 'have it both ways'.

This defence of folk psychology should be abandoned unless there is a notion of narrow content that can be used in formulating a version of the correlation thesis, one whose relationship to wide content can be properly explicated. We will consider such a version of the correlation thesis defence of folk psychology in §8. But there is a better way to defend folk psychology, one that gives us a more complete understanding of folk psychology's place.

## 4. THREE THESES ABOUT FOLK PSYCHOLOGY

One way to approach the alternative I favor is through a brief consideration of Fodor's claim (1987:166, 1989:67–8, 1991c) that one can 'have it both ways' by distinguishing the level at which the *laws* of a special science are stated from the level at which the *mechanisms* of that science are specified. Nomic generalizations in psychology apply in virtue of content in that they quantify over representational entities, whereas the mechanisms in virtue of which such intentional generalizations hold are not representational but computational. Here we have two senses of 'in virtue of'. Psychological laws and generalizations, particularly those of folk psychology, are often stated in intentional language: In this sense, they hold in virtue of content. (In this same sense, biological generalizations, such as 'the closer species are to one another in phylogeny, the more similar they are genetically', hold in virtue of biological properties, such as that of being phylogenetically related.) The mechanisms realizing the processes to which such generalizations refer manipulate tokens in the language of thought in accord with their syntactic properties: Psychological processes operate in virtue of the syntactic features of their constituents. One can accept a computational view of the mechanisms of cognition without holding that the whole of psychology, folk or otherwise, need be computational.

Though I have misgivings about Fodor's particular view (see §5), I want to defend a view of this type as part of a broader conception of folk psychology, a conception that can be developed by articulating three specific theses about folk psychology. I have chosen names for these theses that are informative (and so perhaps memorable), even if they are somewhat inelegant; let us get them out on the table together before discussing each in turn:

The *Not Exhaustively Computational Thesis:* Folk psychological explanation is not exhaustively computational, even if it is in part (and implicitly) computational.

The *Causal Irreducibility Thesis:* Folk psychological explanation, like much explanation in the range of special sciences, is thoroughly causal even though it is not reducible to 'lower-level' explanations.

The *Riches at Face Value Thesis:* Folk psychology's prima facie explanatory riches ought to be taken at face value.

Together these three theses give us what we need for an adequate understanding of the place of folk psychology and allow us to answer the three questions with which the chapter began.

Let me begin with the Riches at Face Value Thesis. It is difficult to deny that our folk psychological explanations of behavior are systematic in a way that accords them the same sort of predictive utility and explanatory coherence that our best scientific theories have. Folk psychology has *predictive utility* in that it reliably – perhaps more reliably than any other theoretical framework that we have ever had – allows us to predict what people will think, feel, want, and do, given particular situations and stimuli (cf. Fodor 1987:ch. 1). Folk psychology has *explanatory coherence* in that it imposes a structure on our view of behavior by relating contents to one another both hierarchically (e.g., the syllogisms of practical reasoning and their instances) and horizontally (e.g., if you believe that the beer is in the refrigerator, then you probably believe that the beer is cold). But not only do predictive utility and explanatory coherence justify viewing folk psychology as a theory; they also justify taking it to be a *good* theoretical framework for explaining human behavior, hence the Riches at Face Value Thesis.

Intuitively, the explanatory depth of folk psychology, its counterfactual rigor, seems *due* partly to its use of the notion of content. We behave as we do *because* of the content of our beliefs and desires: If these contents had been different, then our behaviors would have been different. Jane goes to the *refrigerator,* rather than the closet, because of the content of her belief about the location of golden throat charmers. Had she believed that golden throat charmers were located in the closet instead, she would have gone to the *closet,* not the refrigerator. The different content in these two cases accounts for the different actions. The same is true of the content of desires and other folk psychological states. Putting this together with the previous point: Intentional folk psychological explanations of behavior are systematic and rigorous in a way that suggests that *they* specify real causal factors.

The Causal Irreducibility Thesis relies on a commonly invoked non-reductionist sentiment about causal explanation and provides reasons for accepting the Riches at Face Value Thesis that, in turn, appeal to a broader conception of causal explanation. The special sciences typically contain levels of explanation different from those that specify, in Elster's phrase 'the nuts and bolts, the cogs and wheels' (1985:5).[2] But why? A plausible partial reason is that explanation in many of the special sciences is *functional.* Typically, in functional explanations, *functional* and *implementational* levels of description are distinct. For sciences in which functional explanations are typical (such as evolutionary biology, geology, anthropology, and cognitive psychology), there *are* mechanisms that implement the resulting functional generalizations, but the levels at which many generalizations are pitched are not reducible to the levels at which the implementing mechanisms are described. The corresponding, more familiar onto-

2 Elster himself, although primarily concerned with explanation in the social sciences, is unlikely to be sympathetic to what I say here, as the following fuller quotation suggests: 'To explain is to provide a mechanism, to open up the black box and show the nuts and bolts, the cogs and wheels, the desires and beliefs that generate aggregate outcomes' (1985:5).

logical expression of this point is this: The properties specified at functional levels are *multiply realized* by the properties specified at implementational levels and so cannot be reductively type identified with those properties.

The Causal Irreducibility Thesis further articulates the non-reductive conception of causal explanation introduced in Chapter 5, according to which instantiating explanations are, in some cases, *merely instantiating explanations*. Although instantiating explanations typically provide more causal details than do corresponding higher-level explanations, in *merely* instantiating explanations that detail is not crucial to a broader understanding of the phenomenon being explained. Consider the biological generalizations that highly specialized species tend to extinction in periods of ecological catastrophe, and that the closer species are to one another in phylogeny, the more similar they are genetically. It is true that the investigation of particular cases that fall under these generalizations provides causal detail that supplements our understanding of the natural world. We find out more about what sorts of creatures the generalizations do and do not apply to and why. In one sense, then, such details give us a more complete understanding of the phenomenon of extinction and the nature of phylogeny; to deny this would be to opt for ignorance or mysticism over knowledge. But it is *not* true that those details in themselves satisfy all of the *scientific* interests we have in the phenomena captured by the generalizations because the unity and regularity we seek in science emerge in the higher-level generalization itself, not in any of the instantiating explanations. Because there are cases in which we get generality and unity *only* by describing the phenomena at a level of description articulated in a higher-level science, it is implausible to see the lower-level sciences as having to provide an *explanatory* reductive base for higher-level sciences. And where explanation goes, ontology must follow.

We can thus understand why the Not Exhaustively Computational Thesis, as a claim about folk psychology in particular, is true. Folk psychological explanation is also functional in that it posits functional states, such as beliefs and desires, these being implemented in humans and other organisms in various neural states. The assumption that folk psychological states are computational does not imply that the generalizations and explanations in folk psychology must be non-intentional, for computationalism, if it is true of folk psychology at all, is a truth about the *implementation* of folk psychological states.

Viewing the functional–implementational distinction as the basis for a non-reductive view of causal explanation in the special sciences allows one to vindicate the causal integrity of the intentionality of folk psychology within the computational paradigm. (Note the use of 'allows one' here, for the Not Exhaustively Computational Thesis does not entail folk psychological computationalism. For those who reject folk psychological computationalism, the Not Exhaustively Computational Thesis *may* appear too weak or misleading, though that thesis is independent of the truth of folk psychological computationalism; see §6.)

The Causal Irreducibility Thesis, the general claim about the non-reductive nature of much causal explanation based on its functional nature, is perhaps the most controversial and central of the three theses. I shall consider two challenges to the thesis, the first to the premise that functional explanations are perfectly adequate as scientific explanations, the second to the inference from this premise to the denial of any form of explanatory or ontological reductionism. The dialectic between objection and response here turns, ultimately, on broader issues in the philosophy of the special sciences. Here I will state why I think that each of these challenges should be resisted by identifying my stance on some of these issues.

It has sometimes been thought that there is something prima facie suspect about functional explanation: For example, it does not readily conform to the deductive-nomological model of explanation (Hempel 1965:ch. 11), and it fails to specify mediating mechanisms (Elster 1985:ch. 1). The scientific integrity of disciplines that rely heavily on functional explanation has been subsequently called into question. I think that these views get things backwards: The prevalence of functional explanation in a wide range of sciences is strong (though defeasible) evidence that functional explanations are perfectly good scientific explanations, and this fact should be taken as a basis for rejecting views that have come to serve as a priori constraints on scientific explanation. Such putative constraints, which many sciences do not satisfy, have lost their appeal in the highest court; intuitions, no matter how strong, cannot replace scientific practice as an ultimate arbiter here (cf. Baker 1993b; Burge 1993). Philosophical intuition about the sciences cannot be placed above scientific practice itself.

Someone prepared to grant the premise about functional explanation might not only reject the inference from it to the denial of reductionism but might argue from it to the *acceptance* of reductionism, as Jaegwon Kim (1992, 1993) has. Suppose that functional explanations *are* required because the properties that they specify are multiply realized by properties specified by implementational levels. We need not reject explanatory or ontological reductionism, however; rather, we can and should insist on the necessity of (multiple) *local* reductions, taking the fact of multiple realizability to direct our insistence. To take a stock example, suppose that pain is multiply realized in different properties, $N_1 \ldots N_8$, specified at the neurophysiological level of description. What this implies is that our concept of pain designates a disunified phenomenon: There must be, at least in principle, reductions from instances of pain to each of the properties $N_1 \ldots N_8$. And, correspondingly, explanations that appeal to pain will be reducible to distinct explanations cast in terms of each of $N_1 \ldots N_8$. The one–many relation between functional and implementational levels of description implies the essential *disunity* of the phenomena that the functional level of description apparently unifies.

This second objection to a non-reductive conception of causal explanation appears not to place intuition above scientific practice. However, such an appearance is deceptive. For behind this argument for explanatory and ontological reductionism are powerful metaphysical principles, all of which focus on the intuition that physical phenomena have causal primacy and suffice for complete causal explanations; *none* of these principles derive from an examination of scientific practice. Kim has articulated a series of such principles as part of his challenge to the coherence of non-reductive materialism. For example, the *principle of causal individuation of kinds,* which Kim borrows from Fodor (1987:ch. 2), says that '[k]inds in science are individuated on the basis of causal powers; that is, objects and events fall under a kind, or share in a property, insofar as they have similar causal powers' (Kim 1992:17); and the *principle of causal inheritance* says that '[i]f M is instantiated on a given occasion by being realized by P, then the causal powers of *this instance of* M are identical with (perhaps, a subset of) the causal powers of P' (Kim 1993:208; see also 1992:18).

In Chapter 2, I argued that on the most natural understanding of 'causal powers', according to which the causal powers of $x$ supervene on the intrinsic physical properties of $x$, the first of these principles, the principle of the causal individuation of kinds, is simply false of the kinds in science. Attention to the distinction between the restricted and extended senses of 'causal powers' that I drew there also allows one to see why the *second* of these two principles, the principle of

169

causal inheritance, is either true but inconsequential or false. Assuming the restricted sense of 'causal powers' – which, from Kim's surrounding discussion is, I think, the intended sense – the principle of causal inheritance may be true; but this is of little interest in arguing for a reductive view of causal explanation since many of the causal properties used in scientific taxonomy and explanation are relational, and relational causal properties are causal powers only in the extended sense of 'causal powers'. By contrast, assuming the extended sense of 'causal powers' makes the principle of causal inheritance false. Consider an example of a relational property, such as *being very rich* (M). Suppose that, in a given case, this property is instantiated by a person, Tom, in virtue of instantiating the property of *having a lot of gold coins* (P). The *extended* causal powers of this instance of M can, nevertheless, differ from those of P: Tom's wealth might bring him recognition in his community, whereas his owning a lot of gold coins does not. More generally, instances of higher-level kinds may possess extended causal powers that instances of lower-level kinds do not.

Additionally, the principle of causal inheritance should be viewed with suspicion by someone defending the non-reductionist view I am advocating, since talk of the causal powers of instances is derivative from talk of the causal powers of kinds. Instances of two kinds, M and P, can have identical causal powers only if M and P are individuated by identical sets of causal powers. But if we suppose, with the non-reductive materialist, that M and P are distinct kinds, it is unlikely that this necessary condition is satisfied. This is so even in the case where M is *realized in* instances of P. For example, being a highly specialized organism (M) might be realized, in a particular case, by being a hedgehog (P), but highly specialized organisms and hedgehogs do not have identical intrinsic causal powers.

## 5. WHY NOT 'LAWS' AND 'MECHANISMS'?

The view I am advocating does not mention and does not depend on the distinction between laws and mechanisms; it is thus a view that those sceptical of the appeal to laws and mechanisms can readily accept. But why be so sceptical here? And wouldn't such scepticism, if justified, actually undermine the significance of a non-reductive view of causal explanation, making it little more than hand waving?

Much of the recent discussion of the question of whether there are folk psychological *laws* (Fodor 1987:ch. 1, 1989; Horgan and Tienson 1990; Lepore and Loewer 1987, 1989) reflects, in my view, a misplaced emphasis on the role of laws in scientific explanation. Proponents of the covering-law model of explanation hold that scientific explanations must be 'covered' by laws of nature: Laws are necessary for an explanation to be scientific. In its most clearly articulated form, the deductive-nomological model of explanation, a scientific explanation has the form of a deductive argument from some law or laws of nature and observable conditions to the *explanandum* (Hempel 1965:chh. 9–12). Paradigmatic examples of such laws are drawn from physics and chemistry and are typically quantitative: the Boyle–Charles law, Newton's laws of motion, the law of gravitational attraction, Coulomb's law, Snell's law of refraction, Ohm's law. Such laws allow one to calculate an already observed value for some variable (explanation), as well as predict values that can be tested by independent observation (confirmation). But if being covered by such laws is the mark of a scientific explanation, what of the special sciences? Explanations in the special sciences are covered by laws that only dubiously have observationally confirming predictions and mathematical precision. The 'laws' that cover explanations in the special sciences are, at best, the poor man's substitute for the real thing (see Miller 1987:ch. 1).

Debates over whether there are laws in the special sciences, over whether ceteris paribus laws are sufficient to ground scientific explanation, and over the status of folk psychological laws derive much of their interest from the question of how well the special sciences approximate physics and chemistry. But explanations in the variety of disciplines constituting the special sciences, including *natural* sciences, such as geology and evolutionary biology, are perfectly all right whether or not there are laws that cover them; this being so, the corresponding focus on *folk psychological* laws is misplaced (cf. Kitcher 1984:104; Millikan 1986).

To bring discussion of this point back to the distinction between laws and mechanisms, consider the demarcating roles that an appeal to this distinction plays. If we view the appeal to covering laws as serving to demarcate ideal scientific from less than ideal scientific explanation, then we can also take the appeal to mechanisms as a criterion for distinguishing real scientific laws from pseudo-scientific laws: Real (vs. pseudo) scientific laws are true in virtue of underlying mechanisms. But just as the existence of laws is not necessary for explanation in the special sciences, there need be nothing distinctly 'mechanical' about properties in virtue of which higher-level explanations hold in those sciences.

Consider the theory of continental drift, which holds that the continents were once part of one land mass and have drifted into their current positions over geological time; it explains facts about sea-floor landscapes, the formation of mountains, the distribution of fossils, geomagnetic reversal patterns in volcanic rocks, and the existence of seismic fault lines (see Giere 1988:ch. 8; Runcorn 1962; Wilson 1971). Underlying the phenomenon of continental drift – the causes of the phenomenon – are sea-floor spreading and convection currents in the Earth's mantle. Yet it would be a misleading simplification to suggest that there are two levels of description – one containing laws, the other specifying mechanisms – since the higher-level generalizations constituting the theory of continental drift themselves are mechanical relative to the facts they explain, and generalizations about the mechanisms of continental drift are law-like relative to other lower-level mechanisms. In short, there is a continuous hierarchy of levels of description in the theory of continental drift, each member of which informs us about the causal structure of the world.

The points that this example illustrate are quite general. In a wide range of sciences, one must rationally reconstruct the purported laws *themselves* in order to view existing, acceptable explanations as conforming to the covering-law model of explanation. Unlike many of the sub-disciplines in physics and chemistry, large areas of science are not structured around a set of laws (cf., however, Kitcher 1993:ch. 2). The mixture of home truths and acceptable generalizations one finds in scientific disciplines can often be reconstructed as laws, provided that one is prepared to loosen the concept of a law. Yet with an appropriately liberal notion of a law, one loses law-likeness as a criterion for demarcating sciences from non-sciences. A parallel claim is true of the appeal to mechanisms: To reconstruct the body of knowledge that underlies certain truths in a science as mechanical requires a broadening of the notion of a mechanism, a broadening that defeats the very point of such a reconstruction.

As well as the demarcating roles I have mentioned, appeals to laws and mechanisms also play dual *epistemic* roles. When laws 'cover' putative explanations, there is a sort of guarantee that those explanations identify real causal factors – real because they feature in laws of nature. And when we can cash out putative laws of nature by speci-fying an underlying mechanism (e.g., Mendel's laws in terms of underlying genetic mechanisms), there is a sort of guarantee that those laws quantify over real causal factors – real because they do the causal work. With these epistemic roles in mind, consider the claim that without an appeal to laws and mechanisms, invoking a distinction between higher and lower levels of explanation is just hand waving; and hand waving, no matter how vigorous (or how casual), doesn't solve any puzzle about causality and intentionality. One may well parody my defence as follows: 'You might think that there is a problem about how attributions of *supernatural* properties to persons, such as being a witch or being possessed by the devil, could play any role in causal explanations in a materialistic universe. But there's no problem here, since supernatural properties are specified at a higher level of description, whereas natural properties are specified at a lower level of description.' This is *not* an acceptable defence of the supernatural. Some account of the relation between different levels of explanation is needed, and at least the laws–mechanisms distinction provides us with that much: The relationship between the properties featuring in laws and those in virtue of which the instantiating mech-anisms operate guarantees that such laws describe relations between real causal factors.

What it seems is wanted here is epistemic security guaranteed in an a priori manner; we want (at least) necessary conditions on explana-tion that we can specify a priori, and that will ensure that explanations satisfying such conditions tell us something about how the world really is. I do not believe that there are any such conditions, or that there need be in order to offer a non-reductionist, realist view of scientific explanation. Moreover, the distinction between laws and mechanisms seems to play such a role only if one fudges on what counts as a law or a mechanism. To return to the earlier parodic example, there aren't any supernatural properties (or at least not those cited), and so acceptable causal explanations should not refer to them. But arguments for this conclusion need to be a posteriori, not a priori.

I return now to each of our three initial questions about computa-tionalism, individualism, and narrow content, beginning with the first: How is folk psychology related to computationalism in psy-chology?

## 6. FOLK PSYCHOLOGY AND COMPUTATIONALISM

Someone adopting the view of the place of folk psychology I have articulated could reject the idea that the appropriate implementing level of description for folk psychological states is computational. There are at least two ways in which one might plausibly do so, and I shall sketch each in detail sufficient to convey its plausibility. These alternatives highlight my view as an option for those (e.g., Searle 1980; 1992:chh. 9, 10) sceptical of folk psychological computationalism.

First, one could be cautiously agnostic about folk psychological computationalism. The sort of computationalism that is part of the language of thought hypothesis is a *possible* account of how folk psychological states are causally relevant. But one should not hold that the *truth* of folk psychological generalizations requires this sort of computationalism (see Horgan and Graham 1991). Computationalism might explain why large parts of folk psychology state truths, but we hold these truths on solid enough evidential grounds that, even were computationalism false, we would have little reason to doubt *their* veracity. This view is motivated by the conjunction of a robust commitment to the approximate truth of folk psychology, a less than robust commitment to the approximate truth of the language of thought hypothesis, and some version of the following conservative epistemological principle: The rational acceptance of theories or explanatory frameworks that we have extremely good reason to accept should not depend on views that we do not have extremely good reason to accept.

Second, one could reject folk psychological computationalism altogether by reminding oneself that not all of the various levels of description offered in the *neurosciences* are computational. The sciences to which the catch-all term 'the neurosciences' applies, which primarily inform us about the nature of the causal mechanisms governing cognition, vary themselves in whether they offer computational descriptions of mental states, structures, mechanisms, and transitions. Even if some psychological capacities are best explained at the computational level, there is little reason to think that *all* psychological capacities are to be so explained. Just as no one level describes psychological laws, so too there are multiple levels that describe psychological mechanisms. Perhaps there simply is no computational implementing level of description for folk psychology, and so folk psychological computationalism is just false.

So one need not accept computationalism about folk psychology in order to defend folk psychology along the lines I have suggested. Having said that, I will simply assume the truth of folk psychological computationalism for simplicity in my discussion of our second question: What is the significance of the place of folk psychology for individualism in psychology?

## 7. FOLK PSYCHOLOGY AND INDIVIDUALISM

One point about which Stich and Fodor agree is that computational descriptions of mental states account for the 'mechanics' of mental causation, including folk psychological causation, that is, they describe the ways in which mental processes operate. But because of the many levels of description at which explanations in a discipline are pitched, *even if* folk psychological states are implemented in mechanisms that have a computational description, Fodor is right (although for the wrong reasons) to insist further that this does nothing to impugn intentional folk explanations. The reconciliation of content and computation that I have offered would seem to stand or fall *whether that content is narrow or wide*. Thus, if the defence *does* explain how one can have both a computational and an intentional psychology, then it also explains how one can have both a computational and a *wide* psychology. This implies that even were one to think that folk psychology as it is utilizes both narrow and wide content, one could not appeal to the non-reductive conception of causal explanation selectively so as to explain why *only* narrow content is causally kosher. A conservative use of our defence, one that attempts to employ it within an individualistic framework, requires independent motivation.

This also points to a way in which individualists who are defenders of folk psychology are mistaken. The very reason for thinking that folk psychology is both causal and semantic is also a reason why one should doubt that individualism is a general constraint on psychological taxonomy and explanation. Individualists make precisely the same mistake that Stich makes about computationalism: They make a general claim about the nature of psychological taxonomy and explanation on the basis of a claim that is true of (at best) only *part of* psychology or some particular aspect of it. Let me elaborate.

175

Stich (1983) defends an individualistic view of psychology that is cautiously eliminativist about appeals to content in psychology. Some of Stich's arguments for his eliminativism concern what he views as intrinsic features of our practices of belief attribution: Such attributions are vague, context sensitive, and observer relative, which, in Stich's view, calls into question the suitability of such attributions for cognitive science. But Stich also argues for his eliminativism about content on the basis of his endorsement of the syntactic theory of mind *and* the claim that that theory leaves no explanatory role for intentional explanations to fill. I have rejected the second of these claims in advocating the Not Exhaustively Computational Thesis. And just as folk psychology is not exhaustively computational, neither is it exhaustively individualistic, even if it is in part individualistic.

Thus the view of the place of folk psychology defended here gives us further reason to reject individualism as a constraint on psychological taxonomy and explanation. Our third question is: What is the proper role of the notion of narrow content in folk psychology?

## 8. FOLK PSYCHOLOGY AND NARROW CONTENT

The compatibilist position mentioned in §2 attempts to diffuse the prima facie conflict between folk psychology and individualism by appeal to a concept of *narrow content*. In discussing such compatibilism here, I shall reconsider the correlation thesis defence of folk psychology. In §3, I argued that a strong reading of the correlation thesis, according to which there are law-like relations between a mental state's semantic and syntactic properties, made that thesis false, and that any weaker reading wouldn't show how semantic properties are causally relevant. However, the strong version of the correlation thesis is false only of the relation between *wide* content and syntax; it is true of the relation between *narrow* content and syntax. If one can also adequately explain the relation between narrow content and wide content, then the endorsement of this version of the correlation thesis could be part of a defence of folk psychology, one that does not rely on a perhaps contentious, non-reductive view of causal explanation.

I am sceptical about such defences of folk psychology because of the *dual* role that narrow content must play in them. First, narrow content must satisfy the strong form of the correlation thesis (for even wide content satisfies its weak form) and so supervene on the intrinsic physical properties of the individual. Second, in order to form part of a defence of folk psychology, narrow content must bear some appropriate relation to wide propositional content. There is an inherent tension between these two requirements, one deriving from the two notions that compose the concept of narrow content; 'narrow' and 'content' pull the concept in incompatible directions. Narrow or individualistic psychology taxonomizes the sensory inputs, mental states, and behaviors of physically identical individuals in the same way, no matter how different their environments. The ordinary notion of the content of a mental or linguistic sentence token is at least the *truth conditions* of that sentence (see Boghossian 1990), conditions that are not individualistic. Precisely because our ordinary, intuitive notion of content is deeply tied to notions such as reference and truth conditions, abstraction from the notion of wide content to a notion of narrow content is inherently problematic, for it requires abstracting from the very thing that makes a concept a concept of *content*. Put more forcefully, there is more than a tension in an explanation's being narrow and its being intentional; folk psychological content is *essentially relational,* and so 'narrow content' is an oxymoron. (Or, in the Australian idiom, narrow content is *Clayton's content:* the content you have when you're not having content.)

Does this claim about the essentially relational nature of the concept of content or intentionality beg the question against a proponent of narrow content who wishes to offer a correlation thesis–styled defence of folk psychology? The first point to note is that the appeal to essential relationality is not ad hoc. There is nothing mysterious about concepts that are relational of their nature, such that to abstract from those essential relations is to abstract away from the concept altogether. The mystery here is no greater if we consider *taxonomic* and *explanatory* concepts in science. As I said in Chapter 2, the concepts of planet and species are essentially relational but nonetheless taxonomic in particular sciences; other such essentially relational concepts include continent, ocean, unemployed person, capitalist, and highly specialized organism. There is a sense in which my claim *about intentionality* in particular is question-begging, for this claim will be (and ought to be) rejected by the opponent I envisage. I am articulating a difficulty facing any concept of narrow content, a difficulty I think irresolvable. An existence proof showing that I am mistaken would be an account of narrow content that resolved the putative tension between being narrow and being intentional.

Frank Jackson and Philip Pettit (1993) have recently proposed a view of narrow content that purports to avoid this sort of tension. Their view has three desirable features: It is not part of an overall individualistic view of psychology, and so does not rely on accepting individualism as a constraint on the cognitive sciences; it is not revisionist about folk psychology, and so does not make a reconstructive proposal about explanatory practice; and it identifies a *truth-conditional* notion of narrow content, and so avoids worries that its 'narrow content' is only Clayton's content. With such features, it can be seen as a good dialectical response to my strong claim that 'narrow content' is oxymoronic.

Jackson and Pettit begin with the uncontroversial claims that folk psychology provides a way of identifying patterns in behavior, and that it contains a notion of content that allows us to predict an individual's behavior. They call this content *predictive* content: It is 'the sets of possibilities associated with beliefs and desires' (Jackson and Pettit 1993:269). Predictive content is specified by a 'huge raft of subjunctive conditionals of the form $C_i \rightarrow B_i$,' (p. 273), linking circumstances to behaviors. For example, when Jane is about to go to the refrigerator because she believes it contains golden throat charmers, there is a raft of conditionals true of her: Were the refrigerator to contain no golden throat charmers, Jane would behave differently; were there golden throat charmers at some more convenient place, Jane would go there instead; and so on. The metaphor of a raft of subjunctive conditionals illuminates two aspects of our folk psychological attributions: They explain *patterns* of behavior (a *raft*) and to that extent are holistic, and they imply an interconnected series of links between actual and possible circumstances and behavior (of *subjunctive conditionals;* cf. White 1991:61). As Jackson and Pettit point out, we have access to only a part of this huge raft in making our ascriptions of content (pp. 273–4), and content so ascribed might be indeterminate (pp. 274–5).

The metaphor of a raft of conditionals not only conveys something about the *structure* of the behavioral regularities true of one when one has particular beliefs and desires; it also allows us to see why Jackson and Pettit think that (some) predictive content is a species of *narrow content*. Predictive content is *content* because it is truth-evaluable:

States with it are true just if the set of possibilities that the raft of conditionals specifies includes the way things actually are; and predictive content is *narrow* because the complete raft of conditionals must be shared by doppelgängers in the same possible world.

The narrowness referred to here is what Jackson and Pettit call '*intra-world* narrowness': It is content that an individual and any of her doppelgängers in a given possible world necessarily share. (The contrast here is with *inter-world* narrowness: content that an individual and any of her doppelgängers in *any* possible world necessarily share.) The proposal relaxes the putative inherent tension in the notion of narrow content by claiming that one can have truth-conditional content without having to explain the connection between narrow content and wide content; predictive content is intentional, it has 'aboutness', in and of itself. The crucial question would seem to be this: *Must* the complete raft of conditionals that determines a set of possibilities (and so is truth conditional) be shared by doppelgängers in the same possible world (and so be intra-world narrow)? Only if this is so is predictive content both truth conditional and narrow.

It seems, however, that the answer to this question is 'No'; despite Jackson and Pettit's own claim, predictive content is *not* intra-world narrow. This is because at least the antecedents of some (if not all) of these conditionals must refer to other mental states, and *some* of these mental states are, by Jackson and Pettit's own admission, wide. Even if some of the subjunctives that are part of our folk psychology are purely behavioral in that both the circumstances specified in the antecedent and the behaviors specified in the consequent can be linked together without further reference to mental states, many of these subjunctives are not, at least if they are part of folk psychology as it is. But since the *complete* raft of conditionals for any individual will refer to some mental states that are wide, it is inevitable that the complete rafts for *any* two individuals, even doppelgängers in the same possible world, will differ. Thus the truth-conditional content that such rafts specify is not intra-world narrow.

Consider the subjunctive conditionals true of Jane when she goes to the refrigerator because she wants a golden throat charmer. Although some of these conditionals *may* be purely behavioral, linking circumstance to behavior without mentioning any mental states, many of these do – indeed, must – mention mental states, *wide* mental states. Were Jane to *believe* that the refrigerator was empty, she would behave differently; were Jane to *believe* that there are golden throat charmers at some more convenient place, she would go there instead. The subjunctive conditionals that the folk are committed to typically contain an implicit reference to other mental states, many of which are wide. To put the point another way, the raft of subjunctive conditionals contains at least an implicit reference to the web of mental states that a subject instantiates. Jackson and Pettit have identified a notion of content that is intra-world narrow only if *all* of these states are narrow states. This, in turn, would require the truth of a wide-ranging revisionist thesis about folk psychological content, one that would give Jackson and Pettit's proposal the radical (and controversial) edge that they claim it lacks.

It is true, as Jackson and Pettit say (1993:275–6), that a doppelgänger who *replaces* a given individual will behave in the same way as that individual would behave. But this is a very special case, one concerning the behavior of two individuals who, *ex hypothesi,* are identical both in their intrinsic physical properties *and* in their relational properties: They can differ at most in their historical properties. Yet this is not true of doppelgängers in the same possible world in general. And the *actual* relations that individuals enter into (or simply find themselves in) determine the content of some of their folk psychological states. To take one of Jackson and Pettit's examples (pp. 277–8), Fred, who knows Mary, moves towards her, and had Fred's twin been where Fred was, he too would have moved towards Mary. Yet this does nothing to assure us that Fred's twin *must* have beliefs and desires *about Mary* since Fred, if he is unfortunate, might just be a brain in a vat; for the same reason, it does little to assure us that Fred and every one of his twins have beliefs and desires with the same predictive content. In short, even doppelgängers in the same possible world need not share the same complete raft of subjunctive conditionals, since those rafts must still reflect the doppelgängers' wide folk psychological states, which may differ.

If the view articulated in §4 and §5 is defensible, then one does not need to appeal to narrow content to defend the integrity of folk psychology. And if my claim in this section is right, such an appeal *cannot* allow one to offer a successful defence of folk psychology.

## 9. DENNETT'S INSTRUMENTALISM

Finally, I turn to explain the respects in which the view of the place of folk psychology defended here differs from Dennett's well-known views. Dennett (1978a, 1981a, 1981b) has distinguished three stances one might adopt towards a complex device or organism in explaining its behavior: the *physical* stance, the *design* stance, and the *intentional* stance. In adopting the design stance in explaining behavior – what is primarily done in the cognitive sciences – one ignores the details of physical realization and instead focusses on the design features, which tell you not only what the individual (or a part of the individual) is supposed to do but, in part, *how* she is supposed to do this. But there is another strategy that we employ in explaining behavior, the intentional stance, which Dennett summarizes as follows:

> To a first approximation, the intentional strategy consists of treating the object whose behavior you want to predict as a rational agent with beliefs and desires and other mental states exhibiting what Brentano and others call *intentionality*. . . . [A]ny object – or as I shall say, any *system* – whose behavior is well predicted by this strategy is in the fullest sense of the word a believer. *What it is* to be a true believer is to be an *intentional system,* a system whose behavior is reliably and voluminously predictable via the intentional strategy. (1981a:15)

The view expressed in the final sentence here is often taken to manifest Dennett's instrumentalism about folk psychology. If all there is to being the subject of the propositional attitudes is having your behavior systematically predicted through the positing of folk psychological states, then belief and desire *just are* instruments we use for predicting behavior. Not only are they not relations between an individual and tokens in her language of thought, they are not any type of internal state of the individual at all; rather, they are merely the theorist's fictions.

Like those who accept the language of thought hypothesis, Dennett takes computationalism to provide a basic explanatory framework for understanding mental causation (see Dennett 1981b:61). In adopting the design stance in the cognitive sciences, we view the brain as a computational engine. *Folk* psychology is not defended by appealing directly to computationalism, however, since the design and intentional stances are levels of description that are, respectively, causal and rationalizing.

One should separate what is right in Dennett's view of folk psychology from the instrumentalist strain in his thinking about content. Consider a scenario that Dennett imagines:

> Suppose for the sake of drama, that it turns out that the sub-personal cognitive psychology of some people turns out to be dramatically different

from that of others. One can imagine the newspaper headlines: 'Scientists Prove Most Left-handers Incapable of Belief' or 'Startling Discovery – Diabetics Have No Desires.' But this is not what we would say, no matter how the science turns out. (1987:234–5; cf. Horgan and Graham 1991)

The point that Dennett is making here is correct, and identifies one way in which the debate about folk psychology between capital-R Realists (like Fodor) and die-hard eliminativists (like the Churchlands) has been staked out on a false presupposition.

Empirical details about either the computational or neurophysiological structures that we instantiate are simply too far removed from folk psychology to provide evidence one way or the other about the truth of ascriptions of content. Were one to open up the head and *find* tokens inscribed in mentalese neatly located in the 'belief box' and 'desire box', which were activated in the appropriate ways in practical reasoning, deliberation, behavior, and so on, then not only would folk psychology be vindicated but so too would the language of thought conception of it. But one wants some reason to think that this is more than a bare possibility and the language of thought view simply a graphic way of thinking of the propositional attitudes. The evidence about the structure of mental processing that we actually have is at best distantly related to conclusions about the approximate truth of *folk* psychological explanations of behavior (see also §6).

We might think of this point implicit in Dennett's view as its *negative* component; accepting it does not commit one to the *positive* streak of instrumentalism about mental content that Dennett espouses, at least in places (see Dennett 1987:69–81). Just as the dilemma between Realism and eliminativism about the propositional attitudes is based on a mistaken view about the relation between empirical research and folk psychology, the choice between Realism and instrumentalism about folk psychology is a choice between extreme views (cf. Peacocke 1983:ch. 8), views that presume a conception of causal explanation in psychology that is unduly restrictive. Capital-R Realists think that the language of thought conception of folk psychology is required to understand folk psychological explanation as a form of causal explanation. Dennett, in separating the intentional stance from the design stance, claims that folk psychology posits entities, *abstracta,* different in kind from the causal, theoretical entities posited in design stance theories. For Dennett, intentional systems explanation is idealized, rationalistic explanation, not ordinary causal explanation: Folk psychology, or the appropriately modified version of it that Dennett calls 'pure intentional system theory' (1981b:57), explains behavior instrumentally, not causally.

Each of these alternatives presupposes a restrictive conception of causal explanation. Once one recognizes that not all causal explanation is cast at a level of description that is mechanistic, there is no need to accept *any sort* of instrumentalism in refusing to accept the language of thought conception; to continue with Fodor's vivid (even if misleading) terminology, folk psychological explanation is *law-level* explanation, not *mechanism-level* explanation. On the broad, non-reductive conception of causal explanation that I have been developing in the chapters in Part II, folk psychology is not to be contrasted with other forms of causal explanation; the entities it posits, beliefs and desires, are not merely the theorist's fictions and so different in ontological kind from the entities posited by other forms of causal explanation.

## 10. CONCLUSION

The place of folk psychology is best approached by understanding the character of folk psychological explanations. Folk psychological explanations constitute the most epistemologically solid grasp on folk psychology that we have, and I have focussed on such explanations in an attempt to understand problems facing folk psychology that have a decidedly metaphysical ring to them. Hence I am (unashamedly) using epistemology as a guide to metaphysics, both methodologically and substantively; methodologically, because I take a focus on explanation to *guide* us on metaphysical questions, and substantively because such a focus guides our *metaphysical views*. A well-known pattern of inference is that of *inference to the best explanation,* being an inference from the best of a number of explanations to the *truth* of that explanation. Let me propose a corresponding pattern of inference, *inference to the best ontology,* being an inference from the best understanding of our explanations of a given phenomenon to the adequacy of the ontology that those explanations posit.

I have argued that the best understanding of our folk psychological explanations of human behavior is one that construes them as non-reductive, functional, causal explanations, positing entities such as beliefs and desires. Folk psychology does not posit entities, beliefs and desires, different in ontological kind from the entities posited by other forms of causal explanation; in particular, beliefs and desires are not just the theorist's fictions or merely interpretational objects. Like the rest of psychology, folk psychology describes the internal states that cause behavior at a different level than does physics. What's so puzzling about that?

# Part III

*The case against individualism*

# 8

## The causal depth and theoretical appropriateness of wide psychology

Although the debate over individualism has attended to empirical research in psychology, it has not focussed explicitly on the criteria for evaluating causal explanations. In this chapter I introduce two related aspects to explanatory power, *causal depth* and *theoretical appropriateness*, and offer the following argument against individualism. We do and should, ceteris paribus, prefer causal explanations that exhibit these explanatory virtues. When other things *are* equal, wide psychological explanations of behavior are sometimes causally deeper and more theoretically appropriate than their narrow rivals. Therefore, in at least some cases, we should reject narrow explanations in favor of wide explanations of behavior because of the latter's greater explanatory power.

Some of the details of this argument against individualism also provide reasons for rejecting *neuroscientific* explanations in favor of *intentional* explanations of behavior; the argument is thus secondarily directed at eliminative materialism, particularly versions that concentrate on our folk psychology (P. M. Churchland 1981; P. S. Churchland 1986; Ramsey, Stich, and Garon 1991). Individualists and eliminativists both ascribe primacy to intrinsic physical properties in scientific explanation, and so focus on the issue of how a properly scientific psychology is to be integrated with the developing neurosciences and computer science. This chapter aims to show why this view and the focus it engenders should be rejected.

The complete argument is developed in four stages. First, I provide an account of the explanatory virtues of causal depth and theoretical appropriateness (§1). Second, I examine a class of wide explanations of behavior that clearly possess these explanatory virtues (§2). Although these are not psychological but *evolutionary* explanations, their depth and appropriateness are due to their wide functional nature. Third, I sketch the argument as applied to the case of psychology (§3). Fourth, I defend its premises (§4, §5).

## 1. EXPLANATORY POWER: CAUSAL DEPTH AND THEORETICAL APPROPRIATENESS

Both whole theories and particular explanations can vary in their explanatory power; I focus on explanations rather than theories. Two aspects of explanatory power are causal depth and theoretical appropriateness.

Consider, first, the notion of causal depth. The idea that an explanation must have causal depth (and therefore that better explanations identify causally deeper factors than their rivals) is the idea that causes should be *resilient* across slight counterfactual changes. In circumstances slightly different from the actual circumstances, the causes identified by a causally deep explanation still exist, and the explanation remains true. In the language of possible worlds, a causally deep explanation holds not only in the actual world but also in nearby possible worlds. *Counterfactually rigorous* explanations thus have a degree of necessity indicated by their causal depth. We can think of causal depth as a *vertical* dimension to explanatory power, as a relation between a given explanation and the phenomena explained.

An explanation with causal depth must possess an *implicitly general scope*. A causally deep explanation applies not just to the particular phenomenon being explained but also to phenomena of the same *type* or *kind:* An explanation should be true of a type of entity, process, or event if it really explains *why* an entity or phenomenon came about or did what it did. Explanations with a more extensive scope within the domain being explained are causally deeper explanations. Yet the relative depth of two explanations cannot be determined simply by counting the number of instances to which each applies in the actual world, assigning greater depth to the explanation with the higher number, since some properties and kinds instantiated by only a few entities in the actual world might feature in explanations with a greater scope once one considers both the actual *and* nearby possible worlds. Since uninstantiated kinds are the limiting case of kinds having few instances in the actual world, focussing on the implicitly general scope of an explanation as a part of its causal depth makes it intelligible how causally deep explanations might quantify over uninstantiated kinds. (And if the entities that feature in *idealized* explanations can be thought of as uninstantiated kinds, then we have the beginnings of an account of how such explanations can have causal depth, even though they are, strictly speaking, false.)

Note that implicit generality cannot be all there is to causal depth, since one can gain generality simply by decreasing the amount of information provided in one's *explanans* (e.g., by adding in disjuncts) or by formulating predicates that by stipulation apply to many entities; such ways of making an explanation more general would not give one a causally deeper explanation. Also, in saying that causally deep explanations are implicitly general, I stop short of claiming that deep explanations must be covered by laws. As I said in Chapter 7, I do not think that laws play the central role in science and scientific explanation that has often been ascribed to them. The requirement that explanations have causal depth can be seen as the grain of truth in the regularity theory of causation, according to which singular causal statements must be covered by laws if they are to be genuinely explanatory. Unlike being covered by a law, having causal depth is something an explanation can possess in degrees, and in explanations for which there *are* covering laws, we can understand their explanatory power in terms of the notion of causal depth.

Alan Garfinkel (1981:ch. 2) and Richard Miller (1987:98–104) have both discussed a notion of causal depth; Jackson and Pettit (1990a, 1990b) also rely on this notion in developing their account of 'program explanation'. Consider an example of Jackson and Pettit's. A glass container breaks because the liquid it contains is heated. Although there is a sense in which it breaks because a particular molecule or group of molecules strikes the side of the container, the causal explanation of the breakage in terms of heating is causally deeper, for given the application of heat, it is more or less inevitable that *some* particular molecule or group of molecules will cause the container to break. Thus, even had those molecules that actually caused the breakage not done so – say, because the container was slightly disturbed during heating, so that those molecules were displaced – a breakage would still have occurred. The explanation in terms of the heating of the liquid *programs* for a microphysical explanation. Program explanations are causally deep explanations, although they are not themselves microphysical explanations.

In Garfinkel's vivid terminology, an explanation lacking causal depth is *hyperconcrete*. Garfinkel argues that for explanatory purposes it is often more illuminating to ignore the details provided by microstructural explanations in order to draw out regularities in the phenomena being explained. This point is fairly intuitive when considering explanations in the social sciences, since the object of explanation in the social sciences is often a process or phenomenon that is *merely instantiated* in the actions of particular individuals; such explanations cite only the properties, states, and entities that happen to instantiate some process, where those particular realizers are not essential to the process being explained.

Let us turn now to *theoretical appropriateness*. An explanation is theoretically appropriate when it provides a natural (e.g., non-disjunctive) account of a phenomenon at a level of explanation matching the level at which that phenomenon is characterized. Consider some intuitive cases of theoretical *in*appropriateness. Appealing to a complex change in the quantum state of every sub-atomic particle in a person's body is not the basis for a theoretically appropriate explanation of why a person subsequently makes one decision rather than another, even though such an appeal may accurately identify causal antecedents of that person's decision. Explaining why the proportion of women in graduate programs in philosophy remains fairly small requires explanations drawn from history, sociology, and gender studies, rather than decision theory, even though we might suppose that decision-theoretic explanations tell us why the numbers are as they are. If the intuitive idea that explanations must range over kinds is a way in which the notion of causal depth functions in our commonsense thinking about explanation, then the claim that there are more kinds than those specified by basic physics expresses one way in which our intuitive thinking about explanation is committed to the notion of theoretical appropriateness.

Take Putnam's (1973) well-known example of the explanation of why a square peg goes through a slightly larger square hole, but not through a round hole with a diameter equal to the square hole's width. It is more appropriate to explain this fact in terms of rigidity, size, and geometry than to do so in terms of the microphysical properties of the objects involved. Both types of explanation may make the same predictions about what will happen when you try to put the square peg through the round hole, and the microphysical explanation will provide a more precise specification of what will happen. Nevertheless, the geometric explanation is more theoretically appropriate in this case (cf. Garfinkel 1981:59–61). If causal depth is a vertical dimension to explanatory power, then theoretical appropriateness is a *horizontal* dimension: It concerns the relationship not between explanation and phenomena, but between *explanans* and *explanandum* within the structure of an explanation.

Although Garfinkel and Putnam aim to identify a weakness in reductionist explanations in the social sciences, the application of these concepts is in principle orthogonal to issues concerning reductionism: Causal depth and theoretical appropriateness are features that *any* type of explanation might possess or fail to possess. Consider theoretical appropriateness. Nothing suggests that *micro*structural explanations could not be more theoretically appropriate than their macrostructural counterparts; the same is true more generally of lower-level and higher-level explanations. There are two faces to theoretical inappropriateness, only one of which is emphasized by those espousing a global anti-reductionism about explanation. True to the a posteriori spirit in which the concept of theoretical appropriateness (as well as that of causal depth) has been introduced here, one should view both general reductionist *and* general anti-reductionist views of explanation with some suspicion. Global anti-reductionism thus differs from the *non*-reductionist view of causal explanation defended in Part II.

One can understand the two faces of inappropriateness in terms of an analogy. Corresponding to the two ways in which an image produced by a lens can distort how an object really is, that is, by being either too acute or too obtuse, explanations can suffer from either a certain sort of theoretical myopia – a criticism directed primarily at microstructural explanations – *or* by obscuring features that are shared at some lower level of description – a criticism directed at macrostructural explanations. The same general point holds true of causal depth: Many of our causally deepest explanations *are* microphysical explanations. Like simplicity, precision, and degree of unifying promise as applied to both general theories and particular explanations, causal depth and theoretical appropriateness are pragmatic and context-sensitive constraints on explanation whose content is determined by the details of particular cases.

There are two final points worth making about this pair of notions. First, they provide *defeasible* criteria for evaluating causal explanations. All things considered, an explanation with less causal depth might be a better explanation; likewise for theoretical appropriateness. These criteria may pull in different directions in particular cases, and an overall comparison of two or more competing theories will sometimes involve judgments about the relative importance of each of these criteria. Second, they *tend to* be coinstantiated by the very same explanations. For instance, take Miller's (1987:99) example of the explanation of the Nazis' rise to power in terms of the functional interests of big business, which is causally deeper than an explanation of that rise to power in terms of individual decisions and actions. The functional explanation is also more theoretically appropriate than the narrative explanation in that the causal factors it describes better match the macrosocial phenomenon being explained than do those mentioned in the narrative explanation (cf. also Putnam's square peg example). Were one interested in understanding why the Nazis rose to power *through Hitler's actions,* then the *narrative* explanation would be more theoretically appropriate than the functional explanation; but for such an *explanandum,* the functional explanation would also lack the causal depth that the narrative explanation has. In each of these cases, causal depth and theoretical appropriateness support the same judgment about which of two competing explanations is to be preferred. I shall not attempt here to answer the question of *why* this is true.

## 2. EVOLUTIONARY EXPLANATIONS OF BEHAVIOR

Although the distinction between narrow and wide explanations of behavior derives from the distinction between narrow and wide construals of mental states, and so applies in the first instance to *psychological* explanations of behavior, there is no reason why the distinction should not apply to other types of explanations of cognitive behavior. An explanation of behavior is *narrow* just if it taxonomizes the causes of behavior by reference only to properties that supervene on the intrinsic physical states of the individual whose behavior is being explained; it is *wide* otherwise. By definition, wide explanations violate individualism.

Evolutionary explanations for cognitive behavior explain the existence of a given type of behavior by reference to its evolution by natural selection. Behaviors can be thought of as *phenotypes* that animals, including human beings, possess and can be the object of evolution by natural selection. Evolutionary explanations exist for a broad range of animal behaviors, including the fleeing behavior of gazelles, the 'digging' and 'entering' behaviors of certain species of solitary wasps, the cooperative mimicry behavior of cicadas, the hygienic behavior of honeybees, brood parasitism in cuckoos, and kin preference in monkeys (see Dawkins 1982, 1986, 1989).

Consider a request for an evolutionary explanation of a particular cognitive behavior, say, the fleeing behavior of gazelles when they detect the presence of a predator: Why do gazelles flee from lions? Some evolutionary explanations cite the *selection pressures* that caused that behavior to develop over a period of evolutionary time; they refer to how the phenotypes of the current genetic and biochemical causes of the behavior were selected. Explanations citing the selection pressures causally responsible for a given behavior are wide since selection pressures − such as the relative abundance of competing species, the presence of particular environmental toxins, and the existing physical condition of members of the species − do not supervene on the intrinsic physical properties of individuals. Selection pressures are not intrinsic causal *powers* that individuals instantiate.

Selection pressures are *causally deep* determinants of at least some behaviors. For example, had gazelles not been faced with the selection pressures imposed by predators, the species would not have developed its fleeing behavior. Selection pressures must operate causally through a variety of local causal factors (e.g., the transmission of genes and their complexes), for, as in the psychological case, there is no evolutionary action at a distance. Yet one ought not to suppose that the best causal evolutionary explanations of behavioral patterns can only make reference to these causal factors as these would be typed by an individualist. Many disciplines and sub-disciplines in the biological sciences are not concerned with identifying causal powers, and even disciplines that *are* concerned with identifying the local causes of behavior do not necessarily individuate those causes narrowly. There is nothing wrong with macroevolutionary explanations for behavior. My main point, however, is not the defensive one that wide evolutionary explanations of behavior are perfectly acceptable within the evolutionary sciences. Rather, wide explanations may be or be part of the deepest causal explanations that we have for particular behaviors *because* of their width.

Wide evolutionary explanations may also be more *theoretically appropriate* than narrow explanations of the same phenomena because many evolutionary sciences are interested in explaining behavior described with relative coarseness. Behavior is considered as *fleeing*, or as an organism's *camouflaging* itself, or as *imitating* another species. Precisely how an organism engages in behavior falling under one of these descriptions may vary greatly, even within a given species. Even were narrow explanations to account (in some sense) for the behavior so described, wide explanations would be more theoretically appropriate. To return to the lens metaphor introduced in §1, because evolutionary explanations cast in terms of selection pressures sharpen our focus on behavior described in this coarse way, they are to be preferred to narrow explanations.

One reason for the depth and appropriateness of wide evolutionary explanations derives from a point about the nature of selection. Species are often faced with problems requiring behavioral adaptation. Selection pressures sometimes *force* a solution to a particular survival problem in that had the local causal factors used to solve that problem not been available, the problem would have been solved in some other way: There is a multiplicity of ways in which a survival problem could be solved from which the actual solution is chosen or developed. We might call this the *implementational plasticity* of behavior. Given that some behavior is, in this sense, implementationally plastic, wide explanations will often have more causal depth than their narrow competitors. Also, since one cannot adequately characterize the *explanandum* in terms of the merely instantiating physical movements for such behaviors, explanations that are more theoretically appropriate will feature *explanantia* that are wide. Given implementational plasticity, explanations cast in terms of wide causal roles have a causal depth and theoretical appropriateness that explanations cast in terms of actual, local causal factors lack.

We can draw on Elliott Sober's (1984:ch. 3) distinction between the selection *of* objects and the selection *for* properties to see just why implementational plasticity favors wide rather than narrow evolutionary explanation. Sober claims that natural selection operates on properties or characteristics in an environment, not merely on the things that happen to have those properties. Properties are selected *for* the effects they have, and there is subsequently selection *of* objects instantiating those properties. Evolution selects *roles* rather than particular *occupants* of those roles, where a role is specified in terms of the behavioral output required to solve a given survival problem and the occupants of those roles are the particular ways in which those behaviors are instantiated. The description of the role behavior plays in natural selection is often wide, not narrow, as in our example of the fleeing of gazelles. When many different particular behaviors instantiate the properties or occupy the roles favored by natural selection, the fact that one rather than another such entity was selected is only a *shallow* causal fact about the process of selection; explanations citing such facts are *hyperconcrete*. Wide explanations cast in terms of the properties defining a role that a behavior plays are causally deeper.

Relatedly, the phenomenon of *convergent evolution* demands wide evolutionary explanations. Certain common phenotypes have evolved independently, with species converging on a common solution to a shared evolutionary problem. For example, eyes and eye-like structures have evolved independently in distantly related species many times. To take a behavioral pattern that has also evolved independently many times, consider the evolution of sociality with worker sterility (eusociality) in Hymenoptera, which has evolved independently at least eleven times (Dawkins 1989:ch. 10). Dawkins notes (1989:313–16) that naked mole rats also exhibit eusociality and might be considered the 'social insects' of the mammal world. Perhaps not surprisingly, the evolution of eusociality in mammals occurs in stable environmental circumstances like those of the eusocial Hymenoptera; eusocial insects and mammals share relational ecological properties. Wide evolutionary explanations are required to account for convergent evolution because organisms whose common behavioral phenotypes serve as the *explanandum* do not share relevant intrinsic physical properties. What allows one to explain their behavior in a unified way are common selection pressures.

Individualists might think these points about evolutionary explanations consistent with their views of taxonomy and explanation *in psychology*. I shall call *concessive individualism* the position that rejects individualism about evolutionary explanations while endorsing individualism in psychology. One reason for thinking concessive individualism to be a coherent, defensible position turns on the a posteriori character of causal depth and theoretical appropriateness. I have pointed to general features of the process of natural selection that imply that deep and appropriate evolutionary explanations will often be wide. But if my argument depends on features of the practice of evolutionary explanation, the depth and appropriateness of wide evolutionary explanations should have no real significance for *psychological* explanation.

This train of thought is one with which I have considerable sympathy, for I think that one needs to be wary about drawing substantive general conclusions about science of the basis of one's own enthusiasm for claims about a particular area of science. But concessive individualism is difficult to maintain; it is a view that, I shall argue in §6, is not defensible.

## 3. A STATEMENT OF THE ARGUMENT AGAINST INDIVIDUALISM

One reason causally deep and theoretically appropriate evolutionary explanations of behavior are often wide is that the forces of selection are usually, perhaps even exclusively, *external* to individuals. Since selection pressures are literally *outside* of the individual, there is nothing misleading about expressing the argument for the depth and appropriateness of wide evolutionary explanations in terms of the necessity of external causal factors. The parallel argument for the conclusion that wide *psychological* explanations of behavior are both causally deep and theoretically appropriate, however, *would* be misleadingly expressed in this way. We can explain why by drawing more explicitly on the discussion in Chapter 6.

In distinguishing between the *internal* and *intrinsic* conceptions of mental states in §5 of Chapter 6, I noted that the latter is more satisfactory than the former. On the internal conception, those denying individualism are seen to be claiming that non-local causal factors are required in psychological explanation. One inadequacy of the internal conception is that it suggests that one who denies individualism in psychology claims that much psychological explanation is not really about what is in the head; rather, psychology is the science of identifying the non-local, environmental causes of cognitive behavior. Were one to state my argument against individualism in psychology in terms of the internal conception of mental states, this might imply that I am employing the notions of causal depth and theoretical appropriateness to advocate behaviorism over cognitivism in psychology; it might also be taken to suggest that there is a tension between the criteria of causal depth and theoretical appropriateness. If only to avoid such misunderstandings, I state the argument against individualism in psychology in terms of the *descriptions* of internal mental states that psychology ought to seek, that is, in terms of the intrinsic conception of mental states.

Suppose that both narrow and wide descriptions of neurological states are parts of prima facie satisfactory but distinct psychological theories. The narrow descriptions could be either syntactic or 'nar-

196

rowly contentful', and they may or may not correspond in some systematic way to the wide descriptions. Call the theory embodying the narrow descriptions $N$ and the theory embodying the wide descriptions $W$. If $N$ describes mental states in such a way that the states it specifies vary significantly across individuals, and $W$ describes states that are more widely shared by individuals under various conditions, then, ceteris paribus, $W$ will refer to deeper causal factors than $N$, and so will constitute the basis for a deeper explanation of cognitive behavior than does $N$. Theory $N$ will have neither the implicitly general scope nor the counterfactual rigor of $W$. If $W$ introduces descriptions of the causal factors responsible for behavior that better match the level at which that behavior is to be described than those that $N$ introduces, then $W$ will be more theoretically appropriate than $N$.

The claims that require defence are that in at least some cases (1) wide specifications of the mental states of individuals are more counterfactually rigorous and have greater scope than the corresponding narrow specifications (causal depth), and (2) wide psychological explanations are pitched at a level that better fits the level at which behavior is to be described (theoretical appropriateness). If I am correct in thinking that there is little resistance to the corresponding conclusion about evolutionary explanations of behavior, then resistance to the conclusion in the psychological case derives from thinking that the premises of the argument, (1) and (2), are false.

For a parallel argument against eliminativism, replace 'wide' with 'intentional' and 'narrow' with 'neuroscientific'. Where appropriate, I shall comment on how this argument against individualism also counts against eliminativism and indicate points at which the arguments diverge in their details.

## 4. THEORETICAL APPROPRIATENESS IN PSYCHOLOGY

Consider, first, (2), my claim about theoretical appropriateness. Individualists claim that behavior should be described autonomously (Stich 1983:ch. 8), though they differ amongst themselves on whether this allows psychology to explain behavior described *intentionally*. Autonomous or narrow behavioral descriptions are individualistic: They abstract from historical and relational aspects of behavior so that the behavior they describe supervenes on the current internal physical state of the individual. This claim about behavior can be seen as a recognition of theoretical appropriateness as an aspect of explanatory power: The descriptions of mental causes must 'match' the descriptions of their behavioral effects in that both must be narrow.

The individualist agrees, then, that one should prefer the most theoretically appropriate descriptions of mental states, other things being equal. There is, however, a substantive disagreement about which behaviors *are* the most theoretically appropriate. I think that in at least some cases, wide psychological explanations are more theoretically appropriate than narrow explanations of behavior because they describe mental states in a way that more closely fits our conception of how behavior ought to be described for the purpose of psychological explanation. Psychology explains an agent's *actions,* and the individualist cannot provide an adequate conception of the notion of an action; not all characterizations of the behavioral *explananda* of psychological explanation are narrow descriptions (cf. Taylor 1964:chh. 3, 7).

Although we can state precisely what narrow behaviors are, even paradigmatic, uncontroversial examples of them so defined are difficult to provide. In part, this may be due to the disagreement between individualists about whether narrow descriptions of behavior and mental states are content-free (e.g., syntactic) or intentional. But this dispute to one side, there remain difficulties in fixing on clear cases of narrow behavior. Stich's own example (1983:167–70) of a narrow behavior, that of a robot 'performing a weld' (in contrast to 'performing its 1000th weld'), is not narrow, since although it abstracts from *some* historical and relational facts, it does not abstract from all such facts. Perhaps it is reasonable to expect difficulty in pointing to clear examples of narrow behavior using our ordinary language, and to think instead that descriptions of narrow behavior will be constructed *within* developing individualistic psychological theories; after all, a narrow psychology must differ in important ways from that of common sense.

Individualists and non-individualists should both grant that many wide behaviors warrant psychological explanation, just as many wide behaviors warrant *evolutionary* explanation. As the standard Twin Earth case shows, folk psychological descriptions of behavior are often, even typically, wide. In experimental psychology, particularly cognitive psychology, behavior is often treated as a dependent variable whose value is determined by variations in some independent variable and from which one draws inferences about the underlying mental causes of behavior. Standard types of behavioral paradigms that are incorporated into experimental design, such as preferential-looking, forced choice, and maze navigation paradigms, involve wide behaviors. The crucial questions are: (a) are such behaviors themselves constituted by behaviors that *are* narrow? and (b) is it these narrow descriptions of behavior that adequately characterize the *explanandum* of psychology?

One reason for a negative answer to (b) is that generalizations in psychology sometimes quantify over behaviors constituted by very different narrow behaviors. Consider a vivid example, the phenomenon usually referred to as 'latent learning', whereby an animal may navigate a maze in very different ways, such as running it and swimming it. There is a psychological generalization about the *navigation* of a maze, not simply the *running* of it. A common explanation of the behavior of running and swimming rats presupposes a level of psychological description according to which they are doing the very same thing; such a level of description is wide (cf. Fodor 1965:170). Even if we concede that every wide behavior requiring a psychological explanation is constituted by narrow behaviors, there are psychological generalizations that range over the wide descriptions of behavior; at least some *behavioral* kinds in psychology are wide. This being so, the most theoretically appropriate *psychological* kinds that explain these behaviors must also be wide.

An affirmative answer to (a) does not suffice to show the theoretical appropriateness of narrow descriptions of mental states. The reading of (a) on which both individualists and non-individualists can agree is this: Every wide behavior is constituted in part by some narrow behavior. Yet this reading of (a) tells us nothing about behavioral kinds *in psychology*. Recall from §2 the point that the behaviors of an organism explained by the evolutionary sciences were often described quite coarsely (as *fleeing* or as *camouflaging* itself), without regard to the particular movements in which the behavior is instantiated. This is not to say that there is no narrow description of these behaviors, only that, given the explanatory practice in these sciences as they have actually developed, explanations in terms of selection pressures are more theoretically appropriate for behavior described so coarsely. I suggest an analogous conclusion about *psychological* explanations of behavior; the explanatory interests developed within psychology require wide taxonomies of mental states and behavior.

Were the set of wide behaviors that require psychological explanation isomorphic to some set of narrow behaviors such that one could factor each member of the former set into a member of the latter, then we might have some type of vindication of individualism. Yet the claim that there is such an isomorphism is controversial and, I think, implausible (cf. evolutionary biology).

Consider *skills,* which often involve an individual's acting in the world; having a skill involves bodily know-how constitutively related to possession of the skill. Even when skills can be decomposed into constituent narrow behaviors that *are* the *explananda* of a narrow psychological theory, there are explanatory interests of cognitive psychology that transcend such narrow behaviors. For example, suppose that the skills that compose the ability to play the piano have narrow descriptions. There remain questions of psychological significance not addressed by the existence of such a decomposition: What is it about certain individuals that allows them to reach a level of expertise in their piano playing? Is the development of the skill of piano playing influenced by the development of other skills? Is there a critical period during which certain experiences dramatically influence one's capacity to develop the skill? What is the relationship between possession of the skill at a certain level and more general abilities? In attempting to answer such questions, psychologists taxonomize individuals *not* according to what narrow behaviors they engage in – for example, experts can be extremely diverse in this respect – but in accord with the types of *wide* behavior they exhibit. That the skill can be decomposed into constituent narrow behaviors is of only secondary interest from part of 'the' psychological point of view.

Cognitive behavior is not the only *explanandum* in psychology, which also aims to explain cognitive *capacities.* My defence of (2) can accommodate this, since cognitive capacities are often construed as wide capacities. For example, the capacity to construct a *depth map* (Arbib 1987) representing the depth of items in the visual field explains diverse cognitive processes and behaviors, such as those in human visual processing and prey acquisition behavior in amphibians, and is characterized 'in terms of its relations to the organism's environment and the organism's interaction, visual and motor, with that environment' (Garfield 1988:146). A theoretically appropriate explanation for such a wide capacity will also be wide.

These same considerations show why neuroscientific explanations may not be as theoretically appropriate as wide intentional explanations and so point to a problem for eliminativism: There are explanatory interests in understanding behavior and cognitive capacities described intentionally rather than as a series of bodily movements or computations. Wide intentional explanations are more theoretically appropriate to such an *explanandum*.

## 5. CAUSAL DEPTH IN PSYCHOLOGY

In defending (1), the claim that wide specifications of mental states sometimes identify *deeper* causal factors than the corresponding narrow specifications, I shall consider the cases of folk psychology and subpersonal, cognitive psychology separately. This is because causally deep explanations of each are wide in different ways. Recall that in §2 I said that a narrow explanation of behavior individuates the causes of behavior by reference only to properties supervening on the intrinsic physical states of the individual; it is wide otherwise. From this minimal account of narrow explanation, it follows that there are two types of wide explanation.

First, explanations that taxonomize neither in terms of intrinsic causal powers nor in terms of properties supervening on such powers are wide. Wide explanations of behavior of this type are not narrow *at all*. One could also view the evolutionary explanations discussed in §2 as a special sort of wide explanation of this type: The selection pressures over which they quantify aren't individuated by the intrinsic causal powers of individuals because they are not even *internal* properties of such individuals. Folk psychological explanation is, I think, a species of this type of wide explanation. Second, explanations that are not *exclusively* narrow are wide. The kinds in such explanations are individuated both in terms of intrinsic causal powers *and* in terms of other causal properties. Explanations in subpersonal psychology are a species of this type of wide explanation.

### 5.1. Causal depth (I): folk psychology

Philosophers who think that there is an individualistic vindication of the propositional attitudes are at least implicitly committed to a revision of folk psychology, one cast in terms of narrow content. Let us call this *narrow-folk psychology,* which is the psychology that results from replacing wide content with an appropriate notion of narrow content in folk psychology together with any required adjustments.

By construction, folk and narrow-folk psychology are alike in many respects, differing primarily in that the former is wide, the latter narrow.

Since individuals share beliefs and desires even though they vary in their neurophysiology, folk explanations of behavior must be pitched at a level of description that is not neurophysiological. Likewise, narrow-folk explanations must be pitched at a level of description that abstracts from neurophysiology. Narrow-folk descriptions of mental states, to avoid being chauvinistic and so hyperconcrete, need to be narrow *functional* descriptions, abstracting from the physical details of the state realizations. This is not to imply that narrow-folk psychology is committed to a conceptual role account of narrow content. *Whatever* account of narrow content one favors, narrow content must supervene on the intrinsic physical properties of the individual, and it is more plausible to view narrow content as having a functional-rather than a physical-level description. For the same reason, ordinary, folk psychological states have a (wide) functional rather than a (wide) physical description.

I shall argue that narrow functional descriptions of folk psychological states would be chauvinistic and so hyperconcrete in much the way that neurological descriptions of folk *and* narrow-folk states would be. This implies that folk psychology will have more causal depth than narrow-folk psychology. As in the case of the argument for functionalism over type-type materialism that charges the latter with chauvinism, I shall consider an interspecific case to defend my claims; I shall also help myself to the Riches at Face Value Thesis from Chapter 7, the thesis that the apparent explanatory riches of folk psychology ought to be taken at face value, for the proponent of narrow-folk psychology also assumes this thesis in supposing that narrow-folk psychology has at least folk psychology's riches.

Consider creatures whose behavior, as sophisticated and systematic as our own, is explained by attributing to them *either* folk or narrow-folk psychological states. It would not impugn either of these attributions to discover that such creatures are composed of physical stuff very different from our own cellular, material basis. Furthermore, similar discoveries about the underlying subpersonal, cognitive mechanisms – the 'depth psychology' – of such creatures would not defeat our *ordinary* folk attributions, especially if the wide part of the functional roles of their mental states was the same as ours. Folk psychology is not tied to what McGinn (1989:171ff.) calls *psychotec-*

*tonics,* the study of how to engineer or build a cognitive system; it does not make a substantial claim about the realization or implementation of the states it posits. Consider discoveries about the subpersonal psychology of people from cultures other than one's own. Is there *any* discovery about cross-cultural differences in subpersonal processing mechanisms that could lead us to think that people whose behavior was as sophisticated and complex as ours *did not have beliefs and desires?* I think not. The contrary view reflects a chauvinistic or perhaps an overly specific view of folk psychology, one that does not reflect the huge epistemological gap between investigations in subpersonal, cognitive psychology and the commitments of folk psychology (cf. Dennett 1987:234–5, quoted in Chapter 7, §9).

Would such discoveries about the subpersonal psychology of other beings or other members of our own species defeat our narrow-folk explanations of their behavior? In the following sense, they would not: Simply finding *some* difference in their subpersonal psychology need not imply that they are subject to a different narrow-folk psychology. But if we allow that their subpersonal psychology may vary arbitrarily from our own – and I do not see why we may not – then the following general problem arises. If narrow-folk psychological states are instantiated as subpersonal states $s_1 \ldots s_n$, narrow-folk psychology will not apply to creatures lacking $s_1 \ldots s_n$. Only folk psychology would apply both to us and to such creatures. This implies that for narrow-folk psychology to have the causal depth that folk psychology has, it needs to be tied less closely to subpersonal psychology: It needs to posit narrow functional states that are not tokens in the language of thought, for creatures very much like us in terms of the extensive and sophisticated behavioral regularities they exhibit need not instantiate such tokens.

This leads to a general challenge for the individualist. If those very much like us behaviorally varied from us with respect to *just* the narrow functional structure that one identifies with narrow-folk content, then we could not explain their behavior by a narrow-folk psychology. Such a discovery about their functional distinctness from us would impugn our narrow-folk attributions (but not our *folk* attributions) for the same reason that it would impugn our attributions of particular psychological mechanisms to them. Even if narrow-folk psychology can be multiply realized by creatures with different neurophysiologies – since narrow-folk descriptions abstract away from at least some neurophysiological detail – it cannot be

203

multiply realized by the very narrow functional structures it is identified with. Since such behaviorally sophisticated but neurophysiologically distinct creatures exist in the actual (and nearby possible) worlds, folk psychology has greater causal depth than narrow-folk psychology.

It is the width of folk psychology – precisely what any narrow-folk psychology lacks – that gives folk psychology its causal depth. Since this is precisely what a narrow-folk psychology abstracts away from, *any* narrow-folk psychology will have less causal depth than ordinary folk psychology. The general case I am making here for folk over narrow-folk psychology *may* fail because of details to be completed as part of a narrow content program in philosophical psychology, details that both identified the appropriate narrow functional structures *and* showed these to be shared by behaviorally similar creatures who differ in their general neurophysiology. If such details were forthcoming, they would point to a failure in the argument I offer.

The present argument reminds proponents of the narrow content program that the explanations of a narrow-folk psychology must be causally deeper than those of folk psychology. Since proponents of narrow-folk psychology typically consider folk psychology to have considerable causal depth, this constraint is not trivial. The argument employs a general strategy against those who wish to defend the causal depth of narrow-folk psychology: Show that creatures lacking the narrow functional structures that are to be identified with narrow contents could, nonetheless, share our folk psychological states (cf. Shoemaker 1981: esp. §§IV–VI).

The corresponding argument against eliminativism, which would defend the claim that some intentional psychological explanations have greater causal depth than any non-intentional explanation, divides into two cases: one against non-intentional, *neuroscientific* explanations, the other against non-intentional, *syntactic* or computational explanations. Since eliminativists, unlike advocates of the narrow content program, are typically sceptical about the causal depth of folk psychology, the argument here could not appeal to the Riches at Face Value Thesis, as the preceding argument has done. I shall not develop the argument against eliminativism here, but I do want to note something about each of the two cases.

In the first case, that concerning folk intentional versus neuroscientific explanations, the hyperconcreteness of the latter would have to emerge as a conclusion to the argument rather than serve as a motivating premise. In the second case, that concerning folk intentional versus computational explanations, if one were to consider semantically sanitized versions of folk psychology of the sort that Stich (1983:ch. 8) introduces, then it seems that a slight modification of the present argument would suffice. This is because such a 'folk syntactic' psychology is motivated in much the same way as is a narrow-folk psychology: It takes the Riches at Face Value Thesis for granted and argues that a syntactic, narrow-folk psychology has all the riches of folk psychology *and more* (see also Chapter 9, §3). The more difficult case is that of computational explanations that are *independent* of folk psychology. The problem in this case is that, unlike that of folk versus narrow-folk psychology, since we are comparing explanations that may be extremely different from one another, it will be more difficult to ensure that the ceteris paribus clause in each of the arguments is satisfied.

## 5.2. Causal depth (II): cognitive psychology

Let us now consider explanations in subpersonal psychology. Much of contemporary psychology offers functional analyses and explanations for given capacities, where the object of explanation is a cognitive capacity, such as detecting edges, recognizing faces, remembering names, and drawing valid conclusions. In explaining how agents possess such capacities, we break the capacity into simpler component capacities. The methodology here is *homuncularly functional:* We posit a mechanism (a homunculus) that performs a function that is a necessary part of some larger function the cognitive system performs. The explanatory burden is discharged because each constituent capacity is cognitively simpler than that which it constitutes (see Cummins 1983:ch. 3; Dennett 1978a; Lycan 1981, 1987:ch. 4, 1988:ch. 1).

The prevalence of homuncular explanations in subpersonal psychology might seem to suggest that large parts of psychology must be individualistic. For even when we have wide descriptions of mental states, these can be factored into descriptions of the constituent capacities that are narrow; similar considerations might be adduced in favor of neuroscientific descriptions of constituent capacities. Yet neither of these conclusions follows, and for at least some psychological capacities they are false. I take the weaker of these claims first.

The functions that some homuncular units perform mediate between individuals and their environments in such a way that the subpersonal mechanisms posited are described in terms of their long-armed, world-involving, and often specialized functions. Describing such mechanisms purely in terms of their narrow functional role would not fully express what such psychological mechanisms *do*. Nonetheless, an individualist who claimed that wide descriptions of psychological capacities add nothing to the narrow descriptions of their constituent capacities could at least pose the following challenge: Show me *what* such wide descriptions give us in explanatory terms over and above what the constitutive narrow descriptions give us. My claim is that, in principle and in practice, the answer to the challenge is: additional causal depth.

Let me first make the point abstractly in terms of a comparison of a wide homuncular psychological theory, *WH,* and its closest narrow rival, *NH.* (Roughly, *NH* will be *WH* shorn of its wide homuncular functions.) Theory *WH* may be true in more nearby possible worlds than *NH* and so have greater causal depth because *WH* includes reference to stable relational properties that remain instantiated by individuals in the environments in those worlds. Hence *WH* maintains its truth in these worlds, whereas *NH,* lacking such reference, is false in them. The presupposition is that the constituent capacities (say, $c_1 \ldots c_n$) of *WH* in nearby possible worlds are different than in the actual world, whereas the psychological capacities they constitute in the actual world are the same across these possible worlds. Or, since causal depth comes in degrees and since many of our deepest theories and explanations are not true in *all* nearby possible worlds: $c_1 \ldots c_n$ are instantiated in fewer of the nearby possible worlds than are the wide capacities they constitute in the actual world. I claim that this situation is clearly possible, and its possibility shows that individualism *need not* be a consequence of the reliance of subpersonal cognitive psychology on the homuncular strategy.

To take an example, research in visual cognition suggests that there are special mechanisms for *face recognition* that function to identify either conspecific or familiar faces when oriented in the standard way (see Bruce 1991; Young and Ellis 1989). Our face recognizers are able to recognize faces in the actual world. Although we might find out all sorts of interesting facts about how our face recognizers work – for example, about how they decompose into their constituent capacities and how they are physically realized – *that* way of describing part of our cognitive apparatus is wide, not narrow (cf. §4 on depth maps). Devices in other possible worlds with the same constituent capacities that are not able to recognize faces do not function as face recognizers. Consider the individualist's challenge: What does being a face recognizer add to being the sort of thing that has all of the psychological capacities that constitute being a face recognizer in the actual world? What do we lose if descriptions like 'face recognizer' are not included in our cognitive psychology? *Causal depth.* Face recognition is a psychological capacity that it is likely that *we* (or creatures very much like us) instantiate in nearby possible worlds, and our best explanations of face recognition ought to apply to such creatures.

One reason is that even if our evolutionary history had differed enough so that the particular cognitive capacities that constitute face recognition in the actual world had been different, we would still instantiate face recognizers: Because face recognition is a modular capacity selected for the advantages it confers, it would prevail even if the way it evolved differed. There are nearby possible worlds in which our evolutionary history is such that we have face recognizers constituted by capacities different from those we have in the actual world. The converse is not true: We have those constituent capacities only because they constitute face recognizers, and so in nearby possible worlds in which we lack the capacity to recognize faces, we do not instantiate these constituent capacities. Hence *only* the wide homuncular theory applies to both the actual and these nearby possible worlds, and so the wide homuncular theory is causally deeper. Although parts of our subpersonal, cognitive psychology *would* differ between the actual world and these nearby possible worlds, namely, the parts that are concerned with explaining how our psychological capacities are realized, these parts are not the whole of psychology.

A related point about descriptions of subpersonal psychological mechanisms has been made by Cosmides and Tooby (1987) in discussing evolutionary psychology (see also Chapter 4, §7). Having stated that traditional evolutionary explanations of behavior have largely ignored what they call the 'missing link' between evolution and behavior − the psychological mechanisms that lead to certain behaviors rather than others − Cosmides and Tooby note that when such a missing link has been considered, this has been in terms of physiological rather than psychological mechanisms. On this second point, Cosmides and Tooby say:

Psychological mechanisms can be studied on different descriptive and explanatory levels. Most biologically informed studies of proximate mechanisms have described psychological mechanisms in terms of their physiological underpinnings. . . . But natural selection theory, so far, has made only limited contributions to the investigation of physiology. Just as different kinds of hardware can run the same computer program, different physiological mechanisms can accomplish the same adaptive function. (1987:282)

Cosmides and Tooby are suggesting that an evolutionary psychology is more likely to be stated at a distinctly psychological rather than a physiological level of description, even though its principal concern is to identify and characterize psychological *mechanisms*. For the very reasons that this *is* likely, so too is an evolutionary psychology likely to be wide rather than narrow: Adaptive functions are wide, not narrow. Prima facie, evolutionary psychology is wide, positing cognitive mechanisms individuated both historically and by reference to the (wide) function that those mechanisms serve in a particular evolutionary context.

If the causally deepest explanations for some psychological capacities are evolutionary and wide, why insist that such explanations are not part of cognitive psychology? Differences between disciplines may explain why only some of them are constrained by individualism, but the line to be drawn is *not* that between psychological explanation and evolutionary explanation, since some psychological explanations *are* evolutionary. To put the question another way: What reason is there to think that individualism imposes a constraint on the explanation of psychological capacities and behavior, given that we have the beginnings of wide explanations for some of these?

## 6. PEACEFUL COEXISTENCE AND CONCESSIVE INDIVIDUALISM

Reflection on the case of evolutionary explanations might give one reason to doubt my assumption that narrow and wide explanations of behavior compete with one another. Does one have to choose wide evolutionary explanations over narrow explanations? After all, in the evolutionary and biological sciences there is a sort of *peaceful coexistence* between the two. I think one should adopt precisely this general view of *psychological* explanation: Both wide and narrow explanations have their place in psychology. Yet this is compatible with thinking that in particular cases wide and narrow psychological explanations are rivals, and that they can be profitably compared and evaluated by the criteria of causal depth and theoretical appropriateness. What 'peaceful coexistence' *is* incompatible with, however, is both the acceptance of individualism as a constraint on psychology and neurophilic eliminativism. The evolutionary sciences are inherently pluralistic in their methodology, in their taxonomies, and in the types of explanations they offer. The cognitive sciences should be at least as taxonomically pluralistic as the evolutionary sciences.

If something about explanatory practice in the evolutionary and biological sciences, a feature absent in the cognitive sciences, explained why only *they* were inherently pluralistic, then one could maintain concessive individualism (see §2), adopting individualism as a constraint on taxonomy and explanation *in psychology* while conceding that an analogue to individualism is not a constraint on evolutionary biology. I have said that concessive individualism is a difficult position to maintain. As my preceding comments about peaceful coexistence perhaps suggest, I take the diversity of types of explanation within the biological sciences to be indicative of how diverse psychological explanation is, will continue to be, and ought to be. Although the individual may constitute a boundary for taxonomy and explanation in both evolutionary biology and psychological explanation in some cases, it does not do so for all cases. There appears to be no difference between evolutionary and psychological explanatory practice here, and I suggest that we take these appearances at face value.

A discussion of one purported difference between the evolutionary and cognitive sciences will illustrate some of the general problems facing a concessive individualist. One might think that Dretske's (1988:42–5) distinction between *triggering* and *structuring* causes provides a basis for defending concessive individualism.[1] The triggering causes of a process are those events that initiate or activate that process; its structuring causes are those events that shaped that process in the first place. In Dretske's own terms, where 'C' and 'M' designate events, triggering causes are 'what caused the C *which* caused the M', and structuring causes are 'what caused C *to* cause M rather than something else' (1988:42). Explanations in terms of selection pressures are most plausibly seen as identifying structuring causes, not triggering causes: They explain why, for example, gazelles flee from lions, not why a particular gazelle responds in a particular case in that way.

---

1 This suggestion arose in slightly different forms in comments from Dion Scott-Kakures and in brief, somewhat casual discussions with James Klagge and Sydney Shoemaker. None of these people should be saddled with responsibility for the particular ways the view is developed here.

Psychological explanations, by contrast, do address this latter explanatory question, and when we are interested in identifying the triggering causes of behavior, our explanations must be individualistic, for such causes are always located inside the individual. This suggestion could be developed in at least two ways.

First, one might think that psychology is individualistic because it does not specify the structuring causes of behavior. We can understand the taxonomic pluralism of the evolutionary sciences in terms of their concern with specifying both the triggering and the structuring causes of behavior; psychology lacks this concern and so must be individualistic. Yet the explanatory interests that drive the cognitive sciences make it difficult to characterize them as searching only for triggering causes. For example, cognitive developmentalists who have primary interests in the acquisition and change of an individual's cognitive structures identify both triggering and structuring causes of behavior. To mention two examples, Keil's (1989) study of conceptual shifts throughout childhood and Wellman's (1990) account of the child's development of a theory of mind view concepts and beliefs as both triggering and structuring causes: They trigger particular responses from children on experimental tasks and structure future cognitive changes. Even bracketing areas of psychology that overlap with the evolutionary sciences, this defence of concessive individualism involves a view of psychological explanation that makes little sense of core areas of research in psychology.

Second, one might think that the distinction provides the basis for an account of why certain explanations are individualistic and why others are not and allows one to express an important kernel of truth in individualism: triggering explanations of behavior must be individualistic. Now, unless one also thinks that psychology identifies *only* the triggering causes of behavior, this view doesn't allow one to defend concessive individualism. Even adopting such a view of psychology would not allow one to defend concessive individualism, since we might taxonomize the triggering causes of behavior broadly rather than narrowly. Triggering causes in psychology must be *internal,* local mental states; but they need not be *intrinsic* mental states.

Although the general view of causal explanation in the sciences developed over the last four chapters makes concessive individualism a prima facie plausible view to defend, my scepticism about the prospects for concessive individualism is consonant with that general view. Drawing the required distinction between the evolutionary and cognitive sciences so as to do justice to the explanatory diversity within each and distinguishing the cognitive sciences as individualistic may not be impossible. But attempts to do so look more like efforts to save an a priori thesis about psychological taxonomy and explanation than the result of an a posteriori analysis of psychological explanation in practice.

## 7. TWIN EARTH AND EXPLANATION

Considering the case of doppelgängers might be thought to turn my conclusion for the causal depth of wide explanations on its head (as Dave Robb, Dion Scott-Kakures, and Sydney Shoemaker have each pointed out to me). Suppose that we consider an individual, Rex, and his doppelgänger on Twin Earth, T-Rex. On the standard view, Rex and T-Rex have at least some mental states with different (wide) contents. But, since they are molecularly identical, any narrow psychological explanation that applies to one will also apply to the other. More dramatically, consider not just Rex and T-Rex, but Rex and the total set of his doppelgängers (cf. McGinn 1991:579–81). Then, by parity of reasoning, the wide explanations we can provide for their behaviors will vary in accord with differences in their local environments. Yet narrow explanations for the behavior of one will apply to the behavior of all. If we understand explanatory power in terms of causal depth, a narrow explanation will have more explanatory power than the corresponding wide explanation: Only the narrow explanation, which abstracts away from irrelevant environmental differences, applies across these possible worlds.

I have no quibbles with the conclusion that narrow explanations are in some cases the causally deepest psychological explanations we have. But the preceding reasoning is not valid. As I said in §1, an explanation is not causally deeper merely because it applies to more entities than explanations with which it competes. Generality is an explanatory virtue only insofar as it indicates counterfactual rigor, where we can express this in terms of an explanation's holding in *nearby* possible worlds. For the preceding reasoning to be valid, the set of Twin Earth scenarios just mentioned must form a subset of the set of nearby possible worlds. Yet they do not: Many of the worlds in which doppelgängers exist – for example, those in which Rex's doppelgänger is a brain in a vat – are *very* different physically from the actual world. Think about all of the physical differences between the worlds that Rex and such a doppelgänger live in: Rex's world is like ours, whereas that of the doppelgänger might have only his brain, the vat, and a magic wand for data input. This pair of worlds are not nearby possible worlds (see Heil 1992:142–4). The apparent fact that all the worlds in which Rex's doppelgängers exist *seem to those doppelgängers* to be just as the actual world seems to be to Rex is simply irrelevant to the causal depth of any explanation, be it narrow or wide. This distinction between nearby possible worlds and what we can think of as 'Rex-centered, phenomenologically nearby' possible worlds helps to explain why Earth and Twin Earth are not nearby possible worlds (cf. Heil and Mele 1991); the confusion between the two might also explain the strength of the intuition that narrow psychological explanations *must have* greater causal depth than wide psychological explanations.

Although the criterion of causal depth is context dependent, and so which of two explanations is causally deeper is a function of which contexts one focusses on, one would like some reason for focussing on *only* those contexts in which there exists an individual and (all of) her doppelgängers. After all, we could choose to compare Rex only to a physically very different individual who instantiates the same folk psychological states but exists on a planet that is otherwise *identical* to Earth. In such a case, we might be tempted to think that the wide explanation is causally deeper: *It,* and not its narrow competitors, applies to Rex and his non-doppelgängers. But why focus on *this* context? Likewise, in thinking about psychological explanation, why focus on a context in which only Rex and his doppelgängers exist? Some worlds in which Rex's doppelgängers exist are certainly nearby, for they differ very little from the actual world. Yet focussing only on Rex and T-Rex in such a nearby possible world does not tell you anything about the causal depth of any type of explanation; such a comparison is selective in a way that is inconsistent with how the notion of causal depth should be understood.

An exclusive or primary focus on doppelgängers can lead one to forget that in the actual world in which our psychological explanations are developed, the subjects of psychology are individuals who are not physically identical. These individuals are also (some of) the subjects of evolutionary biology and, as is the case with explanation in evolutionary biology, one should expect psychology to exploit stable relational properties that individuals possess in its attempts to develop causally deep explanations of their behavior. *Folk* psychology has done this for ages; as I argued in §5.2 in this chapter, subpersonal psychology has begun and should continue to do the same.

## 8. CONCLUSION: WIDE EXPLANATION IS EXPLANATION ENOUGH

Although the primary function of my discussion of evolutionary explanations in §2 was to illustrate how the criteria of causal depth and theoretical appropriateness apply to explanations of behavior, the existence of both wide and narrow explanations within an evolutionary framework is suggestive for psychology. Even with the development of various branches of genetics during the twentieth century, explanations offered by these disciplines have not replaced and are extremely unlikely to replace wide explanations that appeal to selection pressures. Likewise, neither folk psychological nor wide functional explanations are used only because we currently lack knowledge about the internal workings of the mind. Wide explanations may be both causally deep and theoretically appropriate and, like wide evolutionary explanations, have these explanatory virtues *because* of their width.

Although I have said something about why concessive individualism is a vulnerable position to attempt to defend, I have done little here to address directly a more radical line of response than concessive individualism, that of someone who agrees that wide psychology and evolutionary biology are on a par but thinks that *both* suffer from related weaknesses. My argument in this chapter adopts a 'partners in crime' strategy: Psychology's reliance on wide explanation is as well motivated as that of evolutionary biology. Someone making the more radical criticism I am envisaging would view my use of the partners in crime strategy as identifying partners *in crime:* Psychology's reliance on wide explanation is *as bad as* that of evolutionary biology! Although wide explanations are ubiquitous in the evolutionary sciences, it might be said that they suffer from a residual Panglossianism about functions, are committed to strong and untenable views of teleology, and are vague and ill-defined. Such a proponent of the radical critique, even one who is open-minded about the prospects for wide, intentional explanation in psychology, is unlikely to be impressed by the argument I have offered in this chapter. (I am grateful to an anonymous referee for *Philosophy of Science* for raising the possibility of this more radical critique.)

My disagreement with such a radical critic can only be resolved by further discussion of both the sorts of a posteriori explanatory virtues and constraints I have articulated here and explanatory practice. To indicate where it seems to me that there is most room for substantial disagreement, let me note that I think that the adoption of an a posteriori perspective on scientific explanation, the *sort* of perspective developed over the last four chapters, cannot reasonably be resisted. The issue to be resolved concerns the status of wide evolutionary explanations *as* scientific explanations.

Since one can understand *why* wide taxonomies and explanations ought to be adopted in some cases in psychology in terms of the criteria of causal depth and theoretical appropriateness, it is difficult to see what is wrong with wide explanation in psychology. In psychology, as in other causal, explanatory sciences, wide explanation is explanation enough.

# 9

## *Individualistic visions of psychology: prospects and problems*

In Chapter 1, I distinguished two questions. The first was whether individualism imposes a constraint on psychology. In Part I, I examined the most influential and interesting arguments for individualism and found them wanting; in Part II, I dug deeper into the intuitions underlying these arguments and did some positive work towards making sense of mental causation without individualism; in Part III thus far, I have provided a more direct argument against individualism. The answer to this first question in light of the discussion to this point appears to be 'No'.

The second question concerned the role of content within psychology: Should psychological explanations refer to an individual's mental contents? Can psychology be intentional or must it be *content-free?* Although I have not discussed this second question explicitly so far, because it is distinct from the first, an individualistic psychology can be either intentional, based on a notion of *narrow* content, or content-free. In broad outline, these are the two positive visions of an individualistic psychology that I shall discuss in this chapter. In §2 and §3, I examine the most clearly articulated and complete expression of the content-free vision of an individualistic psychology, Stephen Stich's syntactic theory of the mind; in §§4–7, I focus on the intentional vision of an individualistic psychology by considering proposals that are part of the narrow content program. To begin, I want to motivate the content-free vision by addressing the question of why one would even want to consider the possibility of a psychology that made no significant use of the notion of content.

## 1. THE PROBLEM WITH CONTENT

The chief reason for contemplating the possibility of a content-free psychology is that the notion that such a psychology eschews, that of mental content, has often been thought to be inherently problematic. But *why* is content problematic? In what way or from which perspective is intentionality considered problematic? (I put to one side here the worries about mental causation discussed in Chapter 6.)

Eliminativism about content has a venerable history, a history in which W. V. O. Quine has played a central role. Notoriously, Quine is ontologically scrupulous, particularly when it comes to entities that are either ill-suited to his austere physicalism or not required by it. In an often-quoted passage in which he remarks that his arguments for the indeterminacy of translation bear a similarity to some of Brentano's arguments for the irreducibility of the notion of intentionality to physical notions, Quine says: 'One may accept the Brentano thesis either as showing the indispensability of intentional idioms and the importance of an autonomous science of intention, or as showing the baselessness of intentional idioms and the emptiness of a science of intention. My attitude, unlike Brentano's, is the second' (1960:221). As the phrase 'the emptiness of a science of intention' suggests, the perspective from which intentionality is problematic for Quine is that of *science*. Ontologically, intentional entities don't fit appropriately into a physicalistic metaphysics; epistemologically, intentional explanations lack the extensionality that Quine thinks scientific explanations must possess.

This is not the place for a detailed exposition of Quine's complicated views or for a critique of them. I want to focus on the claim that a science of intention is, in Quine's terms, empty. Why is the intentional idiom, talk of content, an unsuitable basis for a science? Intentional talk has often been noted to be vague, indeterminate, and holistic (see Stich 1983:chh. 4, 5), and by pointing to these features, we find the beginnings of an answer to this question. When we ascribe mental contents to others – paradigmatically in the ascription of *belief* – we are *interpreting* their behavior; the interpretational nature of content ascriptions makes them vague, indeterminate, and holistic. For, coming back to Quine, there is an indeterminacy of translation whenever we attempt to make sense of behavior through acts of interpretation.

This view of the intentional idiom as essentially interpretational lies behind a variety of views of intentionality. For example, Stich's (1983:ch. 5) view of belief (and, more generally, content) ascriptions as a species of similarity judgment, Dennett's (1987) intentional stance view of folk psychology, and Davidson's (1980, 1984) advocacy of the necessity of the principles of charity and rationality as presuppositions of the coherence of folk psychological ascriptions all build on or develop an interpretationist view of intentionality or content. When coupled with the thesis that interpretations are indeterminate and the claim that scientific claims are not, interpretationism about content leads either to outright scepticism about the notion of content, such as Stich's eliminativism, or to a bifurcated view of intentional and scientific discourses, instances of which include Dennett's trichotomy of stances, Davidson's anomalous monism, and the view expressed by Quine in the passage quoted earlier in this section.

These views all express doubts about of the prospects for an intentional science of the mind. A science of the mind, if there is to be one at all, must thus be content-free. Such a science might be either entirely neuroscientific (P. M. Churchland 1981, 1989; P. S. Churchland 1986) or computational or syntactic (Stich 1983). I shall discuss only the syntactic alternative primarily because only this alternative has been offered as a positive vision of what an *individualistic* psychology would be like; my focus here is driven, secondarily, by a doubt that the first of these alternatives could provide a science that is recognizably psychological or cognitive.

## 2. THE SYNTACTIC THEORY OF MIND

Stich's syntactic theory of mind (STM) is one positive vision of individualistic, content-free psychology. Stich says:

The basic idea of the STM is that the cognitive states whose interaction is (in part) responsible for behavior can be systematically mapped to abstract syntactic objects in such a way that causal interactions among cognitive states, as well as causal links with stimuli and behavioral events, can be described in terms of the syntactic properties and relations of the abstract objects to which the cognitive states are mapped. More briefly, the idea is that causal relations among cognitive states mirror formal relations among syntactic objects. (1983:149).

Although Stich states that the STM is 'officially agnostic' on the question of whether mental states have content, he points out that the official letter of this agnosticism should not mislead one regarding the underlying spirit of the syntactic theory: 'in remaining agnostic on questions of content, the STM is in effect claiming that psychological theories have *no need* to postulate content or other semantic properties, like truth conditions. It sees no psychological work to be done by the hypothesis that mental state tokens or types have semantic properties' (1983:185–6). The STM, then, proposes a model of psychological theory in which there is no significant place for the notion of content.

This model of psychological theory should seem familiar from our discussion of computationalism in psychology in Chapter 3. In fact, Stich thinks that contemporary computational theories are rightly characterized as fitting the model of cognitive theory proposed by the STM (1983:153). Stich takes the STM to offer an abstract characterization of computationalism in psychology; it makes explicit the conception of psychology implicit in the computational paradigm. With this in mind, we can return to Stich's claim, introduced briefly in Chapter 7, that one cannot 'have it both ways', that one cannot consistently endorse both a computational and a representational psychology.[1] Supposing that cognition is computational, and that one does not need the notion of content to account for computational operations, there is no *need* to appeal to the notion of content in psychology. If, as Stich says, 'the most interesting and theoretically powerful generalizations [in cognitive theory] are formal or syntactic ones which simply cannot be stated in the aboriginal language of content' (1983:183), then the cognitive sciences need not burden themselves with the notion of content. This is so even if much existing computational theory happens to be couched in intentional language.

In making explicit the conception of a cognitive theory within the computational paradigm, Stich emphasizes the formal nature not so much of the phenomena being explained but of the explanatory theories. Cognitive theories are to be formal in a sense familiar from logic: They are to consist of a specification of a set of formal primitives, formation rules and rules of inference, and theorems, the last being the hypothesized generalizations that specify formulas derivable in the formal system. The resulting language in which cognitive theories are to be stated is 'no more than an infinite class of complex syntactic objects. *It has no semantics*' (1983:153). This point is central to the STM. As Stich says, '[t]he core idea of the STM – the idea that

---

1 What Stich actually says is that one can't both endorse the formality condition *and* insist on a representational psychology. This points to a tension between a computational and a representational psychology only if the formality condition adequately characterizes computationalism in psychology, which it does not (see Chapter 3, §4).

makes it *syntactic* – is that generalizations detailing causal relations among the hypothesized neurological states are to be specified indirectly via the formal relations among the syntactic objects to which the neurological state types are mapped' (1983:151). Theories constructed in accord with the syntactic model posit only generalizations that refer to formal relations between syntactic objects. In this sense, psychology is to be content-free. To say that neurological states have syntactic properties is to say only that the causal interactions between them of psychological interest can be adequately expressed by an STM-styled cognitive theory.

Like all scientific theories, STM-styled theories must be empirically adequate: They must be able to account for the empirical phenomena in their domain. Precisely which phenomena this includes will depend on broader theoretical considerations. This is important here, for in proposing an abandonment of intentional psychological explanation, the proponent of the STM will, presumably, also propose that we give up attempting to characterize the *explananda* of psychology intentionally: It is only for content-free *explananda* that content-free *explanantia* will be more theoretically appropriate. With this in mind, consider Stich's claim that 'syntactic theories can do justice to all of the generalizations capturable by quantifying over content sentences while avoiding the limitations that the folk language of content impose[s]' (1983:157–8). The first of the claims made here, that theories developed in accord with the syntactic theory are as explanatorily adequate as representational theories, is somewhat puzzling. Since intentional and content-free cognitive theories should have different objects of explanation if they manifest theoretical appropriateness, it is not clear how *either* one can 'do justice to all of the generalizations' of the other.

What sorts of limitations does Stich have in mind when he talks of the 'limitations that the folk language of content impose[s]'? Stich thinks that because folk psychology is a species of similarity judgment, where the standard for comparison is the ascriber's own beliefs, it is unable to generate accurate theories of those who differ from us along any of the dimensions of similarity that determine belief ascriptions. The idea is that STM-styled theories offer the potential for more extensive generalizations than their intentional counterparts because, in Stich's words, STM-styled theories 'eliminate the middleman' (1983:159), the similarity between subject and theorist. Forgoing content and so the ascriber relativity of mental states, STM-styled

219

theories allow generalizations about both those like us and those different from us. Thus Stich says that 'a cognitive science that adopts the STM paradigm can aspire to broadly applicable developmental, clinical, and comparative theories, all of which are problematic for a content-based theory because of the constraints of ideological similarity' (1983:159). Again, to put it in terms of a notion introduced in Chapter 8, Stich thinks that the content-free theories of the STM will have greater *causal depth* than their intentional rivals.

Clearly, the STM articulates a *Cartesian computational* conception of psychology (see Chapter 3, §6). In the next section I shall largely ignore criticisms that others (e.g., Crane 1990; Egan 1989; Horgan and Woodward 1985) have made of the STM in favor of pointing to several key problems with the Cartesian computational conception of psychology that are implicit in the last few chapters. Together they suggest that the prospects for such a psychology are less than rosy.

### 3. PROBLEMS WITH CARTESIAN COMPUTATIONALISM

In discussing the theoretical appropriateness of wide and narrow psychologies in Chapter 8, I argued that since the *explananda* in psychology often cite wide behaviors, the *explanantia* referring to the psychological states of the organism that best match these would also be wide. Even supposing that wide behaviors are completely constituted by behaviors that have a narrow description, since in some cases it is only under the wide description that behaviors count as the *explananda* in psychology, we need wide descriptions of psychological states for theoretically appropriate psychological explanations. Precisely the same point is true of the relationship between intentional and content-free descriptions of behavior and the mental states that cause them.

The claim that computational descriptions of behavior are not always adequate for psychological explanation should be of interest even to those who reject my claim about theoretical appropriateness. Computational taxonomies do not provide an exhaustive characterization of behavioral kinds. In fact, one can defend a stronger claim than this: that computational taxonomies of behavior *rarely* provide the kinds of behavior that feature in psychological generalizations. There is a principled problem with the idea of computational *behav-*

*ioral* kinds for psychology, a problem deriving from a difference between cognitive states and the behaviors they cause.

Computational, individualistic taxonomies of *cognitive* states must specify computational properties that supervene on the current internal physical state of the organism, and so abstract away from environmental properties. Since cognitive states are *internal* in the sense of being *located in* an individual, this is in principle possible. But behavior is not internal to the individual in the same sense: It *involves* an environment, an interaction between the individual and the environment in which she is embedded. This is certainly true of our common, everyday descriptions of actions and behaviors, such as telephoning a friend, reading a book, and flying a kite, and even of more minimal folk descriptions of actions, such as reaching for something, picking something up, and holding an object; I think it is also true of *any* notion of behavior, at least any that cognitive psychology requires. For this reason, the notion of behavior within Cartesian computationalism is incoherent, and even paradigmatic and uncontentious examples of autonomous behaviors are difficult to provide: Behavior is relational, and so partially external to an individual. Thus, the sort of individualistic revision required for autonomous descriptions of behavior is intrinsically problematic. I am not so much denying the existence of behaviors that can be taxonomized in accord with Cartesian computationalism as denying that such behavioral taxonomies pick out a *kind* of behavior.

To clarify what I mean here, I want to draw on a point that Stewart Candlish has made about the notion of a basic action. Candlish says:

It is clear that there must be basic actions. . . . What is not so clear – although those philosophers who have employed the notion of basic action have often been fairly confident on the subject - is that the potentially infinite regress which the basic action arrests is always arrested by the same independently specifiable class of actions. (1984:84)

Candlish goes on to elaborate on an analogy between the role of basic actions in the theory of action and the role of sensory primitives in the theory of perception and urges the following conclusion: 'what we fundamentally perceive, and what we basically do, is going to vary according to the situation and no independently specifiable class can be identified as the basic perceivings or doings' (p. 99). The central point that Candlish makes here about the concepts of sense data and basic actions applies to the notion of behavior required by

Cartesian computationalism. Computational, individualistic behavioral descriptions are likely to vary from situation to situation, and thus the behaviors such descriptions pick out do not constitute a *kind* of behavior or even a conjunction of kinds of behavior from the point of view of cognitive explanation. (And, as in the case of basic actions, this does not imply that behaviors *can't* be given such descriptions.)

But why endorse the strong claim that *any* conception of behavior fit for psychology must recognize behavior as involving an environment, that is, as the behavior of an *embedded* individual? Isn't this precisely the sort of a priori claim about taxonomy in psychology whose denial was a recurrent theme throughout Part II of this book? As a starting point for an answer to both of these questions, note that the sorts of behaviors that are regularly described within existing psychological practice, and that serve as the *explananda* in existing psychological theories, are, like our folk descriptions of behavior, overwhelmingly wide or embedded descriptions. Consider a few examples of behaviors that have played a crucial role in psychological research paradigms in the post-1945 period: the following behavior of goslings in imprinting (e.g., Lorenz), the navigation and exploration of a maze (e.g., Skinner), and preferential looking as part of the perceptual habituation paradigm (e.g., Spelke). The prevalence of embedded taxonomies of behavior within psychology is important, for it implies that the disembedded taxonomies of behavior within the Cartesian computational vision of psychology must form part of an *ideal* psychology, one providing taxonomies cleansed of worldly involvement.

Given the revisionary character of the requisite behavioral taxonomies, proponents of such an ideal psychology face a dilemma. Either the resulting taxonomies of behavior are sanitized versions of existing wide taxonomies, in which case we can argue for the causal depth of wide explanations over these narrow explanations (see Chapter 8, §5), or such ideal taxonomies represent a more radical break from existing taxonomies. The latter alternative typically goes hand in hand with the idea that our folk psychological categories are ill-suited for explanatory work in the cognitive sciences, and thus with the rejection of the Riches at Face Value Thesis. On such a view, the claim that the ideal taxonomy allows one to capture all of the important wide generalizations loses both its plausibility and its point: It is implausible because an ideal taxonomy is extremely likely to carve nature at different joints than do existing wide taxonomies, and it is unnecessary because it is not an explanatory virtue for a theory to allow one to say everything that a radically false theory allows one to say.

But there is a deeper problem with the 'radical break' version of ideal psychology. What ensures that the taxonomies it delivers are *psychological* taxonomies? Given the break not simply with the psychology of the folk but with the folk-like taxonomies that have been appropriated and developed thus far within cognitive psychology, this question is a difficult one for proponents of the radical break view.

The conception of behavior fit for psychology should involve embedded behaviors because embedded behaviors are what exist in developing psychological taxonomies, and both of the revisionary alternatives for disembedded taxonomies are, for different reasons, unpromising. The way my argument for this pair of claims proceeds – from taxonomic practice in psychology to an evaluation of the prospects for a revisionary claim about psychological taxonomy – is a posteriori, not a priori. These claims point to a problem specifically about behavior for the Cartesian computationalist because, unlike psychological states, behaviors are *not* internal to an individual. This means that they do not satisfy a condition necessary for them to be individualistic, and we should expect both taxonomies as they have actually developed to be wide *and* proposed individualistic revisions to be inherently problematic.

The core problem with the Cartesian computational taxonomy of behavior implicit in the STM stems from the *individualistic* nature of such a taxonomy, not from its *computational* nature. Thus, that problem should not exist for a *wide* computational psychology. Perhaps this is right, though it is difficult to tell, because wide computationalism has received little reflective treatment so far and also because once one adopts a wide computational perspective on psychology there is less inhibition in allowing representational taxonomies of both mental states and behavior. In any case, there *is* a prima facie problem with the conception of behavior within Cartesian computationalism deriving from its computational rather than its Cartesian aspect, one that would thus also seem to plague wide computationalism.

One strength of computational theories is in modelling the *inferential* relations between psychological states; after all, the syntactic objects in such theories are related to one another by formal inferential rules. An STM-styled cognitive theory posits inferential relations between the primitives in the theory, these being rules that model the causal relations between the states that those primitives represent; the very structure of such a theory is designed to model causal transitions between states. STM-styled theories are suited to modelling causal transitions between psychological states because it is plausible to see such transitions, including those between the states of a subpersonal, cognitive psychology, as inferences. However, where it is less plausible to see the appropriate causal relations as inferences, STM-styled theories are less plausible. And it is far less plausible to view the causal relations between cognitive states and *behavioral* outputs as inferential. In light of this, computational psychology, whether wide or narrow, is faced with a prima facie problem in taxonomizing behavior.

Since STM-styled theories in the cognitive sciences have typically developed within a Cartesian computationalist conception of the mind, there has been a focus in artificial intelligence on modelling inferential relations between psychological states themselves, with the connections both from perceptual input and to behavioral output viewed as implementational details bracketed off from the computational theory itself (cf. Brooks 1991a, 1991b). On this conception of computational psychology, it *is* problematic to see the relationship between psychological states and behavior as inferential and so computational: One requires a weak conception of computation according to which *any* causal effect that a psychological state has is computational. However, if we give up Cartesian computationalism in favor of wide computationalism, this problem can be resolved. From a wide computational perspective, the overall task of computational psychologists is to provide computational descriptions of an organism's environment and psychological states, formulating algorithms that adequately describe the causal transitions between them. On this conception, since the organism does not mark a significant boundary for psychology, it would be natural to expect computational descriptions of an organism's activities, such as behavior and perception, that are psychological but not purely internal to the individual. Because the wide computationalist sees computational psychology as reaching beyond the individual, the relationship between cognitive states and behavior that she provides is more readily seen as inferential.

## 4. THE NARROW CONTENT PROGRAM: SOME INTRODUCTORY COMMENTS

As I noted in locating our discussion of folk psychology, many philosophers have found themselves sharing a pair of prima facie conflicting intuitions: those motivating individualism and those suggesting that psychological explanation is representational. The most common attempts to reconcile the two sets of intuitions have involved articulating some notion of *narrow content,* an individualistic but intentional notion. Unlike the argument of the previous section, which could focus exclusively on Stich's syntactic theory of mind as the only developed, content-free option for an individualistic psychology, in exploring the prospects for an intentional, individualistic psychology, matters are more complex. Various accounts of narrow content have been offered and, in general, it is less clear what vision of psychology each of these accounts presents. I shall concern myself primarily with a critical examination of the two most widely advocated accounts of narrow content, narrow *conceptual role* semantics (NCRS) and the *narrow function* theory of content.

As a lead-in to these two accounts of narrow content, recall the pre-theoretic doubt about the very notion of narrow content introduced in §8 of Chapter 7, which serves to bring out a tension between an individualistic and an intentional psychology: An individualistic psychology must specify properties that supervene on the intrinsic physical properties of individuals, whereas an intentional psychology will be world-involving because it is truth conditional. Two general ways in which this tension between individualism and intentionality could be relaxed correspond to the two most widely advocated accounts of narrow content. First, one could attempt to characterize content independently of truth conditions; the proposal that narrow content is conceptual role (Block 1986; Field 1978; Loar 1981, 1988a; McGinn 1982) eases the prima facie conflict between individualism and intentionality in just this way. Second, even conceding that there *is* a conceptual connection between our ordinary notion of content and truth conditions, one might still think that one can construct a notion of narrow content that brackets out truth conditions from our ordinary, intuitive notion of content. The narrow function theory (Fodor 1987:ch. 2, 1991a; White 1982, 1991:ch. 2) explores this second option: It concedes that the concept of narrow content is one we grasp, at least ultimately, in terms of truth conditions but claims that there is scope for some notion of content according to which this connection is bracketed.

Either of these accounts of narrow content *could* be offered as part of a pluralistic view of psychology, one that also made room for wide content explanations or even the sorts of wide computational explanations of cognitive behavior that I discussed in Chapter 3. Were the notion of narrow content articulated as part of such a pluralistic framework it would not serve as a *replacement* for wide content; rather, it would be a notion of content for use in those parts of psychology that were individualistic. Thus interest in these versions of the narrow content program extends beyond our interest in individualism as a constraint on taxonomy and explanation in psychology. I shall restrict myself to a consideration of these accounts as part of an individualistic psychology; only as an expression of the intentional vision of an individualistic psychology is the narrow content program relevant to the scope of this book.

## 5. NARROW CONCEPTUAL ROLE SEMANTICS AND THE NARROW FUNCTION THEORY

The basic ideas behind NCRS and the narrow function theory are relatively simple. Consider NCRS. Conceptual role semantics is the view that there is a type of (sometimes *aspect of*) mental content that is a function purely of the conceptual role of the corresponding mental state; what proponents of NCRS add to conceptual role semantics is the view that such a conceptual role is individualistic. Just as there is a type of (aspect of) mental content that is determined by the truth conditions that an attribution of content has, by the proposition that it expresses, so too is there a type of (aspect of) mental content determined by the conceptual connections between a given mental state and other intrinsic states of the bearer of the state. The former of these is wide, the latter narrow.

We can further understand both conceptual role semantics and NCRS in terms of their functionalist pedigree. Functionalists hold that mental states can be defined in terms of the overall functional or causal role that those states have. A mental state's causal role is the totality of potential causes and effects of that state, including both those causes and effects external to the individual and those between internal mental states themselves. Like functionalists, and *unlike* individualists who express their view in terms of the necessity to individ-uate psychological states by their causal *powers,* conceptual role theo-rists, including proponents of NCRS, do not distinguish between the causes and the effects that a mental state has (cf. Chapter 1, §3). Two features distinguish conceptual role semantics from functionalism.

First, conceptual role semantics is a view specifically about the iden-tity of mental *content,* not that of mental states more generally. It is thus possible for someone to endorse functionalism as a view about the na-ture of mental states, especially intentional states such as belief and de-sire, but reject conceptual role semantics as an account of content; since not all mental states are intentional, the converse option – the rejection of functionalism about mental states in general and the accep-tance of conceptual role semantics – would also seem possible.

Second, not *any* functional or causal role is relevant to the identity of mental content, but only those that are conceptual. How we are to understand 'conceptual' here is a question I shall return to in a moment, but we can get an intuitive grasp of what the conceptual role theorist means to exclude as a determinant of content by consid-ering a crude example. Suppose that one of the causal consequences of my believing that Sydney is a large city is that, in a suitable context, I fall off my chair. Even were my falling off my chair a causal effect of this belief, intuitively it is not of the right type to be relevant to the identity of the content of that belief. Likewise with many of the *causes* that such a belief has, such as being hit on the head with a brick. Even supposing that this were how I came to acquire the belief that Sydney is a large city, again intuitively, that causal fact would not be relevant to the identity of the content of the belief. The sorts of causes that are relevant, by contrast, include being told that Sydney is a large city, having the experience of driving in Sydney, and looking at a map of Sydney; the sorts of effects that are relevant include desiring not to drive in Sydney, telling others that Sydney is a large city, and wondering how it compares to other large cities you know.

Staying at an intuitive level, such causes and effects are conceptual, and contrast with other causes and effects, which we might think of as *merely mechanical.* If conceptual role semantics takes a subset of a mental state type's causes and effects (those that are conceptual) as relevant to its content, then NCRS takes a subset of these (those that are narrow). Thus, if the conceptual roles just cited, such as being told that Sydney is a large city and desiring not to drive in Sydney, are to be part of NCRS, they must have individualistic construals.

It is important to see that this makes NCRS stronger (and so harder to derive) than some of its proponents have thought. Drawing again on the distinction between internal and intrinsic mental states, note that it is not sufficient for a conceptual role to be narrow that it be internal to the individual; rather, it must be intrinsic to that individual. That is, according to NCRS, the sorts of conceptual roles that determine content are not simply physically located inside the individual but individuate properties that supervene on the intrinsic physical properties of the individual. Thus, when Ned Block says that for a proponent of NCRS 'conceptual roles stop at the skin' (1986:623), he is stating at most a necessary condition, not a sufficient one, for the identity of narrow content; and he says something misleading in suggesting that one gets these 'short-armed' conceptual roles from 'long-armed' roles by " 'chop[ping] off' the portion of these [long-armed] roles outside the skin" (1986:637).

So much for NCRS for now; let us turn to the other chief account of narrow content. The narrow function theory may be best introduced by a brief discussion of work that inspires it, that of Kaplan (1989) and Perry (1977, 1979) on demonstratives and indexicals in the philosophy of language. Central here is Kaplan's distinction between what he calls the *content* and *character* of a proposition. Consider Kaplan's example of the sentence 'My pants are on fire'. If we think of the content of a sentence as the conditions in which it is true, then because of the indexical 'my', the content of this sentence is determined by reference to the circumstances in which it is uttered. When uttered *by Joe,* it has the content that *his* pants are on fire; it is true just if *Joe's* pants are on fire; when uttered by some other individual, Phil, it is true just if *Phil's* pants are on fire. Although the truth conditions for these two utterances are different, there is something like truth conditions that they share: Both utterances are true just if the speaker's pants are on fire. What they share is their *character,* which we can think of as a rule relating token utterances to truth conditions: Given a token utterance in a context, it provides the conditions under which that token is true. Character is a function from contexts to contents (truth conditions), whereas content is a function from possible worlds to extensions. Thus character can be thought of as a second-order function, a function returning a value (a proposition) that itself is a function (cf. Chapter 5, §2).

Consider the indexical singular term 'I'. The character of 'I' is a linguistic rule: 'I' refers to the utterer or writer. But this rule does not tell us whom 'I' refers to in a particular context; to know *that*, we have to know who the utterer or writer of that token is. Competent speakers of the language use their knowledge of the character of 'I' to determine the extension of particular tokens of it.

Although Kaplan introduces the distinction between content and character as one that applies in the first instance to sentences in natural languages, it would seem equally applicable to mental states. John Perry has argued that character is of particular significance for psychological explanation because the character of mental states explains human action. An example of Perry's illustrates his point:

> When you and I have beliefs under the common character of 'A bear is about to attack me', we behave similarly. We both roll up in a ball and try to be as still as possible. Different thoughts apprehended, same character, same behavior. When you and I both apprehend that I am about to be attacked by a bear, we behave differently. I roll up in a ball, you run to get help. Same thought apprehended, different characters, different behaviors. (Perry 1977:494, as quoted with terminological modification in Kaplan 1989:532)

Perry's point is that character – what *he* calls the *sense entertained* – is used to individuate mental states when we are interested in predicting and explaining behavior. The character of thought fixes the psychological role that mental states play in the causation of behavior; as Perry says, same character, same behavior. To return to Kaplan's example, when you and I both think '*My* pants are on fire', we engage in the same behavior, namely, attempts to extinguish the blaze in our own pants. This would not be so had we both simply grasped the same content of the thought that *A*'s pants are on fire, where *A* designates one of us (cf. Block 1986:623, 668–9).

The narrow function theory attempts to generalize Kaplan's notion of character as an account of content appropriate for psychological explanation: Narrow content is a function from contexts to wide contents. If a mental state's narrow content is one of its intrinsic causal powers, it is a power to produce a semantically evaluable content, a proposition. Given a context, the narrow content that a mental state has specifies its propositional content. The identity conditions for functions are *extensional:* Two functions defined for the same arguments that determine the same values for each argument are the same function.

To see how the narrow function theory works in a familiar case, consider the standard Twin Earth case and the beliefs that Rex and

T-Rex would express by saying 'Water is wet'. If the context is Earth and the belief Rex's, then the belief expressed by 'Water is wet' has the content $H_2O$ is wet; if the context is Twin Earth and the belief T-Rex's, the belief has the content XYZ is wet. The narrow content of that belief is what remains constant across these contexts, and so is shared Rex and T-Rex. Indeed, narrow content is shared by doppelgängers across *all* possible contexts, the idea being that for any context in which Rex has beliefs about water, were T-Rex to be in that same context, he would have beliefs about water. So, although Rex and T-Rex may have beliefs with different contents because of their different contexts, they share beliefs with the same narrow contents. This is no different from two identical knives that bring about different effects (only one cuts) because of their different contexts (only one has force applied to it); the knives still have identical causal powers, such as being sharp, across these contexts.

Since my central criticism of the conception of behavior within the syntactic theory of mind turned on that theory's individualistic nature, that criticism will also apply to the conception of behavior within both NCRS and the narrow function theory. Rather than modify my argument from §3 and so adapt this criticism, I want to introduce some general, prior problems for each of these accounts of narrow content. As with my discussion of the content-free vision of an individualistic psychology, I shall not attempt to recount existing criticisms of NCRS (e.g., Fodor 1987:ch. 3; Fodor and Lepore 1992:ch. 6; Harman 1988) and the narrow function theory (Adams, Drebushenko, Fuller and Stecker 1990; Block 1991; Stalnaker 1989), focussing instead on criticisms implicit in this book thus far. Advocates of narrow content are correct to insist on the need for an intentional psychology. The problems that both NCRS and the narrow function theory face are testimony to the depth of the prima facie tension between an individualistic and an intentional psychology; they are evidence that the only intentional psychology we are likely to have is wide.

## 6. NARROW CONCEPTUAL ROLE: TOO MUCH, TOO LITTLE . . .

In §5 of Chapter 8, I argued for the causal depth of ordinary, wide *folk* psychology over what I called *narrow-folk* psychology, an individualistic version of folk psychology. Although the form of narrow-folk psychology for which this argument is clearest is the language of thought conception, according to which narrow-folk states are instantiated as subpersonal states, I suggested that the argument applies to *any* narrow-folk psychology that identifies narrow-folk states and their contents with narrow functional structures. NCRS, as applied to folk psychology, is such a type of narrow-folk psychology, and here I want to show how this objection applies to NCRS.

I begin with a quick recap of the basic idea of the argument. Since folk psychology is in large part wide, it is able to express generalizations that hold between creatures who differ arbitrarily in the details of their internal workings. Although a narrow-folk psychology would be able to capture some of these regularities, it could not do so in cases in which the creatures concerned differed in precisely the narrow functional structures that were to be identified with narrow contents. Since creatures in the actual world who are behaviorally similar to us may differ significantly in their neurophysiology, folk psychology has greater causal depth than narrow-folk psychology. Now, consider a narrow-folk psychology that identifies the narrow content of the states it posits with their narrow conceptual role. Since folk-like states are taxonomized in part by their content, when the narrow conceptual role differs, the states taxonomized will differ. Individuals could differ in the narrow conceptual role that their folk-like states have, yet still be the subjects of common behavioral and psychological regularities. Only wide folk psychology offers a common explanation of such regularities.

This gets us to a conclusion about causal depth, however, only if we consider folk psychology and such a narrow-folk psychology in the actual and nearby possible worlds (see Chapter 8, §7). Focus initially on the nearest of all possible worlds, the actual world. Why think that narrow conceptual roles vary between people in the actual world? (One cannot simply suppose that they do, for to do so would be to beg the question at issue.) One reason is that people's mental states vary not only in their *wide* conceptual roles but also in their *functional* roles more generally. I consider this a serious problem for functionalist views of type identity, and to see the problem that NCRS inherits from its functionalist pedigree, I must explain why.

It is no accident that those proposing type functionalism typically mention a few causes and effects of a given mental state and then, implying that the specification of the functional role could be completed, stop.[2] For were they to attempt completeness, one would be able to see that type functionalism does not adequately define commonsense psychological terms. As soon as the list of defining causes and effects for a given mental state goes beyond a few stock items, it seems pretty doubtful that a mental state's *complete* functional role could define that state; very few states of the same psychological kind share complete functional roles.

To see this, consider a typical example of a mental state defined by its functional role. What is it to have the belief that *there is a leopard in that tree above?* According to the functionalist, it is to be in an internal state of belief that is typically caused by seeing a leopard in a tree above one, and typically causes one to enter other mental states (e.g., fear, excitement) and make certain responses, such as running back to the Jeep (if that is close by), reaching for one's gun (if one is, say, a hunter), or remaining very quiet. These connections between perceptual stimuli, other mental states, and behavioral responses constitute the functional role of the state of believing that there is a leopard in that tree above, a belief state with the content 'there is a leopard in that tree above'. As the three disjuncts on the effect side suggest, a complete specification of the functional role of that state will be extremely detailed, involving many conditionals; the same will be true on the cause side, once the reference to typical causes is appropriately unpacked. Complexity in the taxonomic criteria itself is no problem, provided that the state so taxonomized is one that individuals share. But here is the catch: The more complete the specification of the functional role, the more particular the state taxonomized is to a given individual *because* the complete functional roles of folk psychological states typically vary across individuals. Since intentional states are typically dispositional, and so the appropriate functional definitions highly conditional, the variation here need not be as radical as one might think (e.g., from individual to individual). But since the conditionals must be conjoined for them to specify a common state, instantiation of the resulting functional definition is unlikely to be widespread. For some beliefs, the variation here may be minimal enough for generality to be purchased through idealization: There *are* typical causes and effects for some beliefs, and for these

2 In Ramsey-styled formulations of functionalism that Lewis (1970, 1972) introduced and that Shoemaker (1981) relies on in contrasting analytic functionalism and psychofunctionalism, note the ' . . . ' featuring in the Ramsified expressions. Cf. Putnam (1988:chh. 5, 6) on functionalism.

perhaps the tension between completeness and causal depth can be relaxed through idealization. Yet such beliefs tend to be the exception rather than the rule.

Continuing with our example, there is no one set of causes and effects instantiated by individuals who believe that there is a leopard in the tree above: What causes and effects that state has depend on the sort of person who has it (a coward, a nervous person, an aggressive person), the social role of that person (a hunter, a tourist, a prisoner), and her circumstances (in the jungle, at the zoo, reading a book). Individuals who vary with respect to all of these parameters could still instantiate the belief that there is a leopard in the tree above; they do so even though their instantiations of that belief have very different conceptual roles. Even the *stated* components of the functional role do not *need* to be present in anyone who believes that there is a leopard in the tree above. There is not even one thing that people with this belief *must* also believe in virtue of having that belief.

The idea that only our ignorance about the causes and effects of folk psychological states stops us from specifying their complete functional roles should be turned on its head: We know enough about how various the causes and effects of a given folk psychological state can be to know that folk states are not taxonomized by their functional roles. *Complete* functional roles provide too fine-grained a taxonomy of psychological states for folk psychological purposes. Even idealizations of incomplete functional roles are likely to leave us with a taxonomy of psychological states that is hyperconcrete.

In one respect, the situation with NCRS is worse and raises a second problem that NCRS faces. For although we can talk with some plausibility of idealizing about a given state's wide functional role, idealization about that state's narrow conceptual role is more problematic. The reason is that many of the causes and effects of mental states that *are* shared by individuals who, intuitively, instantiate the same kind of state are external to those individuals, and such causes and effects cannot be part of a narrow conceptual role. For example, one typical cause of the belief that there is a leopard in the tree above is that there *is* a leopard in the tree above; one typical effect of that belief is that one communicate this fact to others if they are present. Neither this cause nor this effect are part of the *narrow* conceptual role of that belief. Yet precisely these sorts of causes and effects are likely to be shared by individuals with that belief, given the actual circumstances in which individuals possess it. This raises the question of why we should think that narrow conceptual roles specify contents at all.

We can summarize the chief problem with NCRS by saying that there is *too much* in the narrow conceptual role that a folk-like psychological state has for it to be what is shared by physically distinct individuals in common environments, and so what provides the basis for causally deep psychological explanations of their behaviors. Much the same point is true of the states of a subpersonal psychology. To return to an example of Kim Sterelny's mentioned at the end of Chapter 3, both an owl and a bat may instantiate a perceptual state with the content 'mouse down there,' even though its causal relations internal to each animal are very different. It is plausible to think that because owls and bats function with different sense modalities, they differ in the narrow conceptual role that their 'mouse down there' states have. Nonetheless, such states can be caused by the same stimulus, that is, a mouse, and can cause the same behavioral response, and for some explanatory purposes should be viewed as being of the same psychological kind. A wide taxonomy of psychological states gives us the causal depth that one based on NCRS is ill-suited to provide.

Sterelny's example can also be used to illustrate the second problem I have posed: that abstracting away from a psychological state's full conceptual role leaves one with *too little* to specify narrow content. Precisely because owls and bats are likely to vary in their internal psychological details, in abstracting away from both the external causes and effects, and so much of the complete causal role that their 'mouse down there' states have, one loses just what makes the states of the same *intentional* kind. We are left with causal (even computational) relations between the state and other internal states, but why do these relations suffice to give the states intentional content, let alone the same intentional content? We attribute shared intentional states to both owls and bats, and make generalizations about them not because of the state's narrow conceptual role but because of its wide causal role.

It is important to be clear about what this argument against NCRS as an account of narrow content purports to show. First, the argument's primary conclusion is not that the general notion of narrow content articulated by NCRS is incoherent or oxymoronic; rather, it is that a psychology using such a notion of narrow content is explanatorily more limited than a wide intentional psychology. There may be a way to abstract away from the details of a state's narrow conceptual role and preserve causal depth in some cases, but there is reason to think that this is not possible in general. Because of this, even if NCRS does articulate an adequate notion of narrow content for some purposes, it cannot provide the basis for a complete individualistic vision of an intentional psychology. Thus NCRS is most plausibly seen as part of two-factor conceptual role semantics (Block 1986; McGinn 1982); such a two-factor view gives up on the individualistic vision of psychology.

Second, the argument provides *some* reason for accepting the stronger claim that the notion of narrow content suffers from an inherent tension. One could see the argument as showing that narrow conceptual role provides neither necessary nor sufficient conditions for intentionality. The first problem – that there are cases in which we have two states of the same psychological kind, despite those states having different narrow conceptual roles – is a denial of the necessity of identity in narrow conceptual role for shared intentionality. The second problem is a denial of the sufficiency of identity in narrow conceptual role *for intentionality at all,* where the narrow conceptual role being considered is one that idealizes away from many of the causal details that constitute complete narrow conceptual roles.

Attempting to express the state's narrow content with its narrow conceptual role is very much like attempting to express the concept 'narrow planet' in terms of the intrinsic physical properties of massive astronomical bodies or the concept 'narrow species' in terms of the intrinsic physical properties of individuals. The prospects for going narrow in each case do not look promising because the intrinsic causal powers of the entities taxonomized vary in a way that problematizes the relationship between the original and revised concepts. This is what one would expect of an essentially relational concept; it is what one would expect were content essentially relational. And if content *is* essentially relational, then narrow content is an oxymoron.

## 7. NARROW FUNCTIONS AND PSYCHOLOGICAL EXPLANATION

The worry about the adequacy of NCRS for specifying a notion that is intentional at all is one that also arises for the narrow function theory. If narrow content is a function from contexts to propositions,

235

then specifying the context of an individual's belief determines its propositional content. But precisely the same is true of *computational* mental states, states that may not be intentional: Specifying their context determines what they represent. Thus it cannot be qua function from contexts to propositions that narrow content is intentional.

A second problem concerns the *expressibility* of narrow content on the narrow function theory. If narrow content is a type of causal power that is semantically evaluable relative to a context, this suggests that narrow content is not itself semantically evaluable and so expressible. There is, of course, an intuitive conception of what narrow content is: It is the sort of content that Rex and his Twin Earth doppelgänger T-Rex share in virtue of which they engage in behaviors of the same kind. The trick is to move from this intuitive conception to a way of expressing such content, for it is only as it is expressed that it can feature in psychological generalizations.

Suppose that we want to express the narrow content that T-Rex has when he is thinking about twater. If, to take the simplest case, we say that T-Rex has thoughts *about twater,* then although our attribution is true it is not an attribution of narrow content, for the state specified is not one shared by T-Rex and Rex (Rex does *not* have thoughts about twater). An early proposal of Fodor's for expressing narrow content illustrates the general problem. Fodor says:

> [B]y the content of a belief I mean approximately what we would specify if we were asked to write down its logical form, with constants for the predicate terms. So, the content of the phenomenological belief is something like: (x)(x is drinkable, transparent, sailable-on . . . etc. only if x is wet). (1982:111)

Fodor claims that such a conception of content – what he refers to as the content of *phenomenological* beliefs – is narrow:

> When somebody on Earth believes that water is wet, he holds a universally quantified belief with approximately the content: *all the potable, transparent sailable-on . . . etc., kind of stuff is wet.* And when somebody on Earth$_2$ believes that water$_2$ is wet, what he holds is a belief with that *very same content.* (1982:112)

For the content to be narrow, however, it must apply not just to Rex and T-Rex, but to Rex and *all* of his doppelgängers. But, given that the environments of these doppelgängers can vary arbitrarily, it is extremely unlikely that *any* conjunction of descriptions will express a content they all share, for such a conjunction will almost certainly include descriptions of features that can vary across the environments. For example, consider a doppelgänger of Rex existing in a world in which what is called 'water' doesn't have *any* properties specified in the phenomenological content of water for Rex.

Fodor's proposal is an attempt to articulate how an individual conceives of and describes her own intentional states. This might seem a relatively straightforward task, but it is not if one is constrained by individualism. For how an individual conceives of her own *intentional* states is just how she conceives of how she conceives of the world, and so in describing her own intentional states it is inevitable that she offer wide descriptions. If I want to describe my belief that water is wet, then I describe it as the belief that water is wet. But this description is wide, not narrow, one that may not accurately describe the beliefs of my doppelgängers.

Consider the prima facie inexpressibility of narrow content as a challenge for narrow content theorists, one to be met by proposals about narrow content (cf. Jackson and Pettit 1993; White 1991:ch. 2). If narrow content *is* inexpressible, this is a deep problem for the narrow function theory. Fodor, who in other work concedes that narrow content itself is inexpressible, does not seem to think so. He says:

> What I share with my Twin − what [local] supervenience *guarantees* that we share − is a mental state that is semantically evaluable relative to a context. Referring expressions of English can therefore be used to pick out narrow contents, via their *hypothetical* semantic properties. So, for example, the English expression 'the thought that water is wet' can be used to specify the narrow content of a mental state that my Twin and I share (even though, qua anchored to $H_2O$, it doesn't, of course, *express* that content). In particular, it can be used to pick out the content of my Twin's 'water'-thought via the truth conditions that it *would have had* if my Twin had been plugged into my world. (1987:51)

There are at least two distinct points that Fodor is making here.

First, the semantic evaluability of a mental state relative to a context is sufficient for that state's being taxonomic in an intentional psychology. This constitutes a response to the claim that the strict inexpressibility of narrow content entails that narrow content is not suitable for psychological explanation. Second, and subsequently, relational expressions in English can be used to refer to narrow contents without themselves expressing those contents. This is because these expressions have the truth conditions that the states they pick out would have had had they been instantiated on Earth, where English (rather than, say, Twin English) is spoken. I think that Fodor is mistaken on both points and that these mistakes are significant for the plausibility of the narrow function theory more generally.

Take Fodor's first point about the insignificance of narrow content's inexpressibility. I do not see how one can accept a criterion of taxonomic individuation for psychological states that is inexpressible, for such criteria give us the kinds that feature in psychological generalizations, and inexpressible generalizations are not generalizations at all. This point holds true for *any* taxonomy. More particular to the case of psychological states, when we are dealing with doppelgängers, we can be sure that they will instantiate states with the same narrow content – by definition, if we like – but without a way to express narrow content in general, there is no reliable way to determine whether two arbitrarily chosen individuals have psychological states with the same narrow content.[3]

Fodor's second point, his claim that relational expressions can be used to refer to narrow contents without themselves expressing those contents, might be thought to temper this objection. His claim turns on the idea that propositional clauses function in the way proponents of the causal theory of reference claim that descriptions associated with natural kind terms function: Such descriptions are reference-fixing, not essence-identifying. And, as with the causal theory of reference, the expectation here is that the appropriate essences will be specified by an underlying empirical theory. In the case of psychology, the essences are intrinsic causal powers, narrow contents, that are semantically evaluable relative to a context and picked out (identified by) propositional clauses.

This second point clarifies the broader conception of psychological taxonomy invoked by the narrow function theorist. Individuating psychological states by their propositional contents does not yield a taxonomy suitable for psychology. Rather, propositional clauses provide reference-fixing descriptions of internal mental states that will be taxonomized by a developing empirical theory articulating narrow contents. If there turns out to be a close enough fit between the kinds and generalizations in our folk psychology and those in the to-be-

---

3 In this connection, note that Stephen White's (1982:esp. 357) account of narrow content is explicitly restricted to the case of doppelgängers; in White's terms, it is an account of *partial* character. White's (1991:ch. 2) development of the narrow function theory still seems restricted to an account of partial character.

arrived-at narrow theory, then one can reasonably talk of factoring folk psychology into a narrow-folk psychology, and so defend the former by the latter.

I shall not offer a direct argument against this conception of psychological taxonomy. Rather, I simply want to contrast it with the alternative conception of taxonomy in psychology developed throughout this book. Taxonomies both in science and in common sense are often rough and lack precision, and often do not specify essences, if these are conceived of as intrinsic causal powers. Taxonomic schemes are as good as are the generalizations their kinds feature in and need not conform to general a priori constraints on taxonomy. Developing and future sciences may, of course, offer various improvements on both existing folk and scientific taxonomies, but they are seldom the epistemic yardstick by which the explanatory value of existing taxonomic schemes are measured. This is because many of our existing taxonomies have already earned their own epistemic keep; they are on solid enough ground themselves that their failure to reduce (in some suitable sense) to new and exciting scientific theories simply provides further a posteriori evidence for the truth of a non-reductive view of the structure of our folk and scientific explanatory frameworks. From this perspective, ideal taxonomies, such as those offered by the narrow function theory, are motivated by a mistaken epistemology of science.

## 8. CONCLUSION

Let me first review my chief conclusions about two versions of the narrow content program, NCRS and the narrow function theory. Against NCRS I posed the 'too much, too little' dilemma: On the one hand, states taxonomized by their complete narrow functional roles were too fine-grained to serve in intentional explanations with more causal depth than their wide rivals; on the other, idealization about narrow functional roles is likely to leave one with no intentional psychology at all. Against the narrow function theory, I made three points about the notion of narrow content it specifies. First, it is not intentional; second, it is inexpressible (and this is unacceptable); and third, it is part of a larger conception of taxonomy and explanation to which I have provided an alternative and preferable conception.

Proponents of NCRS and the narrow function theory should

probably put their in-house differences to one side and develop their views as *complementary* parts of the narrow content program; NCRS and the narrow function theory are, I think, best seen as mutually supporting perspectives on narrow content. NCRS attempts to articulate a notion of narrow content by attending exclusively to the rich internal conceptual relations between psychological states; it is an account of content *without the outer*. The narrow function theory proposes a notion of narrow content that can be factored out of ordinary wide content without saying anything substantive about the conceptual relations between psychological states; it is an account of content *without the inner*. If the narrow content program is to be completed, narrow content theorists need to say something both about the conceptual relations between mental states *and* about how narrow content relates to wide content.

Part of my aim in discussing the content-free and intentional individualistic visions of psychology represented by Stich's STM and the narrow content program is to articulate the positive conceptions of psychology that individualists have in mind. The aim of this chapter has been to convey something of the prospects and problems for individualistic visions of psychology, though it would be misleading to imply that I take myself simply to be offering a survey of some options and tentatively pointing to some problems with them. I think that individualism is false, that it should be rejected as a constraint on psychology, and that the generality and depth of the problems that an individualistic psychology faces constitute strong evidence for these conclusions. My strategy of discussing broad options for an individualistic psychology and developing objections that have their seeds in earlier chapters of this book, although less definitive than one that examines in detail a series of specific proposals, claims, and arguments, is useful in challenging the intuitions and assumptions that motivate such proposals, claims, and arguments. And it is these intuitions and assumptions that, in my view, need challenging in thinking our way beyond individualism in psychology.

# 10

## Conclusion: Cartesian psychology and the science of the mind

We do not need an individualistic or Cartesian psychology in order to develop satisfactory psychological explanations for the workings of the physical mind. More pointedly, there are various ways in which a Cartesian psychology would be explanatorily impoverished relative to its wide rivals, and this makes individualism not only unnecessary but implausible. Part of my general argument has involved bringing out non-individualistic strands to existing psychological explanations, using these as a check on the normative claims that individualists have made about psychological explanation and mental causation; part has involved rethinking the more general claims on which individualists have based their views about psychology in particular. Since one of the central motivations for individualism is a commitment to some form of physicalism or materialism about the mind, many of these more general claims have been made about the nature of science and scientific explanation, these being paradigms of triumphs in our attempts to understand the physical world.

In arguing that a science of the mind does not require a Cartesian psychology, I have neither rejected materialism nor claimed that individualists suffer from so-called scientism about psychology, that is, a faith in science to provide all of the answers that it is reasonable to ask about the mind. This book expresses no scepticism about the cognitive sciences, only a reluctance to accept all that has been claimed on their behalf and a rejection of certain construals of what an interdisciplinary, scientific understanding of the mind must be like. It is not an external critique of individualism but a challenge to individualism on its own terms.

Viewing individualism as a constraint on psychology construes individualism as a thesis that applies to psychology in general. Does anyone *really* accept such a strong construal of individualism (cf. Rowlands 1991; Segal 1991)? Putting this question aside for a moment, suppose that one abandoned individualism as a constraint on psychology and opted instead for some more restricted or limited individualistic thesis (see Patterson 1991). Wouldn't the most vexing problems concerning the nature of psychological explanation and mental causation survive this sort of concession? For example, if one were to think individualism true of *computational* taxonomies in psychology but not of psychological taxonomy more generally, a version of the problem of making sense of mental causation would still arise. Given that, how significant for philosophical psychology is the rejection of individualism as a constraint on psychology? Focussing on a strong version of individualism has certainly made the argument easier in places than it might have been. But there are three reasons for the focus, and for thinking that a rejection of the strong view is both more than shadow boxing and of general significance for philosophical psychology.

First, in Part I we saw that arguments for individualism turned on more general claims; in particular, the argument from causal powers discussed in Chapter 2 has a premise about the nature of taxonomy in science, and at least one version of the computational argument examined in Chapter 3 made a claim about the nature of computational individuation. In each chapter in Part II we examined quite general, a priori claims and intuitions sometimes invoked in support of individualism (and against its rejection). These sorts of appeals would be out of place were individualism not held as a general constraint on psychology. It is only so conceived that one would expect such frequent and varied reliance on a priori arguments for individualism.

Second, it is difficult to see many of the positions and views that individualists find problematic *as* problematic unless one construes individualism as a general, normative constraint on psychological taxonomy and explanation. The clearest case that comes to mind is that of folk psychology: Given that most individualists are not wholesale eliminativists about folk psychology, their doubts about the scientific integrity of folk psychology (and hence their advocacy of the narrow content program) must stem from a view of folk psychology as violating some more general constraint; if individualism were held as a thesis about parts of psychology, or about some specifiable aspects to psychological explanation, then why should there be even a prima facie problem with folk psychology? In light of folk psychology's apparent explanatory successes, surely the correct inference to draw when faced with folk psychology's non-individualistic character would be that it is not one of those parts of (or aspects to) psychology that is individualistic. *No problem.*

Individualism was taken to be so intuitive in the late 1970s and early 1980s that explicit arguments for it were developed only later. Stich remarked (1983:165) that when he first formulated the principle of autonomy, he didn't think that it required an argument at all; Fodor's (1980a) defence of the doctrine of methodological solipsism proceeds almost entirely negatively, that is, as an argument against the possibility of a 'naturalistic' psychology. The uncritical use of such a principle and doctrine indicates that a general thesis about psychology was being discussed.

Third, one of my central concerns has been to uncover some of the many underlying intuitions that motivate individualism. I do not see individualism as a knee-jerk consequence of a simplistic philosophical view; rather, as my reference in Chapter 1 to both Cartesian and physicalist motivations for individualism may have indicated, I take individualism to be a deeply intuitive view precisely because it draws on a hodgepodge of intuitions – about the natures of the mind, science, explanation, causation, and content. My interest, in part, is in uncovering the general conception of the mind and psychology that many have found so intuitive, and for this reason I have tended to bracket or ignore all but the most striking expressions of individualism.

That said, the investigation of individualism as a constraint on psychology has shed light in many places on more cautious versions of individualism. For example, in considering the computational argument for individualism in Chapter 3 we detected an a priori strand to that argument, and I argued that once this strand is removed and the computational argument is presented as a thoroughly empirical argument, both of its premises are in prima facie conflict with existing explanatory practice in (some) computational psychology. Suppose now that we were to consider a version of the computational argument claimed to support not individualism in psychology in general but a conclusion of a more restricted scope, say, individualism about certain aspects of computational psychology. So, for example, consider the following argument: *Insofar as* computational psychology attempts to characterize the mechanisms underlying modular cognitive capacities, since computational states supervene on the physical states realizing them and computational *psychological* states are realized in internal neural states, computational psychology is individualistic. I think that the sort of critique I have developed of the computational argument also sets the stage for rejecting this argument for a more restricted conclusion: I have questioned the inference from modularity to individualism in Chapter 4, and provided the basis for challenging the claim about supervenience in Chapters 5 and 6. Our consideration of individualism as a constraint places us in a good position to take up related but more restricted individualistic theses and views.

Although I think that this general point is also true of my argument in Part III, the details of that argument would *not* survive a shift from a view of individualism as a constraint to a more restricted view of individualism. My argument in Chapter 8, although directed at specific types of narrow psychology, casts a shadow on the more general prospects for an individualistic psychology. The criteria of causal depth and theoretical appropriateness allow us to compare causal explanations when other things are equal, and I was able to ensure that this condition was met in the details of my argument for wide over narrow psychology by considering only versions of narrow psychology that were very much like existing wide psychology. But what of narrow psychological explanations that mark a radical departure from existing wide explanations? Although the argument presented in Chapter 8 itself does not apply to such explanations, I have used that argument as a foot in the door in assessing the prospects and problems for an individualistic psychology more generally in Chapter 9. For someone who thinks either that the narrow content program can be completed or that the syntactic theory of mind provides an adequate vision of psychology, there are the challenges introduced in Chapter 8, and I have suggested that these are unlikely to be met by an overarching individualistic vision of psychology. Since many of the points made in Part III point to the limits of an individualistic psychology rather than its incoherence, I see no obvious reason to think that the core of my argument there would be likely to apply to individualism when construed as a more restricted thesis. The irony is that were one to advocate a more restricted thesis about the place of individualism in psychology, in so doing one would be giving up on an individualistic *vision* of psychology.

## 2. INDIVIDUALISM AND BEHAVIORISM

In Chapter 1, I alluded to an analogy between individualism and behaviorism, and now we are in a position to replace the allusion with a more concrete comparison of the two views. The initial point of comparison, recall, was that both behaviorism and individualism could be viewed as constraints on psychological taxonomy and explanation, though I left open just what sort of constraint each was. As a reminder of why it is plausible to view behaviorism as such a constraint, consider J. B. Watson's concluding claim in an influential early paper:

Psychology as behavior will, after all, have to neglect but few of the really essential problems with which psychology as an introspective science now concerns itself. In all probability even this residue of problems may be phrased in such a way that refined methods in behavior (which certainly must come) will lead to their solution. (1913:177)

Behaviorism in psychology delimits a space of admissable possibilities, and in so doing constrains psychological theory.

Thinking of both behaviorism and individualism as constraints on psychological taxonomy and explanation brings out an interesting contrast between them: Behaviorists hold that the referents of psychological terms that lie within the organism ought to be taxonomized by reference to (observable) external states of the organism and its environment, whereas individualists hold just the opposite – that the referents of psychological terms ought to be taxonomized *without* reference to what is external to a given individual. Both behaviorists and individualists view the boundary of the organism as significant for psychological taxonomy. They differ in what each brackets off in taxonomizing psychological states: What is inside of that boundary (behaviorism) or what is outside of it (individualism).

Like behaviorism, individualism comes in a variety of flavors that vary along the a priori–empirical dimension. Take the two varieties of behaviorism at each end of this continuum, starting with philosophical or *analytical* behaviorism, the view that mental states *are* behavioral dispositions. At the height of the influence of language-focussed approaches to philosophy in the 1940s and 1950s (including both 'ordinary language' philosophy and the positivism expressed in Carnap's writings), this point was expressed as a semantic thesis about the *meaning* of mental terms and was typically defended as a conceptual truth; in addition, the sorts of arguments given for it were a priori in that they proceeded largely through an appeal to intuitions and thought experiments, and without direct reference to research in empirical psychology. For all the talk of individualism as either a presupposition of cognitive science or an inevitable consequence of the adoption of a physicalistic conception of mental phenomena, the most influential arguments for individualism share this feature with arguments for philosophical behaviorism.

By contrast, psychological or *methodological* behaviorism holds that psychologists ought to treat mental states as if they were definable as sets of stimulus–response pairs, for it is only by doing so that an intersubjective science explaining behavior will be possible (see Mackenzie 1977). Typical arguments for methodological behaviorism were empirical in that they appealed either to the methodological futility of non-behavioristic approaches to psychology or to the particular explanatory successes of existing behavioristic approaches. In Chapters 3 and 4 we discussed arguments for individualism of both of these types.

One apparent disanalogy between behaviorism and individualism, perhaps best conceived as a sociological difference, concerns the relationship of each to psychological practice. Behaviorism was articulated and developed *within* psychology itself; as a consequence, it was not simply a thesis or proposition for which arguments could be given, but something more like a Kuhnian paradigm within psychology. Although individualism is manifest in certain approaches to psychology, it is first and foremost a philosophical thesis, and its various formulations use terms particular to philosophical discourse, such as 'supervenience', 'Twin Earth', and 'individuation'. Even if there are distinctly philosophical versions of behaviorism, behaviorism has a home in psychological practice in a way that individualism does not. In light of this difference, isn't it misleading to imply (or even to suggest) that individualism in psychology, and so its rejection, has anything like the significance *for psychology* as did behaviorism and its rejection?

Although I am tempted to think that the difference identified here *is* important, the issues here are complicated by a number of factors.

One is that 'philosophical' and 'psychological' behaviorism have been intertwined; another is that purely a priori and empirical arguments for both behaviorism and individualism are similar philosophical fictions. In addition, I am inclined to think that the methodological characterization of the distinction between individualism and non-individualism in psychology discussed in Chapter 4 (roughly, Fodor's 'rationalism' and 'naturalism') does distinguish two actual research traditions that embody different conceptions of what psychology ought to be like. The idea that intelligence and mentality can be investigated in large part independently of both their neural realizations and the environments in which organisms happen to be located – that one can embrace a disembedded, Cartesian perspective in studying intelligence and mentality – has certainly been a guiding light in much research in artificial intelligence and cognitive science. Likewise, although the individualistic visions of psychology discussed in Chapter 9 are very much philosophical sketches of an ideal psychology that raise some prima facie problems for individualists, it would be a mistake to view such visions simply *as visions,* for they take their cue from much existing psychological explanatory practice.

## 3. OTHER INDIVIDUALISMS

The term 'individualism' has been used to refer to a number of distinct views, and in some quarters it has become a term with a distinctly negative connotation. I want to say something brief about these other uses of 'individualism' in order to clarify the relationship between individualism in psychology and these views, and so locate individualism in psychology in a broader intellectual context. I shall focus on three other forms of individualism: methodological individualism in the social sciences, individualism in evolutionary biology, and individualism or 'atomism' in political theory in the liberal tradition.

Methodological individualism in the social sciences is a normative, reductionist view; it is the view that explanations in the social sciences ought to be reducible, at least in principle, to explanations cast in terms of the intentional states and behaviors of individuals (Elster 1986; Popper 1952; Watkins 1957). For example, in considering why there was a series of rebellions and revolutions in Europe in the middle of the nineteenth century, one ought to be able to reduce any acceptable explanation to the intentions, desires, beliefs, and behaviors of the individual agents involved. One implication of method-ological individualism is that holistic explanations in the social sci-ences that are not so reducible – and here methodological individualists typically have had in mind Marxist–Hegelian explana-tions in terms of factors such as the force of history, the class struggle, and the relationship between productive forces and the relations of production – should not be entertained as acceptable, falsifiable scien-tific explanations. Thus, methodological individualism constrains so-cial scientific explanation.

As my agreement in Chapter 8 with critics of methodological individualism, such as Garfinkel (1981) and Putnam (1973), might suggest, I think that individualism in psychology and methodological individualism ought to be rejected for much the same reason: The pragmatics of explanation shows each to be an unduly restrictive constraint on explanation and so taxonomy (cf. Bhargava 1992:chh. 4, 5). My own positive view of explanation differs from those of these critics, though, in its more explicit endorsement of explanatory pluralism; if Putnam and Garfinkel *are* ecumenical in their view of explanation, this is obscured by their at times trenchant anti-reductionism. This is not to say that one could not reject individual-ism in psychology and endorse methodological individualism, or vice versa; indeed, Philip Pettit (1993) has embraced the first of these options. In discussing concessive individualism in §6 of Chapter 8, I suggested caution in proposing constraints that apply across scientific disciplines, and to this extent I am sympathetic to Pettit's general approach (see Wilson 1994c). Nonetheless, the rejection of both individualism in psychology and methodological individualism is a much less strained view than the 'reject-accept' option; recall that this was also my conclusion about the 'reject-accept' option that conces-sive individualism expresses.

Individualism in evolutionary biology is the view that the individ-ual organism is the largest unit that can be usefully viewed as a unit of selection: Natural selection operates on entities as small as genes and as large as organisms, but not on *groups* of organisms (e.g., species). Groups of organisms have differential survival value, but we can explain this adequately in terms of the relative adaptedness of individuals and their biological constituents. Importantly, we don't need to posit a process such as group selection, which accords selec-tive efficacy to units larger than the individual. The most extreme form of individualism in evolutionary biology – the selfish gene view defended by Dawkins (1982, 1989) and Williams (1966) – has had particular influence in applications of evolutionary thought to human behavior and society. Again, like individualism in psychology and methodological individualism, this form of individualism is a normative constraint on explanation, and one difficult to reconcile with many of the diverse phenomena that fall within the province of evolutionary biology. As with my similar claim about methodological individualism, the defence of this claim requires a detailed examination of explanatory practice in evolutionary biology (see D. S. Wilson 1989; Wilson and Sober 1994). But I have said enough to indicate why these three forms of individualism – in psychology, in the social sciences, and in evolutionary biology – are constraints of a kind, and the sorts of considerations relevant to evaluating each of them.

Turning from the philosophy of the special sciences to normative political theory, communitarians (Sandel 1982; Taylor 1985) have criticized the liberal tradition for what they see as an undue emphasis on political values that are built on an individualistic conception of individuals. The liberal tradition – construed broadly so as to include both classic liberals and libertarians – views isolable, insular, 'atomistic' individuals as an ultimate location of political value, as shown in its emphasis on values such as individual freedom and decision making that attach to individuals, and on the value of a state that remains neutral between competing individual conceptions of the good life. The communitarian critique is that such a conception of individuals is *politically* mistaken because state neutrality does not adequately reflect the indebtedness of individuals to particular social structures: Our values ought to be embedded within and protected by the state and society, since it is only by such active structuring of our social world that individuals can lead valuable lives. Such a conception is also *metaphysically* mistaken because the view of the self as standing beyond or apart from society is false: Selves just are not like that. The idea of an individual who is separable from the society she is in – of an individual who merely happens to find herself located in a particular society – is a philosophical fancy.

Even a general relationship between this political individualism and individualism in psychology is more difficult to discern than in either of the other two cases I have recounted. This is *not* because these other individualisms are factual views, whereas political individualism is a normative view. Rather, options here are largely open because the contrast between communitarians and the liberals they criticize is much less clear than it needs to be for one to determine whether one could coherently reject (accept) individualism in psychology and opt for (reject) political individualism. For example, the rejection of political individualism is often taken to go hand in hand with political pluralism and diversity, and were this so, then there would be at least an ecumenism shared by those who reject both individualisms. But it is far from clear that the rejection of political individualism *does* go so naturally with political pluralism, or that its acceptance is in any tension with such pluralism (Kymlicka 1989, 1990). A proper under-standing of the relationship between individualism in psychology and political individualism requires, in my view, further discussion.

The beginnings of this discussion are already underway. For exam-ple, Naomi Scheman has argued that one reason individualism in psychology has such a strong grip on our thinking is because of its connection to 'the notion of the self embodied in the ideology of liberal individualism' (1983:230). Scheman's claim is that the atomis-tic conception of the self found in liberal political theory functions as part of an ideology, liberalism, in that it gives a sheen of naturalness to views that are in fact 'expression[s] of a historically specific way of structuring some set of social interactions' (1983:231). Individualism in psychology compels because it is part of or a complement to such liberal ideology. Scheman's argument for this claim is complex and in part implicit, so it will pay to step through it slowly.

For the liberal, social entities such as communities and the state are composed of individuals, individuals who are self-determining and have their own private interests to satisfy. The political values that attach to such social entities are derivative from those that attach to individuals. To take two central social values, liberal and egalitarian societies are valued because they promote individual liberty (or hap-piness, or flourishing, or virtue). Thus, at the foundation of liberal ideology is a conception of individuals as the ultimate bearers of value. But were individuals (and what is valuable about them) to be constituted, in turn, by *their* social relations, their location in the social world, we would not have the conception of individuals as self-determining or self-defining that liberal ideology demands. In addition, a liberal requires a conception of the individual that ensures that there is a fact of the matter about what it is to be self-determining, and this pushes one in the direction of realism (vs. social constructivism) about psychological states. As Scheman says:

250

The problem is this: if individuals, their identities and life-plans are to be identifiable independently of forms of social organization (as the liberal needs them to be), then we are hard pressed to come up with anything that could make this identification non-arbitrary – unless we accept psychological realism. The idea that psychological states are definite particulars is the natural mirror to the liberal conception of individuals, since on this conception we are deprived of anything to guide the choosing and the weighing that would need to be involved were these states to be seen as constructions. (1983:233–4; footnote omitted)

I want to note a number of ways in which Scheman's argument, interesting as it is, is problematic by drawing on some of our earlier discussion.

First, as Scheman acknowledges (1983:225–6), it is often not clear what 'individualism' as applied to psychology means. I have argued that individualism is a putative constraint on taxonomic individuation in psychology. One consequence of this claim is that it is misleading to think of individualism as the view that mental states are in the head, for, as I made explicit in Chapter 6, mental states can be *internal* to individuals even if they are not *intrinsic* to them. Furthermore, although individualism is readily expressed as a view about psychological states as mental particulars – most clearly in the language of thought conception of them – I have also argued that such a view of psychological states is neither necessary nor sufficient for an individualistic conception of mental states. If one accepts these clarifications of 'individualism' in psychology, then its connections to liberalism become more complicated than those Scheman suggests. And if the same sorts of clarifications are required of the concept of *liberalism,* then the relationships between the two individualisms will likely be multifarious and complex.

Second, in Scheman's argument as I have reconstructed it, assumptions are made that are not themselves part of the conception of the self implicit in liberal ideology and are only questionably a necessary part of liberalism. The most important of these is a foundationalist moral epistemology, one that seeks a pyramid of justification with individual values at its base. Just how crucial a role this assumption and its variants play is a difficult issue, one that I shall not discuss here. In light of Rawls's (1971) explicit rejection of foundationalism in favor of his reflective equilibrium model of political justification, however, it would seem an error to view liberalism and foundationalism as too intimately connected. The more general point is that the

251

very fact that one has to introduce additional views to connect individualism in psychology and the political individualism we find in liberal ideology reflects the considerable inferential gap between the two views.

Third, an emerging theme throughout this book has been that many intuitively plausible inferences – from views about causal powers or causation to individualism, for example – are actually invalid because (in part) of some of the distinctions I have already mentioned. When one attempts, as Scheman does, to broaden the intellectual landscape and shift from seeking *justifying* reasons to seeking *explanatory* reasons for individualism in psychology, one should expect the number of parameters to one's discussion to increase, perhaps dramatically. And with such an increase, the required arguments become more complicated and thus less likely to be sound.

One criticism of these three points turns on the claim that I have misunderstood the nature of Scheman's philosophical project in linking liberal ideology and individualism in psychology. When one shifts from a discussion of arguments from *A* to *B* to one of how *A* and *B* 'hang together' – from justifying to explanatory reasons – there is a shift in goal. The goal is no longer to construct an *argument* from *A* to *B,* but to develop a *narrative* shedding light on the connections between *A* and *B.* The standards of evaluation for such a goal differ from those for the evaluation of arguments; to try to identify additional complexities, hidden premises, and mistaken inferences is to fail to recognize just this point.

Exploring the issues that a complete response to this objection involves is something I look forward to doing in future work. My hunch is that *whatever* their exact differences, the languages of argumentation and narrative are not so distinct as to operate on mutually exclusive intellectual planes; more particularly, the points I have made in the language of argumentation could also be stated without any conceptual strain in the language of narrative. Recognizing differences between argumentation and narrative is important; insisting on their incommensurability, however, would be a mistake.

## 4. BETWEEN SCIENCE AND COMMON SENSE

Finally, a more metaphilosophical concluding note. We can think of this discussion of individualism in psychology as located between science and common sense. As I have tried to make clear in the introduction to this chapter, much of what I have said in favor of rejecting individualism as a constraint on psychology views psychology as the (or at least *a*) science of the mind. Yet many of the points I have made about individualism so viewed stem from fairly mundane, commonsense reflections on explanation and its relationship to other concepts, such as causation and taxonomy. There is also a strand of commonsense realism that runs throughout the book, one that abides by a variation on the maxim 'If it looks like a cat, smells like a cat, and sounds like a cat, then it *is* a cat'; this commonsense realism is manifested perhaps most clearly in the view of folk psychology I have developed in Chapter 7.

At the end of Chapter 1, I said that I take the issue of individualism to be an issue located primarily in the philosophy of science. Commonsense realism figures in my discussion because I see the philosophy of science very much through the lens of common sense. Much of twentieth-century philosophy of science has consisted of 'rational reconstructions' of existing scientific practice in accord with a priori philosophical ideals, and although the ingenuity and systematic rigor of many such reconstructions deserve respect in their own right, they have often left commonsense thinking behind. As my discussion in Part III perhaps suggests, I view individualistic visions of psychology in a similar light. It is not so much that they cannot be made coherent – although I have expressed some doubts about this – but that an alternative understanding of the relationship between explanation and more metaphysical notions makes such visions are unnecessary.

What of the intuitive motivations for individualism with which we began, motivations that suggest that individualism itself is a part of commonsense thinking about the mind and our science of it? I have suggested that some of our philosophically sophisticated views about science need to be given up, as do some of the intuitions about science on which they are based. The same is true of a strand to commonsense thinking about the mind: Not only should philosophical refinements of commonsense, individualistic views be given up, but so too should some of the intuitions on which individualism in psychology is based. Even were the inferences from commonsense intuitions to individualism valid, those intuitions themselves are candidates for rejection. And so, although common sense is a source for individualistic views in psychology, it is not a sturdy foundation from which to defend those views.

253

# References

Adams, F., D. Drebushenko, G. Fuller, and R. Stecker. 1990. 'Narrow Content: Fodor's Folly', *Mind and Language* 5:213–29.

Antony, L. 1990. 'Semantic Anorexia: On the Notion of "Content" in Cognitive Science', in Boolos 1990.

Arbib, M. 1987. 'Modularity and Interaction of Brain Regions Underlying Visuomotor Coordination', in J. Garfield, ed., *Modularity in Knowledge Representation and Natural-Language Understanding.* Cambridge, MA: MIT Press.

Astington, J., P. Harris, and D. Olson, eds. 1988. *Developing Theories of Mind.* New York: Cambridge University Press.

Bach, K. 1982. 'De Re Belief and Methodological Solipsism', in Woodfield 1982.

Baker, L. R. 1993a. 'What Beliefs Are Not', in S. Wagner and R. Warner, eds., *Naturalism: A Critical Appraisal.* Notre Dame, IN: University of Notre Dame Press.

1993b, 'Metaphysics and Mental Causation', in Heil and Mele 1993.

Barkow, J., L. Cosmides, and J. Tooby, eds. 1992. *The Adapted Mind.* New York: Oxford University Press.

Bennett, J. 1964. *Rationality.* London: Routledge and Kegan Paul; 1989: Indianapolis, IN: Hackett.

Bhargava, R. 1992. *Individualism in Social Science.* New York: Oxford University Press.

Blackburn, S. 1984. *Spreading the Word.* Oxford: Oxford University Press.

Block, N. 1978. 'Troubles with Functionalism', in Savage 1978. Reprinted in Block 1980.

ed. 1980. *Readings in the Philosophy of Psychology, Vol. 1.* Cambridge, MA: Harvard University Press.

1986. 'Advertisement for a Semantics for Psychology', in French et al. 1986.

1990. 'Can the Mind Change the World?', in Boolos 1990.

1991. 'What Narrow Content Is Not', in Loewer and Rey 1991.

Boghossian, P. 1990. 'The Status of Content', *Philosophical Review* 99:157–84.

Boolos, G., ed. 1990. *Meaning and Method: Essays in Honor of Hilary Putnam.* New York: Cambridge University Press.

255

Boyd, R. 1988. 'How to Be a Moral Realist', in G. Sayre-McCord, ed., *Essays on Moral Realism*. Ithaca, NY: Cornell University Press.

1989. 'Realism: What It Implies and What It Does Not', *Dialectica* 43:5–29.

1990. 'Realism, Approximate Truth, and Philosophical Method', in C. W. Savage, ed., *Scientific Theories: Minnesota Studies in the Philosophy of Science 10*. Minneapolis: University of Minnesota Press.

Boyle, R. 1744. 'The Origins and Forms of Qualities', in *The Works of the Honourable Robert Boyle,* Vol. ii (1744). London: A. Millar.

Braun, D. 1991. 'Content, Causation, and Cognitive Science', *Australasian Journal of Philosophy* 69:375–89.

Brooks, R. 1991a. 'Intelligence Without Representation', *Artificial Intelligence* 47:139–59.

1991b. 'Challenges for Complete Creature Architectures', in J. Meyer and S. W. Wilson, eds., *From Animals to Animats*. Cambridge, MA: MIT Press.

Bruce, V., ed. 1991. *Face Recognition*. Hillsdale, NJ: Lawrence Erlbaum.

Burge, T. 1979. 'Individualism and the Mental', in P. French, T. Uehling, Jr., and H. Wettstein, eds., *Midwest Studies in Philosophy,* Vol. 4: *Metaphysics*. Minneapolis: University of Minnesota Press.

1982a. 'Two Thought Experiments Reviewed', *Notre Dame Journal of Formal Logic* 23:284–93.

1982b. 'Other Bodies', in Woodfield 1982.

1986a. 'Individualism and Psychology', *Philosophical Review* 95:3–45.

1986b. 'Cartesian Error and the Objectivity of Perception', in Pettit and McDowell 1986.

1988. 'Individualism and Self-Knowledge', *Journal of Philosophy* 85:649–63.

1989. 'Individuation and Causation in Psychology', *Pacific Philosophical Quarterly* 70:303–22.

1992. 'Philosophy of Language and Mind: 1950–1990', *Philosophical Review* 100:3–51.

1993. 'Mind–Body Causation and Explanatory Practice', in Heil and Mele 1993.

Campbell, F. W., and J. G. Robson. 1968. 'Application of Fourier Analysis to the Visibility of Gratings', *Journal of Physiology* 197:151–66.

Candlish, M. S. 1984. 'Inner and Outer Basic Action', *Proceedings of the Aristotelian Society* 84:83–102.

Carey, S. 1985. *Conceptual Change in Childhood*. Cambridge, MA: MIT Press.

Carnap, R. 1928. *The Logical Structure of the World,* trans. by R. George, 1967. Berkeley: University of California Press.

Child, W. 1994. *Causality, Interpretation, and the Mind*. New York: Oxford University Press.

Chomsky, N. 1957. *Syntactic Structures*. The Hague: Mouton.

1965. *Aspects of the Theory of Syntax*. Cambridge, MA: MIT Press.

1980. *Rules and Representations*. New York: Columbia University Press.

Churchland, P. M. 1979. *Scientific Realism and the Plasticity of Mind*. New York: Cambridge University Press.

1981. 'Eliminative Materialism and the Propositional Attitudes', *Journal of Philosophy* 78:67–90.

1989. *A Neurocomputational Perspective*. Cambridge, MA: MIT Press.

Churchland, P. S. 1986. *Neurophilosophy*. Cambridge, MA: MIT Press.

Clark, A. 1989. *Microcognition*. Cambridge, MA: MIT Press.

1993. *Associative Engines*. Cambridge, MA: MIT Press.

Cosmides, L. 1989. 'The Logic of Social Exchange: Has Natural Selection Shaped How Humans Reason? Studies with the Wason Selection Task', *Cognition* 31:187–276.

Cosmides, L., and J. Tooby. 1987. 'From Evolution to Behavior: Evolutionary Psychology as the Missing Link', in J. Dupre, ed., *The Latest on the Best*. Cambridge, MA: MIT Press.

1992. 'Cognitive Adaptations for Social Exchange', in Barkow, Cosmides and Tooby 1992.

Crane, T. 1990. 'The Language of Thought: No Syntax Without Semantics', *Mind and Language* 5:187–212.

1991. 'All the Difference in the World', *Philosophical Quarterly* 41:1–25.

Cummins, R. C. 1983. *The Nature of Psychological Explanation*. Cambridge, MA: MIT Press.

1989. *Meaning and Mental Representation*. Cambridge, MA: MIT Press.

1991. 'Methodological Reflections on Belief', in R. Bogdan, ed., *Mind and Common Sense*. New York: Cambridge University Press.

Davidson, D. 1970. 'Mental Events'. Reprinted in Davidson 1980.

1980. *Essays on Actions and Events*. Oxford: Oxford University Press.

1984. *Inquiries into Truth and Interpretation*. Oxford: Oxford University Press.

1987. 'Knowing One's Own Mind', *Proceedings and Addresses of the American Philosophical Association* 60:441–58.

Davies, M. 1991. 'Individualism and Perceptual Content', *Mind* 100:461–84.

Dawkins, R. 1982. *The Extended Phenotype*. Oxford: Oxford University Press.

1986. *The Blind Watchmaker*. New York: W. W. Norton.

1989. *The Selfish Gene,* 2nd ed. Oxford: Oxford University Press.

Dennett, D. C. 1978a. *Brainstorms*. Cambridge, MA: MIT Press.

1978b. 'Current Issues in the Philosophy of Mind', *American Philosophical Quarterly* 15:249–61.

1981a. 'True Believers: The Intentional Strategy and Why It Works', in A. F. Heath, ed., *Scientific Explanation*. New York: Oxford University Press. Reprinted in Dennett 1987.

1981b. 'Three Kinds of Intentional Psychology', in R. Healey, ed., *Reduction, Time and Reality*. New York: Cambridge University Press. Reprinted in Dennett 1987.

1987. *The Intentional Stance*. Cambridge, MA: MIT Press.

Devitt, M. 1990. 'A Narrow Representational Theory of the Mind', in Lycan 1990.

1991. 'Why Fodor Can't Have It Both Ways', in Loewer and Rey 1991.

Donald, M. 1991. *The Origins of the Modern Mind*. Cambridge, MA: Harvard University Press.

Dretske. F. 1988. *Explaining Behavior*. Cambridge, MA: MIT Press.

Egan, M. F. 1989. 'Discussion: What's Wrong with the Syntactic Theory of Mind', *Philosophy of Science* 56:664–74.

———. 1991. 'Must Psychology Be Individualistic?', *Philosophical Review* 100:179–203.

———. 1992. 'Individualism, Computation, and Perceptual Content', *Mind* 101:443–59.

Elster, J. 1985. *Making Sense of Marx*. New York: Cambridge University Press.

———. 1986. *An Introduction to Karl Marx*. New York: Cambridge University Press.

Elugardo, R. 1993. 'Burge on Content', *Philosophy and Phenomenological Research* 53:368–84.

Evans, G. 1982. *The Varieties of Reference*. New York: Oxford University Press.

Field, H. 1978. 'Mental Representation', *Erkenntniss*, 13:9–61. Reprinted in N. Block, ed., *Readings in the Philosophy of Psychology*, Vol. 2. Cambridge, MA: Harvard University Press, 1981.

Fisher, R. A. 1930. *The Genetical Theory of Natural Selection*. Oxford: Dover rev. ed., 1958.

Fodor, J. A. 1965. 'Explanation in Psychology', in M. Black, ed., *Philosophy in America*. London: George Allen and Unwin.

———. 1974. 'Special Sciences', *Synthese* 28:77–115. Reprinted in Fodor 1981a.

———. 1975. *The Language of Thought*. New York: Thomas Y. Crowell.

———. 1978a. 'Propositional Attitudes', *The Monist* 61:501–23. Reprinted in Fodor 1981a.

———. 1978b. 'Computation and Reduction', in Savage 1978. Reprinted in Fodor 1981a.

———. 1980a. 'Methodological Solipsism Considered as a Research Strategy in Cognitive Psychology', *Behavioral and Brain Sciences* 3:63–73. Reprinted in Fodor 1981a.

———. 1980b. 'Methodological Solipsism: Replies to Commentators', *Behavioral and Brain Sciences* 3:99–108.

———. 1981a. *Representations*. Cambridge, MA: MIT Press.

———. 1981b. 'Introduction: Something on the State of the Art', in Fodor 1981a.

———. 1982. 'Cognitive Science and the Twin-Earth Problem', *Notre Dame Journal of Formal Logic* 23:98–118.

———. 1983. *The Modularity of Mind*. Cambridge, MA: MIT Press.

———. 1987. *Psychosemantics*. Cambridge, MA: MIT Press.

———. 1989. 'Making Mind Matter More', *Philosophical Topics* 17:59–79.

———. 1991a. 'A Modal Argument for Narrow Content', *Journal of Philosophy* 87:5–26.

———. 1991b. 'You Can Fool Some of the People All of the Time, Everything Else Being Equal: Hedged Laws and Psychological Explanations', *Mind* 100:19–34.

———. 1991c. 'Replies', in Loewer and Rey 1991.

Fodor, J. A., and E. Lepore. 1992. *Holism: A Shopper's Guide*. Cambridge, MA: Basil Blackwell.

Fodor, J. A., and B. McLaughlin. 1990. 'Connectionism and the Problem of Systematicity: Why Smolensky's Solution Doesn't Work', *Cognition* 35:183–204.

Fodor, J. A., and Z. Pylyshyn. 1988. 'Connectionism and Cognitive Architecture: A Critical Analysis', *Cognition* 28:3–71.

French, P., T. Uehling, Jr., and H. Wettstein, eds. 1986. *Midwest Studies in Philosophy,* Vol. 10: *Philosophy of Mind.* Minneapolis: University of Minnesota Press.

1990. *Midwest Studies in Philosophy,* Vol. 15: *The Philosophy of the Human Sciences.* Notre Dame, IN: University of Notre Dame Press.

Gallistel, C. R. 1989a. 'Animal Cognition: The Representation of Space, Time and Number', *Psychology Annual Reviews* 40:155–89.

1989b. *The Organization of Learning.* Cambridge, MA: MIT Press.

Garfield, J. 1988. *Belief in Psychology.* Cambridge, MA: MIT Press.

Garfinkel, A. 1981. *Forms of Explanation.* New Haven, CT: Yale University Press.

Gauker, C. 1991. 'Mental Content and the Division of Epistemic Labour', *Australasian Journal of Philosophy* 69:302–18.

Geach, P. 1969. *God and the Soul.* New York: Schocken.

Gibson, J. J. 1979. *The Ecological Approach to Perception.* Boston: Houghton Mifflin.

Giere, R. 1988. *Explaining Science.* Chicago: University of Chicago Press.

Goldman, A. 1993. 'The Psychology of Folk Psychology', *Behavioral and Brain Sciences* 16:15–28.

Gopnik, A. 1993. 'How We Know Our Own Minds: The Illusion of First-Person Knowledge of Intentionality', *Behavioral and Brain Sciences* 16:1–14.

Gordon, R. 1986. 'Folk Psychology as Simulation', *Mind and Language* 1:158–71.

Gould, S. J. 1981. *The Mismeasure of Man.* Middlesex, England: Penguin.

Grimm, R., and D. Merrill, eds. 1988. *Contents of Thought.* Tucson: University of Arizona Press.

Hamilton, W. D. 1964. 'The Genetical Evolution of Social Behavior I and II', *Journal of Theoretical Biology* 7:1–52.

Hardwig, J. 1985. 'Epistemic Dependence', *Journal of Philosophy* 82:335–49.

Harman, G. 1973. *Thought.* Princeton, NJ: Princeton University Press.

1987. '(Nonsolipsistic) Conceptual Role Semantics', in E. Lepore, ed., *New Directions in Semantics.* London: Academic Press.

1988. 'Wide Functionalism', in S. Schiffer and D. Steele, eds., *Cognition and Representation.* Boulder, CO: Westview Press.

Haugeland, J., ed. 1981a. *Mind Design.* Cambridge, MA: MIT Press.

1981b. 'Semantic Engines: An Introduction to Mind Design', in Haugeland 1981a.

1991. 'Representational Genera', in W. Ramsey, S. Stich, and D. Rumelhart, eds., *Philosophy and Connectionist Theory.* Hillsdale, NJ: Lawrence Erlbaum.

Heil, J. 1992. *The Nature of True Minds.* New York: Cambridge University Press.

259

Heil, J., and A. Mele. 1991. 'Mental Causes', *American Philosophical Quarterly* 28:61–71.

    eds. 1993. *Mental Causation*. New York: Oxford University Press.

Hempel, C. G. 1965. *Aspects of Scientific Explanation*. New York: Free Press.

Hobbes, T. 1655. *De Corpore*, Vol. 1 of *The English Works of Thomas Hobbes*, ed. by W. Molesworth. London: John Bohn, 1839.

Horgan, T. 1987. 'Supervenient Qualia', *Philosophical Review* 96:491–520.

    1993. 'From Supervenience to Superdupervenience: Meeting the Demands of a Material World', *Mind* 102:555–86.

Horgan, T., and G. Graham. 1991. 'In Defense of Southern Fundamentalism', *Philosophical Studies* 62:107–34.

Horgan, T., and J. Tienson. 1990. 'Soft Laws', in French et al. 1990.

Horgan, T., and J. Woodward. 1985. 'Folk Psychology Is Here to Stay', *Philosophical Review* 94:197–226. Reprinted in Lycan 1990.

Hornsby, J. 1986. 'Physicalist Thinking and Conceptions of Behavior', in Pettit and McDowell 1986.

Jackson, F., and P. Pettit. 1988. 'Functionalism and Broad Content', *Mind* 97:381–400.

    1990a. 'Program Explanation: A General Perspective', *Analysis* 50:107–17.

    1990b. 'Causation in the Philosophy of Mind', *Philosophy and Phenomenological Research* 50:195–214 (suppl.).

    1993. 'Some Content Is Narrow', in Heil and Mele 1993.

Kaplan, D. 1989. 'Demonstratives', in J. Almog, J. Perry, and H. Wettstein, eds., *Themes from Kaplan*. New York: Oxford University Press.

Keil, F. 1989. *Concepts, Kinds, and Cognitive Development*. Cambridge, MA: MIT Press.

Kim, J. 1982. 'Psychophysical Supervenience', *Philosophical Studies* 41:51–70.

    1984. 'Epiphenomenal and Supervenient Causation', in P. French, T. Uehling, and H. Wettstein, eds., *Midwest Studies in Philosophy*, Vol. 9: *Causation and Causal Theories*. Minneapolis: University of Minnesota Press.

    1987. " 'Strong' and 'Global' Supervenience Revisited", *Philosophy and Phenomenological Research* 48:315–26.

    1989a. 'Mechanism, Purpose, and Explanatory Exclusion', in Tomberlin 1989.

    1989b. 'The Myth of Nonreductive Materialism', *Proceedings and Addresses of the American Philosophical Association* 63:31–47.

    1992. 'Multiple Realizability and the Metaphysics of Reduction', *Philosophy and Phenomenological Research* 52:1–26.

    1993. 'The Non-Reductionist's Troubles with Mental Causation', in Heil and Mele 1993.

Kitcher, Patricia. 1984. 'In Defence of Folk Psychology', *Journal of Philosophy* 81:89–106.

    1985. 'Narrow Taxonomy and Wide Functionalism', *Philosophy of Science* 52:78–97.

Kitcher, Philip. 1993. *The Advancement of Science*. New York: Oxford University Press.

Kripke, S. 1980. *Naming and Necessity.* Cambridge, MA: Harvard University Press.

Kymlicka, W. 1989. *Liberalism, Community, and Culture.* New York: Oxford University Press.

1990. *Contemporary Political Philosophy.* New York: Oxford University Press.

Lepore, E., and B. Loewer. 1986. 'Solipsistic Semantics', in French et al. 1986.

1987. 'Mind Matters', *Journal of Philosophy* 84:630–42.

1989. 'More on Making Mind Matter', *Philosophical Topics* 17:175–91.

Leslie, A. 1987. 'Pretense and Representation: The Origins of "Theory of Mind" ', *Psychological Review* 94:412–26.

Lewis, D. K. 1970, 'How to Define Theoretical Terms', *Journal of Philosophy* 67:427–46. Reprinted in his *Philosophical Papers,* Vol. 1. New York: Oxford University Press.

1972. 'Psychophysical and Theoretical Identifications', *Australasian Journal of Philosophy* 50:249–58.

Loar, B. 1981. *Mind and Meaning.* New York: Cambridge University Press.

1988a. 'Social Content and Psychological Content', in Grimm and Merrill 1988.

1988b. 'Reply: A New Kind of Content', in Grimm and Merrill 1988.

Locke, J. 1694. *An Essay Concerning Human Understanding,* ed. by A. C. Fraser. New York: Dover edition, 1959.

Loewer, B., and G. Rey, eds. 1991. *Meaning in Mind: Fodor and His Critics.* Cambridge, MA: Basil Blackwell.

Lycan, W. 1981. 'Psychological Laws', in J. Biro and R. Shahan, eds., *Mind, Brain, and Function.* Norman: University of Oklahama Press, 1982.

1987. *Consciousness.* Cambridge, MA: MIT Press.

1988. *Judgement and Justification.* New York: Cambridge University Press.

ed. 1990. *Mind and Cognition.* Cambridge, MA: Basil Blackwell.

Mackenzie, B. 1977. *Behaviourism and the Limits of Scientific Method.* London: Routledge and Kegan Paul.

Macnamara, J. 1992. 'Logic and Cognition', in J. Macnamara and G. Reyes, eds., *The Logical Foundations of Cognition.* Oxford: Oxford University Press.

Maloney, J. C. 1989. *The Mundane Matter of the Mental Language.* New York: Cambridge University Press.

Marr, D. 1982. *Vision.* San Francisco: Freeman.

Mayr, E. 1942. *Systematics and the Origin of Species.* New York: Columbia University Press, 1982 edition.

1982. *The Growth of Biological Thought.* Cambridge, MA: Harvard University Press.

McDowell, J. 1977. 'On the Sense and Reference of a Proper Name', *Mind* 86:159–85.

1984. 'De Re Senses', in C. Wright, ed., *Frege: Tradition and Influence.* Oxford: Basil Blackwell.

1985. 'Functionalism and Anomalous Monism', in E. Lepore and B.

261

McLaughlin, eds., *Actions and Events: Perspectives on the Philosophy of Donald Davidson*. London: Basil Blackwell.

1986. 'Singular Thought and the Extent of Inner Space', in Pettit and McDowell 1986.

McGinn, C. 1982. 'The Structure of Content', in Woodfield 1982.

1989. *Mental Content*. Cambridge, MA: Basil Blackwell.

1991. 'Conceptual Causation: Some Elementary Reflections', *Mind* 100:573–586.

McLaughlin, B. 1989. 'Type Epiphenomenalism, Type Dualism, and the Causal Priority of the Physical', in Tomberlin 1989.

Miller, R. W. 1987. *Fact and Method*. Princeton, NJ: Princeton University Press.

Millikan, R. G. 1986. 'Thoughts without Laws: Cognitive Science with Content', *Philosophical Review* 95:47–80.

Newell, A., and H. Simon. 1976. 'Computer Science as Empirical Inquiry: Symbols and Search', *Communications of the Association for Computing Machinery* 19:113–26. Reprinted in Haugeland 1981a.

Noonan, H. 1986. 'Russellian Thoughts and Methodological Solipsism', in J. Butterfield, ed., *Language, Mind, and Logic*. New York: Cambridge University Press.

Owens, J. 1993. 'Content, Causation, and Psychophysical Supervenience', *Philosophy of Science* 60:242–61.

Palmer, S. 1978. 'Fundamental Aspects of Cognitive Representation', in E. Rosch and B. Lloyd, eds., *Cognition and Categorization*. Hillsdale, NJ: Lawrence Erlbaum.

Patterson, S. 1990. 'The Explanatory Role of Belief Ascriptions', *Philosophical Studies* 59:313–32.

1991. 'Individualism and Semantic Development', *Philosophy of Science* 58:15–35.

Peacocke, C. 1981. 'Demonstrative Thought and Psychological Explanation', *Synthese* 49:187–217.

1983. *Sense and Content*. Oxford: Oxford University Press.

Perry, J. 1977. 'Frege on Demonstratives', *Philosophical Review* 86:474–97.

1979. 'The Problem of the Essential Indexical', *Nous* 13:3–21.

Pettit, P. 1993. *The Common Mind*. New York: Oxford University Press.

Pettit, P., and J. McDowell, eds. 1986. *Subject, Thought and Context*. Oxford: Oxford University Press.

Popper, K. 1952. *The Open Society and Its Enemies,* 2nd ed. Princeton, NJ: Princeton University Press.

Putnam, H. 1973. 'Reduction and the Nature of Psychology', *Cognition* 2:131–46. Reprinted with modification in Haugeland 1981a.

1975. 'The Meaning of "Meaning" ', in K. Gunderson, ed., *Language, Mind and Knowledge*. Minneapolis: University of Minnesota Press. Reprinted in H. Putnam, *Mind, Language, and Reality: Philosophical Papers,* Vol. 2. New York: Cambridge University Press.

1988. *Representation and Reality*. Cambridge, MA: MIT Press.

Pylyshyn, Z. 1984. *Computation and Cognition*. Cambridge, MA: MIT Press.

Quine, W. V. O. 1960. *Word and Object*. Cambridge, MA: MIT Press.

Ramsey, W., S. Stich, and J. Garon. 1991. 'Connectionism, Eliminativism, and the Future of Folk Psychology', in J. Greenwood, ed., *The Future of Folk Psychology*. New York: Cambridge University Press.

Rawls, J. 1971. *A Theory of Justice*. Oxford: Oxford University Press.

Recanati, F. 1993. *Direct Reference*. Oxford: Basil Blackwell.

Robinson, D. 1992. 'Epiphenomenalism, Laws, and Properties', *Philosophical Studies* 66:61–94.

Rollins, M. 1989. *Mental Imagery*. New Haven, CT: Yale University Press.

Rowlands, M. 1991. 'Towards a Reasonable Version of Methodological Solipsism', *Mind and Language* 6:39–57.

Runcorn, S. K., ed. 1962. *Continental Drift*. London: Academic Press.

Salmon, W. 1984. *Scientific Explanation and the Causal Structure of the World*. Princeton, NJ: Princeton University Press.

Sandel, M. 1982. *Liberalism and the Limits of Justice*. New York: Cambridge University Press.

C. W. Savage, ed. 1978. *Perception and Cognition: Issues in the Foundations of Psychology, Minnesota Studies in the Philosophy of Science 9*. Minneapolis: University of Minnesota Press.

Scheman, N. 1983. 'Individualism and the Objects of Psychology', in S. Harding and M. Hintikka, eds., *Discovering Reality*. Dordrecht, the Netherlands: D. Reidel.

Schiffer, S. 1981. 'Truth and the Theory of Content', in H. Parret and J. Bouveresse, eds., *Meaning and Understanding*. New York: de Gruyter.

1991. 'Ceteris Paribus Laws', *Mind* 100:1–17.

Schofield, C. B. S. 1979. *Sexually Transmitted Diseases,* 3rd ed. New York: Longman.

Searle, J. 1980. 'Minds, Brains, and Programs', *Behavioral and Brain Sciences* 3:417–24. Reprinted in Haugeland 1981a.

1983. *Intentionality*. New York: Cambridge University Press.

1992. *The Rediscovery of the Mind*. Cambridge, MA: MIT Press.

Segal, G. 1989a. 'Seeing What Is Not There', *Philosophical Review* 98:189–214.

1989b. 'The Return of the Individual', *Mind* 98:39–57.

1991. 'Defence of a Reasonable Individualism', *Mind* 100:485–94.

Sekuler, R., and R. Blake. 1990. *Perception,* 2nd ed. New York: McGraw-Hill.

Shoemaker, S. 1979. 'Identity, Properties, and Causality'. Reprinted in Shoemaker 1984.

1980. 'Causality and Properties'. Reprinted in Shoemaker 1984.

1981. 'Some Varieties of Functionalism'. Reprinted in Shoemaker 1984.

1984. *Identity, Cause, and Mind*. New York: Cambridge University Press.

Smolensky, P. 1988. 'On the Proper Treatment of Connectionism', *Brain and Behavioral Sciences* 11:1–74.

1991. 'Connectionism, Constituency, and the Language of Thought', in Loewer and Rey 1991.

Sober, E. 1980. 'Evolution, Population Thinking, and Essentialism', *Philosophy of Science* 47:350–83. Reprinted in Sober 1993.

1984. *The Nature of Selection*. Cambridge, MA: MIT Press.

263

ed. 1993. *Conceptual Issues in Evolutionary Biology,* 2nd ed. Cambridge, MA: MIT Press.

Sokal, R., and T. Crovello. 1970. 'The Biological Species Concept: A Critical Evaluation', *American Naturalist* 104:127–53. Reprinted in Sober 1993.

Spelke, E. 1990. 'Principles of Object Perception', *Cognitive Science* 14:29–56.

Sperber, D. 1994. 'The Modularity of Thought and the Epidemiology of Representations', in L. Hirschfeld and S. Gelman, eds., *Domain Specificity in Cognition and Culture.* New York: Cambridge University Press.

Stalnaker, R. C. 1989. 'On What's in the Head', in Tomberlin 1989.

1991. 'How to Do Semantics for the Language of Thought', in Loewer and Rey 1991.

Sterelny, K. 1989. 'Computational Functional Psychology: Problems and Prospects', in P. Slezak and W. Albury, eds., *Computers, Brains, and Minds.* Dordrecht, the Netherlands: Kluwer.

1990. *The Representational Theory of Mind.* Oxford: Basil Blackwell.

Stich, S. 1978a. 'Autonomous Psychology and the Belief–Desire Thesis', *Monist* 61:573–91. Reprinted in Lycan 1990.

1978b. 'Beliefs and Subdoxastic States', *Philosophy of Science* 45:499–518.

1983. *From Folk Psychology to Cognitive Science.* Cambridge, MA: MIT Press.

1991. 'Fat Syntax Meets Skinny Semantics', in Loewer and Rey 1991.

Taylor, C. 1964. *The Explanation of Behaviour.* London: Routledge and Kegan Paul.

1985. 'Atomism', in his *Philosophy and the Human Sciences: Philosophical Papers,* Vol. 2. New York: Cambridge University Press.

Tomberlin, J., ed. 1989. *Philosophical Perspectives,* Vol. 3: *The Philosophy of Mind and Action.* Atascadero, CA: Ridgeview.

Trout, J. D. 1992. 'Theory Conjunction and Mercenary Reliance', *Philosophy of Science* 59:231–45.

Unger, P. 1983. 'The Causal Theory of Reference', *Philosophical Studies* 43:1–45.

1984. *Philosophical Relativity.* Minneapolis: University of Minnesota Press.

van Gulick, R. 1989. 'Metaphysical Arguments for Internalism and Why They Don't Work', in S. Silvers, ed., *Rerepresentation.* Dordrecht, the Netherlands: Kluwer.

Watkins, J. W. N. 1957. 'Historical Explanation in the Social Sciences', *British Journal for the Philosophy of Science* 8:104–17.

Watson, J. B. 1913. 'Psychology as the Behaviorist Views It', *Psychological Review* 20:158–77.

Wellman, H. 1990. *The Child's Theory of Mind.* Cambridge, MA: MIT Press.

White, S. 1982. 'Partial Character and the Language of Thought', *Pacific Philosophical Quarterly* 63:347–65.

1991. *The Unity of the Self.* Cambridge, MA: MIT Press.

Wiggins, D. 1980. *Sameness and Substance.* Oxford: Oxford University Press.

Williams, G. C. 1966. *Adaptation and Natural Selection.* Princeton, NJ: Princeton University Press.

Williams, M. 1990. 'Social Norms and Narrow Content', in French et al. 1990.

Wilson, D. S. 1989. 'Levels of Selection: An Alternative to Individualism in Biology and the Human Sciences', *Social Networks* 11:257–72. Reprinted in Sober 1993.

Wilson, D. S., and E. Sober. 1994. 'Re-introducing Group Selection to the Human Behavioral Sciences', *Behavioral and Brain Sciences* 17:585–608.

Wilson, J. T., ed. 1971. *Continents Adrift*. San Francisco: W. H. Freeman.

Wilson, R. A. 1992. 'Individualism, Causal Powers, and Explanation', *Philosophical Studies* 68:103–39.

1993. 'Against *A Priori* Arguments for Individualism', *Pacific Philosophical Quarterly* 74:60–79.

1994a. 'Causal Depth, Theoretical Appropriateness, and Individualism in Psychology', *Philosophy of Science* 61:55–75.

1994b. 'Wide Computationalism', *Mind* 103:351–72.

1994c. Review of Pettit 1993, *The Philosophical Review* 103:716–718.

Woodfield, A., ed. 1982. *Thought and Object: Essays on Intentionality*. Oxford: Oxford University Press.

Yablo, S. 1992. 'Mental Causation', *Philosophical Review* 101:245–80.

Young, A. W., and H. D. Ellis, eds. 1989. *Handbook of Research on Face Processing*. New York: Elsevier.

# Index

ecological optics, 96
ecumenism, *see* pluralism
Egan, F., xii, 31, 39, 61, 67–8, 68n, 79, 87,
    91, 103, 106, 220
eliminative materialism, 161, 176, 182,
    187, 197, 204–5, 242–3; *see also* physi-
    calism
eliminativism about content, 215–17
Ellis, H., 206
Elster, J., 166, 166n, 168, 247
Elugardo, R., 13
embeddedness, 84, 94–5, 113, 222
epiphenomenalism, 77, 149–50, 149n; *see
    also* causal efficacy
epistemic dependence, *see* mercenary reli-
    ance
Evans, G., 16–17
evolutionary
    biology, 4, 39, 43, 124, 200, 213, 248–9
    explanations, 124, 132–5, 165–6, 187,
        192–6, 198, 208–9
    psychology, 108–12, 207–8
explanatory power, *see* causal depth, theo-
    retical appropriateness
extended vs restricted senses of causal pow-
        ers, 46, 53–4, 56, 59, 117, 135, 169–
        70
    genuine properties, 125
    psychological mechanisms, 144–5
external storage systems, 111
externalism, 2, 22–3

face-recognition, 108, 206–8
Field, D., xii, 80n
Field, H., 15n, 97, 101, 154, 162n, 225
Fisher, R. A., 74n
Fodor, J. A., 1, 7, 15n, 31–5, 37n, 39, 47–
    51, 52–8, 52n, 61, 62, 71, 79, 79n,
    94–100, 106–7, 127, 130, 139–41,
    143, 148, 149n, 154, 156, 162–5,
    169, 175, 183, 199, 225, 230, 237–9,
    247
folk psychological computationalism, 162,
    168, 174–5; *see also* folk psychology
folk psychology, 100–2, 130, 154, 212,
    253
    computationalism about, 62–3, 100–1,
        159, 162–4, 174–5; *see also* language
        of thought
    and explanation, 56, 140, 159, 164–7,
        174, 201–5, 219–20
    explanatory coherence of, 165
    and individualism, 10–14, 159–60

instrumentalism about, 26, 180–4
    predictive utility of, 165
    as a theory, 10–11, 160
formal
    operations, 68
    properties, 71–3, 83, 90, 95, 163
    structure to an environment, 70, 83–6,
        99
    systems, 69, 71–2, 75, 82, 85, 90
formality
    of cognition, 71, 88–91
    condition, 71, 164, 218n
    systemic conception of, 72–3, 75
Fuller, G., 230
functional analysis, *see* functional explana-
    tion
functional explanation, 166–9, 192, 205–8,
    213
functionalism, 156, 202, 226–7, 231–3
    and computationalism, 89
    homuncular, 205–6
    and individualism, 9–10
    Ramsey-styled formulations of, 232n

Gallistel, C. R., 82–4, 85–7
Garfield, J., 200
Garfinkel, A., 188–91, 248
Garon, J., 187
Gauker, C., 102
Geach, P., 119n, 124
Gibson, J. J., 96, 99
Giere, R., 172
Ginet, C., xii, 35n
global individualism, 32, 41–2, 48–52, 59,
    94, 117
    argument for, 33–5
    as a constraint on science, 36, 40, 54, 58,
        139
Goldman, A., 10
Gopnik, A., 10
Gordon, R., 10
Gould, S. J., 43
Graham, G., 174, 182, 203

Hamilton, W., 74n
Hardwig, J., 102
Harman, G., 68, 162n, 230
Harris, P., 106
Haugeland, J., 63, 65
Heil, J., xii, 146, 149n, 212
Hempel, C., 168, 171
Henry, W., xii
Hobbes, T., 24n

materialism, *see* physicalism, eliminative materialism, supervenience

McDowell, J., 17n, 152

McGinn, C., 6–7, 15n, 16, 18n, 22–3, 23n, 31, 64, 130–5, 136, 139, 148–9, 150n, 202, 211, 225, 235

McLaughlin, B., 63, 149n

Mayr, E., 44, 44n

mechanisms, 141, 144, 164, 166, 168, 170–3, 244; *see also* psychological mechanisms

Mele, A., 149n, 212

mental causation, 8, 25–6, 139–41, 147, 153, 157–8, 215
  and wide content, 140–5, 148–50, 157–8

mental representation, 6, 14–15, 66, 85, 95, 144, 162–3
  and representational psychology, 16, 82–4, 86–7, 97, 113, 164, 218

mercenary reliance, 102, 102n
  and epistemic dependence, 102–5
  and Loar's examples, 103–5

mere-Cambridge
  causal powers, 55–7
  change, 119n, 123
  properties, 119–24, 119n, 125–6, 129–30

methodological solipsism, 1, 2n, 6, 12, 17–19, 243
  vs methodological individualism, 47–8

Miller, R., 171, 189, 191

Millikan, R., 171

modularity, 79n, 97, 108–12, 207, 244
  and central processes, 79–80, 111–12
  and computational psychology, 66–7, 79–80, 105–8, 155

Moore, J., xii

multiple realization, 89, 156, 167, 168–70, 203–4; *see also* implementation, instantiation, realization

multiple spatial channels theory, 80–2, 84, 95; *see also* perception, form

narrow content, 15, 154, 161, 164, 176–80, 225–6; *see also* content, intentionality, psychological content
  as a causal power, 227, 229, 236, 238
  expressibility of, 236, 237
  and narrow conceptual role semantics (NCRS), 226–7, 230–5, 239–40
  narrow function theory of, 227–30, 235–9, 238n, 239–40

an oxymoron, 177–8, 234–5
  program, 204, 215, 225–6, 239–40, 243, 244

narrow explanation(s), 192, 194, 201, 211, 244

narrow-folk psychology, 201–2, 203–5, 230–5

narrow psychological states, 1, 179

narrowness
  intra- vs interworld, 179

naturalistic psychology, 96–100, 243, 247

neuroscience(s), 88, 90, 148, 160, 174, 187; *see also* eliminative materialism

Newell, A., 62–3

Noonan, H., 17n

Not Exhaustively Computational Thesis, 165, 167–68, 176

007 Principle, 110

Olson, D., 106

Owens, J., 31, 118

Palmer, S., 85

Patterson, S., 103, 242

peaceful coexistence, 208–9; *see also* pluralism

Peacocke, C., 17n, 182

perception, 70, 79, 89, 108, 110, 224, 234
  form, 80–2, 84, 95; see also multiple spatial channels theory
  Gibsonian views of, 96, 99

Perry, J., 228–9

Pettit, P., 161, 178–80, 189, 237, 248

physical symbol system hypothesis, 62

physicalism, 78, 156, 216, 241; *see also* eliminative materialism
  identity theories, 89, 155–7
  and mental causation, 147
  as a motivation for individualism, 10, 17–20, 243

planets, 47, 51, 54, 58, 99, 145, 177
  'narrow planets', 235

pluralism
  about explanation, 112–14, 208–10, 226
  in methodology, 96–7, 113–14
  political, 250

Popper, K., 247

possible worlds, 130, 180
  and counterfactual rigor/causal depth, 36, 188, 197, 204
  and explanation, 127, 188, 206–7, 211–13, 231–2

principle of autonomy, *see* autonomy

principle of the causal individuation of
    kinds, 169–70
principle of causal inheritance, 169–70
principle of charity, 216
program(s), 76, 78, 90
program explanation, 188
projectibility, 9, 33, 36–7, 37n, 98
properties
    causal theory of, 119–30
    genuine (vs mere-Cambridge), 119–24,
        125–6, 129–30, 135
    historical, 33–5, 142–4, 146, 180
    relational, 33–9, 53, 123–5, 132–5, 142–
        4, 206, 212; see also relational taxo-
        nomies
    as second-order functions, 121
propositional attitudes, see folk psychology
psychological content
    as narrow content, 103–5
psychological mechanisms, 141, 144n,
    144–5, 207–8; see also mechanisms
Putnam, H., 2n, 3, 12, 150n, 190–2, 232n,
    248
Pylyshyn, Z., 61, 63, 107

Quine, W. V. O., 216–17

Ramsey, W., 187
rationalist psychology, 96, 247
Rawls, J., 251
realization(s), 73, 109, 156, 170, 207, 244,
    247; see also implementation, instantia-
    tion, multiple realization
    conditions, 103–4
    function(s), 68
Recanati, F., 2
reductionism, 165, 167–70, 239, 247
reference, 101, 148, 177
reference-fixing, 37, 238
relational taxonomies, 39–46, 55, 177–8;
    see also properties
    and corpuscularism, 127–9
    incompatibility with individualism, 42–
        5, 47–52, 56, 136
    revisionism about, 32, 35–9, 40–1, 50–2
    and science, 42–5, 58–9, 123–5, 132–8,
        170, 238–9
replacements, 7–8; see also doppelgängers
representational psychology, see mental rep-
    resentation
revisionism
    about behavior, 200, 222–3
    about content, 15–16, 160–1, 180, 235

about folk psychology, 13, 100–1, 151,
    153–4, 160–2
about relational taxonomies, 32, 35–9,
    40–1, 47, 50–2, 59, 124–5
about species, 51–2, 177, 235
Riches At Face Value Thesis, 165–6, 202,
    204–5, 222
Robb, D., xii, 211
Robinson, D., 149n
Robson, J., 80
Rollins, M., 72
Rowlands, M., 242
rule-guided
    vs regular behavior, 76–8
Runcorn, S., 172
Russell's Principle, 16–17

Salmon, W., 127
Sandel, M., 249
Scheman, N., 250–2
Schiffer, S., 37n, 152, 162n
Schofield, C., 40
science
    and commonsense, 36–7, 239, 252–3
    taxonomy in, 36, 39–46, 100, 102,
        135–7
scientific laws, see laws, scientific
Scott-Kakures, D., xii, 209n, 211
Searle, J., 13, 72, 174
Segal, G., 15n, 17n, 61, 66–7, 67n, 78, 84,
    242
Sekuler, R., 80–2
selfish gene, 74–5, 74n, 248–9
semantic relativity, 13
Shoemaker, S., xi, 35n, 48, 55, 119n, 120–
    1, 120n, 123, 204, 209n, 211, 232n
sibling's disease, 57
Simon, H., 62–3
Sismondo, S., xii
Skinner, B. F., 222
Smith, B., xii
Smolensky, P., 63
Sober, E., 44, 194, 249
sociology, 42–3
Sokal, R., 44n
species, 39, 43–5, 44n, 124, 167, 194–5,
    248; see also revisionism
Spelke, E., 88, 222
Sperber, D., 110–11
Stalnaker, R., xi, 22, 38, 48, 230
Stecker, R., 230
Stein, E., xi
Sterelny, K., 6, 89, 234

272

Stich, S., 2, 8, 10–11, 15, 63, 90, 151, 154, 163–4, 175–6, 187, 198, 205, 215–20, 218n, 240, 243
strong singular thought theory, 17n
subpersonal psychology, 63, 158, 162–3, 181, 213, 224,
  and causal depth, 201–6, 234
supervenience, 2–3, 7, 64, 143, 221, 244, 246
  and causal powers, 7, 31, 35, 41, 50, 53–4, 125, 169
  and content, 14–15, 17, 160–1, 163
  local vs global, 54, 145–8, 237
  and materialism, 145–8
  violation of, 26, 139–41, 145, 154
syntactic properties, 154, 164–5, 176, 217; see also formal properties
syntactic psychology, see syntactic theory of the mind
syntactic theory of the mind, 15, 176, 215, 217–20, 240, 244

taxonomy, see individuation, relational taxonomies; science, taxonomy in
Taylor, C., 198, 249
theoretical appropriateness, 187–92, 195–6, 208–9, 244
  in evolutionary biology, 93–5
  in psychology, 197–201, 220–2
Tienson, J., 37n, 171
Tooby, J., 111–12, 207–8
transformational grammar, 95

Trout, J. D., xi, 102n
truth conditions, 15, 100, 103, 177, 237
  and content, 217, 225, 226, 228
Twin Earth, 12, 14–15, 104, 155, 163, 198, 246; see also doppelgängers
  and explanation, 211–13, 229–30

Unger, P., 13

van Gulick, R., 31, 39

Watkins, J., 247
Watson, J. B., 245
weight, see mass
Wellman, H., 10, 210
White, S., 15n, 178, 225, 237, 238n
wide computationalism, 64–71, 74–5, 91–2, 109, 113, 154, 223–4
  and the computational metaphor, 76–8
  in cognitive psychology, 80–7
  objections to, 67–8, 70–1, 76–80, 84–7
  and wide functionalism, 68–9
Wiggins, D., 23
Williams, G., 74n, 249
Williams, M., 31, 118
Wilson, D. S., 249
Wilson, J. T., 172
Wilson, R. A., 248
Woodward, J., 220

Yablo, S., 149n
Young, A., 206